THE NAZIS
IN THE
BALKANS

The Nazis in the Balkans

*A Case Study
of Totalitarian
Politics*

DIETRICH ORLOW

*University
of
Pittsburgh
Press*

▲▲ | **Preface**

WHEN the Third Reich collapsed in the spring of 1945, it left behind a vast number of official documents dealing with virtually every facet of German life. Almost all of this primary material is now available to scholars, but owing in large part to its sheer bulk, much of it has remained unexplored. This is particularly true of material covering the activities of organizations that were not constantly bathed in the glaring light of National Socialist or Allied propaganda. The neglect is unfortunate for a number of reasons. An analysis of the growth and activities of such agencies is often quite rewarding, not only for the insight it may yield into the routine operation of the National Socialist totalitarian system but also because such organizations often had a surprising amount of policy-making authority; the work of the secondary agencies at times involved far more than merely the execution

v

of centrally directed policies at the local or regional level. This study is of one such organization, the *Südosteuropa-Gesellschaft* (SOEG). It describes the agency's internal development, its interaction with other agencies, and its role in planning and executing the Third Reich's blueprint for the New Order in Southeastern Europe.

An in-depth analysis of a lower echelon agency carries with it the obvious danger of distorting or exaggerating the agency's influence within the system as a whole. For this reason it may be useful at the outset to delineate the areas of inquiry in which an analysis of the SOEG's history can and cannot add significantly to the knowledge of National Socialist totalitarianism. This study of the SOEG does not pretend to encompass the entire complex field of German-Balkan relations in World War II. Rather, the SOEG was for the most part a recipient only of economic policy directives and had very little contact, for example, with the German military agencies in Southeastern Europe. Neither did the SOEG determine Germany's wartime policies in the Balkans. This, too, was done at higher levels; the Society was expected to execute the directives without feedback.

On the other hand, as an integral part of the National Socialist political system, the SOEG's history does provide significant new insights into the workings of that system. To begin with, substantively the SOEG had a specific grant of authority to draw up blueprints for Germany's postwar New Order in the Balkans. The project was never completed, but the extant records reveal very detailed plans for the postwar exploitation of an important area of Europe. In addition the SOEG, precisely because it was a lower echelon agency, interacted on an almost daily basis with other components of the National Socialist power structure. The interaction reveals not only a great deal about the plans and projects of these other agencies—the SS, the Foreign Ministry, the Party, the agricultural interest group—but, above all, provides an inside view of totalitarian politics. It is a commonplace, of course, that the Third Reich was never as monolithic as Goebbels' propaganda described it. Much has been written about the

great rivalries of Bormann and Himmler, of Goebbels and Göring, yet the history of the SOEG shows that this too is a distorted picture. Politics at the lower levels were not massive
struggles for power, but an unending series of guerrilla engage-
ments often punctuated by spontaneous, symbiotic armistices
and alliances that had little relation to the status of the major
battles raging in Berlin.

*   *   *

It is a pleasant duty to acknowledge the many institutional
and personal debts of gratitude that I have incurred in the course
of completing this analysis of the SOEG.

The bulk of the study is based upon the *Südosteuropa-Gesellschaft's* unpublished records, and I wish to express my gratitude to the Horace H. Rackham School of Graduate Studies
at the University of Michigan for a grant that enabled me to
purchase most of these records on microfilm. I would also like
to express my appreciation to the College of William and Mary
for a Faculty Research Grant that enabled me to devote the
summer of 1964 to the task of revising the original manuscript.

During a stay in Germany, I was able to use the collections
of the Staats-und Universitätsbibliothek, the Hamburgisches
Weltwirtschaftsarchiv, the Seminar für öffentliches Recht und
Staatslehre, the Seminar für auswärtige Politik (all in Hamburg); the Institut für Weltwirtschaft in Kiel; and the Österreichische Nationalbibliothek in Vienna. I would like to express
my appreciation to these institutions for allowing me to use
their facilities. In addition, I would like to thank the Wiener
Library in London for the preparation of photostats of some
pertinent materials from its collection, and to the new
Südosteuropa-Gesellschaft in Munich (which, incidentally, is
not a neo-Nazi successor organization) for information on the
whereabouts of some of the wartime SOEG's officials.

During the same European sojourn I had the privilege of dis-
cussing the SOEG's history with three individuals who had been
intimately associated with the Society's work: Mr. August Heinrichsbauer, the Society's former executive secretary; Dr. Erika

Hanel, formerly Mr. Heinrichsbauer's personal secretary; and Professor Hermann Gross, during the early forties an executive with I. G. Farben Industries in Vienna. Their willingness to relate their personal impressions of the SOEG is gratefully acknowledged, though a reading of the study will make it readily apparent that they would in all likelihood not agree with many of the findings and conclusions.

I would also like to express my appreciation for unfailing kindness and archival assistance to Miss Mary Rollman of the University of Michigan Libraries, Dr. Arnold H. Price of the Library of Congress, and Mr. Robert Wolfe of the National Archives. Furthermore, two of my former colleagues at the College of William and Mary, Professors Anthony J. Esler and Joseph L. Brent, III, were kind enough to read and criticize portions of the manuscript.

I acknowledge with particular gratitude the pungent criticisms and ever-ready advice I received from my teacher at the University of Michigan, Professor Gerhard L. Weinberg. This study owes its inception as a Ph.D. thesis to Professor Weinberg's suggestion, and his willingness to answer questions and suggest new avenues of research made considerably easier the task of revising and expanding the original manuscript into its present form.

My thanks also go to Miss Virginia Dixon for her very efficient editorial assistance and to Mrs. Margherite Smith and Mrs. Grace Jones for typing parts of the manuscript.

Finally, this study would not have been completed without the sort of encouragement and criticism that only a wife can give. For this I would like to thank her publicly.

D. O.

Syracuse, New York
September, 1967

Contents

1 | Introduction

In January 1933 Adolf Hitler became Chancellor of the German Reich; the Nazis had come to power in Germany, and the era of dynamic and aggressive National Socialist activities began. The countries of Southeastern Europe quickly became objects of major interest for a regime that made German hegemony on the European Continent its ultimate goal.

During the 1930's, the Balkan nations were ill prepared to resist German encroachments on their political and economic independence. The aftermath of World War I had left the region divided into two sharply opposed groups: the revisionist and antirevisionist powers. The former included the losers in the war—Bulgaria and Hungary; the latter, the victors and beneficiaries of the treaties of Neuilly, Trianon, and St. Germain—Rumania, Yugoslavia, Czechoslovakia, and Greece. The victors

1

had an obvious common interest in preserving the status quo established by the World War I peace settlement, and they quickly forged an alliance system that, on paper at least, assured the continued political and military preponderance of the saturated powers. The Little Entente of 1922 joined Czechoslovakia, Rumania, and Yugoslavia in a common front against the major revisionist nation, Hungary, and a series of bilateral treaties between the Entente partners and France made France, in turn, the guarantor of the Balkan peace settlement.

The picture of postwar political and territorial stability in Southeastern Europe was deceptive, however. While the alliance system presumably was a guarantee against a Hungarian or an Austrian attack on the Entente partners, the Entente in no way solved the internal nationality and social problems plaguing all of the nations in Southeastern Europe and most acutely the territorially saturated powers.[1] The nations of Southeastern Europe also had to deal with very serious problems of social polarization among their populations, and the already sharp economic antagonisms between the urban and rural populations were at times aggravated by differences in their ethnic background. In some instances, religious differences added to the social and nationality problems. Finally, the historic territorial claims of the Balkan peoples had as much or as little relation to the actual areas of ethnographic settlements as ever; these irreconcilable claims had plagued the Austro-Hungarian Empire for many years and were a part of the inheritance the old Empire bequeathed to its successor states.[2]

1. For instance, in Yugoslavia friction existed not only among the three "official" peoples—the Serbs, the Croats, and the Slovenes—but also between these peoples and the other minority groups settled within Yugoslavia's territorial boundaries. See Gerhart Wolfram, "Die Völker und Nationalitäten," in *Osteuropa-Handbuch: Yugoslavien,* ed. Werner Markert (Cologne, 1954), p. 21. For a vivid description of antagonism between Croats and Serbs in the postwar era, see Vladko Maček, *In the Struggle for Freedom,* tr. Elizabeth and Stjepan Gazi (New York, 1957), chs. 7, 8 (especially pp. 120–21, 125–26), 9.

2. Martin Wright, "Eastern Europe," in *Survey of International Affairs 1939–1946: The World in March 1939,* ed. Arnold Toynbee and Frank T. Ashton-Gwatkin (London, 1952) (hereafter cited as *Survey, March 1939*), p. 222; and Maček, *Struggle,* p. 115.

Despite its defects, the alliance system preserved some degree of stability in the early years of the decade after the war. After 1922, however, the narrowly anti-Magyar and anti-Habsburg viewpoint of its framers rendered the system little short of anachronistic. The Little Entente and later the Balkan Pact[3] provided safeguards only against the ambitions of Bulgaria, Hungary, and Austria. Actually, after 1922 the danger to Balkan independence came not from within Southeastern Europe but from Fascist Italy.[4] Mussolini's anti-French policy in the Balkans significantly affected the balance of power in the region and noticably lessened the original value of the antirevisionist alliances.[5] Unwittingly, Italy's Francophobia and "consistently malignant policy"[6] prepared the road for the National Socialist drive into Southeastern Europe after 1933. During the 1920's Mussolini actively championed the "have nots," particularly Hungary, and thereby widened the chasm between the two blocs in the Balkans. The Fascist state encouraged the national antagonisms within the borders of the Balkan nations; Yugoslavia's domestic problems, for example, were greatly intensified by Italy's clandestine support for the Croat extremists. And, quite apart from such overt disturbance of Balkan tranquility, Fascist Italy, by its very form of government, served as an alternative to French political influence. The Italian authoritarianism stirred considerable admiration among Southeastern European rightist circles, and may well have prepared them for their favorable reaction to the new Nazi state some years later.

The economic consequences of World War I left the nations of Southeastern Europe with equally formidable problems. One of the area's most pressing needs was that of finding employment

3. See p. 7, below.
4. John A. Luckacz, *The Great Powers and Eastern Europe* (New York, 1953), p. 60.
5. See the statement of Stoyadinovitch to Ciano as quoted in Ciano, "Conversation with Yugoslav Prime Minister Stoyadinovitch, Belgrade, March 26, 1937," in Count Galeazzo Ciano, *Ciano's Diplomatic Papers*, ed. Malcolm Muggeridge and tr. Stuart Hood (London, 1948) (hereafter cited as Ciano, *Diplomatic Papers*), p. 99.
6. Wright, "Eastern Europe," in *Survey, March 1939*, p. 249.

for its surplus rural population, and all of the Balkan nations inaugurated programs of rapid industrialization to cope with the problem. Since the capital resources of the Balkan countries were inadequate for a massive industrialization effort, the nations had to accept the burden of high foreign debts. Once established, the infant industries had to be protected by substantial tariffs, which in turn led to high domestic prices and adversely affected the export possibilities of the agricultural surpluses the countries continued to produce.[7] In addition, the industrialization schemes often showed evidence of being dominated more by political and nationalistic motives than by an appreciation for economic realities.[8] All of this rendered the results of the crash programs generally unsatisfactory; the rural population problem was not notably alleviated by the industrialization.[9]

The effect of the world depression upon the weak and imbalanced Balkan economies was catastrophic. A few figures may serve to illustrate. From 1928 to 1932 the foreign trade of Southeastern Europe, virtually the only source of foreign exchange for the Balkan countries, declined as follows:[10]

Country	Imports (Millions of $)		Exports (Millions of $)	
	1928	1932	1928	1932
Albania	11	8	5	2
Bulgaria	87	42	76	41
Hungary	358	97	244	99
Rumania	332	116	278	170
Czechoslovakia	961	374	1062	367
Turkey	193	69	150	81
Yugoslavia	233	78	192	83

7. Leo Pasvolsky, *Economic Nationalism of the Danubian States* (New York, 1928), pp. 554–55.

8. *Ibid.*, p. 552; and Paul Einzig, *Hitler's 'New Order' in Europe* (London, 1941), p. 105.

9. For statistics on the rise of the peasant population in Czechoslovakia, Hungary, Yugoslavia, Rumania, and Bulgaria after World War I, see Doreen

By 1933 then, when the Nazi drive toward domination of Southeastern Europe began, the Balkan countries were faced with problems of political and social disunity,[11] heavy financial obligations as a result of too-rapid industrialization, a grave rural overpopulation problem, and a seemingly indisposable surplus of agricultural goods. Any effective solution to these problems, even when offered by the Nazis, could only be eagerly welcomed in the Balkans.

The advent of the Nazi dictatorship in Germany ushered in a new phase of history in Southeastern Europe. From the beginning the Nazis were determined to play a much more active role in the area than the Weimar Republic had ever envisioned. Nazi policy was pursued along two separate but parallel routes: the essentially subversive work of the NSDAP among the *Volksdeutsche* (ethnic Germans) and the indigenous Fascist or Nazi-like parties in the Balkans, and the more orthodox channels of intergovernmental diplomacy and economic policy.[12] The basic goal was the same: to increase Germany's influence in South-

---

Warriner, *Economics of Peasant Farming* (London, 1939), p. 47. Agricultural reforms, which were promised for purposes of internal political consolidation, if for no other reason, in all of the Southeastern European countries after the war, were equally ineffective. The actual amount of land involved in the redistribution schemes was quite small, and a significant change in the prewar social composition of the countries was not achieved. See Slavcho D. Zagaroff, Jenö Vegh, and Alexander D. Bilimovich, *The Agricultural Economy of the Danubian Countries, 1935-1945* (Stanford, Cal., 1955), p. 40, and the tables on pp. 113-15.

10. League of Nations, Economic Intelligence Service, Economic, Financial and Transit Department, *Europe's Trade* (Geneva, 1941), p. 83.

11. The depression also had its effect on the political structure of the area. Its most significant political result was the growth of indigenous Fascist and extreme nationalist groups in the Southeast European countries. See Lukacz, *Great Powers*, p. 26.

12. See Minister in Yugoslavia to the Foreign Ministry, "Tel. Nr. 106 vom 13. April," 13 April 1939, in United States Department of State, *Akten zur deutschen auswärtigen Politik* (Baden-Baden, 1956) (hereafter cited as *ADAP*), Series D (hereafter cited as D), VI, Doc. 192, p. 195; State Secretary to Minister Fabricius (Rumania), "Zu Pol IV 3465" (secret), 7 June 1938, *ibid.*, V, Doc. 207, pp. 238-39; Alan Bullock, *Hitler, a Study in Tyranny* (New York, 1951), p. 436; Andreas Hillgruber, *Hitler, König Carol und Marschall Antonescu* (Wiesbaden, 1954), pp. 11ff., 157; and Wilhelm Sattler, *Die deutsche Volksgruppe im Unabhängigen Staat Kroatien* (Graz, 1943), p. 51.

eastern Europe to the point where it assumed the Reich's political and economic hegemony in the area.[13]

Germany's diplomatic activity in Southeastern Europe after 1933 was consistently ambiguous. Negatively, the policy was designed to prevent any economic or political union of the Balkan countries either directed against Germany or dominated by any nation other than the Third Reich. Thus, Germany was as interested as Italy in dissolving the Little Entente.[14] Unlike the Italians, however, the Germans were determined not to identify themselves with either the antirevisionist or the prorevisionist bloc in Southeastern Europe. In Ribbentrop's telling phrase, Germany had to "keep both irons [Rumania and Hungary in this particular case] in the fire and to shape matters in the German interest according to the way the situation develops."[15]

The policy of naked opportunism and cynicism was particularly apparent in the National Socialist attitude toward territorial revisions in Southeastern Europe. Alfred Rosenberg, chief of the Nazi Party's Foreign Policy Office, publicly insisted that each revisionist claim must be examined on its own merits; a collective judgment was not possible.[16] However, such expressions of policy did not prevent Hitler from speaking to statesmen who "wished to hear it" of a basic dualism in Europe between the "have" and the "have-not" nations, and to hint broadly that the "have-not" nations must stand together.[17]

13. The German activity after 1933 was not entirely unwelcome in the Balkans. To some, perhaps already conditioned by admiration for Mussolini's work, the new Germany was a symbol of progress and dynamism, characteristics that such circles compared favorably with what they felt to be Western stagnation. See Lukacz, *Great Powers,* pp. 36–37.

14. Meissner, "Aufzeichnung über den Empfang des ungarischen Ministerpräsidenten von Daranyi und des ungarischen Aussenministers von Kanya beim Führer und Reichskanzler am 25. November 1937, zu Pol I 6353g Rs." (top secret) [25 Nov. 1937], *ADAP,* D, V, Doc. 149, p. 170.

15. Ribbentrop, "Zusatz des Reichsaussenministers = Unterredung des Führers mit dem rumänischen König im Beisein des Reichsaussenministers, Berchtesgaden, 24. Nov. 1938," *ibid.,* Doc. 245, p. 285.

16. See Alfred Rosenberg, "Unterdrückte Völker und Revisionen," *Völkischer Beobachter* (North German ed.), 15 Nov. 1936, pp. 1–2.

17. Schmidt (of the Büro RAM), "Aufzeichnung über die Unterredung zwischen dem Führer und dem Bulgarischen Ministerpräsidenten Kiosseivanoff in der

The persistent lack of political and economic unity among the Balkan nations greatly facilitated the success of Germany's Machiavellian operations. The weakness of the Little Entente has been pointed out. In 1934 Greece, Turkey, and Yugoslavia concluded a second Southeast European alliance, the Balkan Pact. This too, however, was not a reliable bulwark against German aggression but merely another narrowly conceived barrier against a Balkan revisionist power, in this case Bulgaria.[18] Indeed, the fear of Bulgarian and Hungarian revisionism among the neighbors of the two countries was not formally abated until 1938, and by that time the balance of power in Southeastern Europe had shifted so completely in favor of Germany that the gesture of restoring the right of armament parity to Sofia and Budapest had no important consequences.

Diplomatic events outside the Balkans also played into Germany's hands. France, the country toward which the Little Entente powers gravitated, concluded an alliance with the Soviet Union in 1935. Since most of the politically powerful forces in the Balkans were on the right of the political spectrum, the Franco-Soviet Pact could hardly increase their sympathy for France. In 1936 the Spanish Civil War broke out. Again Germany and Italy were on the rightist, nationalist, anti-Soviet side while the West's sympathies lay with the Russian-supported loyalists, a point German propaganda skillfully exploited.[19]

By the latter part of the 1930's Germany's political and economic policies[20] had assured the Reich a position of considerable

---

Reichskanzlei in Berlin am 5. Juli 1939, in Anwesenheit des Reichsaussen-ministers von Ribbentrop, des Deutschen Gesandten in Sofia von Richthofen, des Bulgarischen Gesandten in Berlin Droganoff und des Direktors der Politischen Abteilung Gesandten Altinoff, RAM 40," 5 July 1939, *ADAP*, D, VI, Doc. 617, p. 848.

18. Some of the participants have since realized the defects of the alliance. See Alexander Papagos, *The Battle of Greece, 1940–41,* tr. Pat. Eliascos (Athens, Greece, 1949), pp. 42–43.

19. Lukacz, *Great Powers,* pp. 82–83.

20. For the German economic policies in the Balkans after 1933, see below, pp. 10–11.

importance in the future history of Southeastern Europe.[21] The
Nazis were not content to participate in a partnership that
shaped the destiny of Southeastern Europe. Germany was unwilling to share control of Southeastern Europe with either her
Axis partner or the Soviet Union. Although the Nazis assured
Italy on numerous occasions that they regarded the Mediterranean as an Italian sea[22] and never openly rejected Italian requests for a specific demarcation of spheres between the Axis
partners, they did effectively evade a serious discussion of such
plans. There was no lack of Italian requests for specific demarca-
tions; indeed, the requests grew more insistent as Germany became the preponderant Axis partner. Ciano, for instance, noted
on March 22, 1939, that Mussolini wanted a definite division,[23]
and nine days later the Italian ambassador in Berlin made the
Italian position unmistakably clear. According to the State Secretary of the German Foreign Ministry, Weizsäcker, the ambassador noted: "It was . . . necessary to formulate afresh and
put into writing our mutual interests within the framework of
the Axis. [Moreover] . . . though the Mediterranean had certainly been assigned by us to the Italians, the adjacent countries
and the Danube basin also belonged to this area. . . ."[24]
Weizsäcker did not reply to this broad hint; further documents
do not indicate that the Italians ever received an answer to
their plea.

The problem of dividing Southeastern Europe into spheres
of interest was also acute in connection with the negotiations
leading to the German-Soviet Nonaggression Pact of August
1939. The formula used in the secret protocol to express the
respective German and Soviet interests in Southeastern Europe,

21. See, for example, Minister in Rumania (Fabricius), "Aufzeichnung des
Gesandten in Bukarest z. Zt. Berlin, Pol IV 5085," 7 Oct. 1937, *ADAP*, D, V, Doc.
145, p. 165.
22. Ribbentrop to Ciano (personal), 20 March 1939, *ibid.*, VI, Doc. 55, pp.
52–53. The letter is also reprinted in Ciano, *Diplomatic Papers*, pp. 278–79.
23. Ciano, *The Ciano Diaries, 1939–1943*, ed. Hugh Gibson (Garden City,
N.Y., 1946), p. 50.
24. Weizsäcker, "Aufzeichnung des Staatssekretärs, St. S. Nr. 301" (secret),
31 March 1939, *ADAP*, D, VI, Doc. 140, p. 145.

that is, that Germany had no political interests in the area, but recognized the Soviet interest in Bessarabia,[25] was intentionally vague, primarily to remove a possible impasse in the negotiations themselves,[26] but also to enable Germany to aspire further to a protectorate in the Balkans, without forcing her to state these aspirations in a written agreement.

Germany saw no reason to clarify her position until September 1940. By this time, when the balance of power in Europe had further shifted in Germany's favor, Ribbentrop had apparently convinced himself that the paragraph of the secret protocol relating to the Balkans referred to Soviet interest in Bessarabia and her complete disinterest in the rest of Southeastern Europe. Conversely, Germany had no interest in Bessarabia, but was vitally interested in the rest of the Balkan region.[27] Ribbentrop also rejected a plan, which the Russians indicated they would favor,[28] for the peaceful division of the Balkans between Italy, the Soviet Union, and Germany. As reason for the rejection of such a plan the Germans gave the platitude which they always employed when they were asked to define precise spheres: "in principle," Ribbentrop informed Moscow, Germany had no territorial ambitions in the Balkans.[29] This, however, was quite far from the truth. During the visit of the Japanese Foreign Minister Matsuoka in the spring of 1941, Ribbentrop indignantly told

25. The clause relating to the Balkans is embodied in paragraph 3 of the "Geheime Zusatzprotokoll zum Nichtangriffsvertrag zwischen Deutschland und der Union der Sozialistischen Sowjetrepubliken," 23 Aug. 1939, in United States Department of State, *Das Nationalsozialistische Deutschland und die Sovietunion,* ed. E. M. Carroll and F. T. Epstein (Berlin, 1948) (hereafter cited as *NSD*), Doc. 55, p. 86.

26. Gerhard L. Weinberg, *Germany and the Soviet Union, 1939–1941* (Leiden, 1954), p. 48.

27. Memorandum contained in Reich Foreign Minister to German Ambassador in the Soviet Union, "Tel. Nr. 1580," 3 Sept. 1940, *NSD,* Doc. 172, p. 205. It is true that Ribbentrop mentions only Germany's vital economic interest, but it must be remembered that the German ambassador was expected to inform the Russians of Ribbentrop's interpretation.

28. German Ambassador in the Soviet Union (Schulenburg) to Foreign Ministry, "Tel. Nr. 1079," 6 June 1940, *ibid.,* Doc. 133, p. 162.

29. Reich Foreign Minister to German Ambassador in the Soviet Union, "Tel. Nr. 1007," 16 June 1940, *ibid.,* Doc. 137, p. 166.

him that the Russians had demanded among other things, " 'positions of strong influence (*starke Einflusspositionen*) in the Balkans.' " He added, " 'the Führer does not go along with that sort of thing.' "[30] In effect, the Nazis' pious reiterations of their political disinterest in Southeastern Europe signified no more than a temporary unwillingness to reveal their true policy aims with respect to the Balkans. It was a policy of hypocrisy, not disinterest.

Germany's economic policy in Southeastern Europe after 1933 was subordinated to her long-range political aims. The essence of the Reich's economic policy until June 1940 was a very conscious attempt to use economic means—even to the extent of sacrificing immediate economic benefits for Germany—in order to create a favorable political climate in the Balkans. The image of a Nazi Germany using her economic dominance in the Balkans for purposes of purely economic exploitation is a distorted and to some extent naive picture of Nazi policies. Germany had long-range political and economic plans for Southeastern Europe; short-term economic exploitation was not in her interest.

Germany's acute, high-level[31] economic interest in Southeastern Europe as well as her basic policy of subordinating economic

30. Quoted in Paul Schmidt, *Statist auf diplomatischer Bühne* (Bonn, 1949), p. 530. These exact words are not used in Schmidt's official reports on the Ribbentrop-Matsuoka conversations; instead, the German Foreign Minister's views are paraphrased as follows: "[Germany] could not permit the penetration of the Balkans by the Russians." See "Aufzeichnung über die Unterredung zwischen dem RAM und dem japanischen Aussenminister Matsuoka in Berlin am 29. März 1941, Aufz. RAM 19/41," 31 March 1941, *NSD,* Doc. 226, p. 341.

31. For example, there are reports that economic relations with the Danubian countries was the major topic of discussion during the first Hitler-Mussolini meeting. See Ulrich von Hassel, *Südosteuropa—Bemerkungen zum Ausgleich der deutschen und italienischen Wirtschaftsinteressen* ([Berlin] 1941), p. 34, in National Archives Microcopy No. T-84 (hereafter cited as T-84), roll 79, frame 1367282. Hassel was the German ambassador to Italy at the time. The Foreign Ministry's report of the conversation, however, did not agree with his view. It claimed the Balkans had hardly been mentioned. See Neurath, "Memorandum by the Foreign Minister, RM 681," 19 June 1934, in United States Department of State, *Documents on German Foreign Policy, 1918–1945* (Washington, 1957) (hereafter cited as *DGFP*), Series C (hereafter cited as C), III, Doc. 19, p. 50.

profits to political goals began within the first year of the Nazi era. A memorandum written in 1938 by Carl Clodius, then deputy director of the Economic Policy Department of the German Foreign Ministry, contains the revealing notation that "the German government [has made efforts] since 1933 to develop systematically (*planmässig*) economic and thereby political relations with the countries of Southeastern Europe."[32] Examples of German economic sacrifices in her dealings with Southeastern Europe abound. As early as 1934, the Reich negotiated trade treaties with Yugoslavia and Hungary which contained some financially disadvantageous terms. Moreover, while a confidential Foreign Ministry memorandum explained that this was done in the interest of German foreign policy in the Balkans and was not intended to become general policy,[33] the practice of sacrificing financial or commercial gain for political considerations continued.

In general, German trade policies were remarkably subtle. There was the long-range expectation that political alignments would follow routinely satisfactory economic relations;[34] only rarely did the Germans exert particularly vigorous efforts to counteract momentary French or British economic offensives,[35]

32. Clodius, "Aufzeichnung über die deutsch-jugoslawischen Wirtschaftsbesprechungen für etwaige Besprechungen mit dem jugoslawischen Ministerpräsidenten Stojadinowitsch, W III SE 136," 7 Jan. 1938, *ADAP*, D, V, Doc. 159, p. 183. See also "Note sur les Relations économiques Germano-hongrois," 18 Nov. 1937, *Documents Secrèts du Ministère des Affaires éstrangères d'Allemagne,* tr. Madeleine and Michel Éristov (Paris, 1946) (hereafter cited as *Documents Secrèts*), II, Doc. 1, pp. 15–18.

33. "Circular of the Foreign Ministry," 18 June 1934, *DGFP*, C, III, Doc. 13, p. 36.

34. Minister in Rumania to Foreign Ministry, "Inhalt: Verhandlungen der deutschen und rumänischen Regierungsausschüsse in Bukarest, W III SOE 9066, Tgb. Nr. 332 IC4," 18 Nov. 1937, *ibid.*, Doc. 147, p. 168.

35. See, Minister in Bulgaria (Rümelin) to Foreign Ministry, "Tel. Nr. 83, 5. Nov. 1937, W 361g," 5 Nov. 1937, *ADAP,* D, V, Doc. 146, p. 167; Minister in Rumania, "Inhalt: Die Geschäfte von Rheinmetall mit Reschitza [Resita] [sic] betr.: Flakgeschütze und Werkzeugmachinen für Rüstungsindustrie, W 688g," 15 July 1938, *ibid.*, Doc. 121, p. 243; Deputy Director of the Economic Policy Department to Embassy in Turkey, "Telegramm Nr. 134 zu W III 7009," 15 Sept. 1938; *ibid.*, Doc. 552, pp. 619–20; Funk to Schwerin-Krosigk, 2 Sept. 1938, as quoted in *ibid.*, p. 620, n. 1.

or to assure political success for a Balkan statesman who was
considered friendly toward the Reich.[36] Only one commodity,
arms and munitions, was expected to return immediate political
dividends. Bulgaria's price for an arms credit was to be her signature on the Anti-Comintern Pact,[37] and Yugoslavia, in return
for similar German services, was strongly urged to do the same
as well as dissociate herself from the Balkan Entente.[38]

Neither Italy nor the Southeastern European nations were
unaware of the dangers of German predominance in the Southeastern European countries,[39] and at least some of the Balkan
countries attempted to maintain a degree of independence by
reducing their trade in strategic goods with Germany.[40] However,
there was relatively little that the Balkan nations could do, un-
aided, against the growing shadow of German hegemony in

36. Clodius, "Aufzeichnung für die am 30. Juni beginnenden deutsch-türkischen
Wirtschaftsverhandlungen," 29 June 1939, *ibid.,* Doc. 545, pp. 608–09.

37. Weizsäcker to the Legation in Bulgaria, "Telegramm Nr. 104 Pol IV,"
9 June 1939, *ADAP,* D, VI, Doc. 500, p. 573.

38. See the memorandum by Weizsäcker, "St. S. Nr. 545," 8 July 1939, *ibid.,*
Doc. 637, p. 741; the memorandum by the director of the Political Department
(Woermann), 15 July 1939, *ibid.,* Doc. 675, pp. 778–79; Foreign Ministry to
Legation in Yugoslavia, "W 290g" (secret), 27 Feb. 1939, *ibid.,* V, Doc. 307,
p. 339. This discussion of the German economic policy in Southeastern Europe
in the thirties has been deliberately restricted to a discussion of some specific
examples of the subordination of German economic aims to political considerations in order to show the existence of long-range German political aims even
at this date. The general subject of Nazi economic tactics in the area has
been described in previously published works. See particularly the excellent
article by Wilhelm Treue, "Das Dritte Reich und die Westmächte auf dem
Balkan," *Vierteljahrshefte für Zeitgeschichte,* I (Jan. 1953), 45–64.

39. The German ambassador in Italy reported Mussolini's distrust of German
policy in the Balkans as early as 1934. See, Hassel to Foreign Ministry, "Tel.
No. 242 of Oct. 23," 23. Oct. 1934, *DGFP,* C, III, Doc. 266, p. 524. See also Ciano,
Ciano's Hidden Diary, 1937–1938, ed. and tr. Andreas Mayor (New York, 1953)
(hereafter cisted as *Ciano Diary, 1937–38*), entries 16 May 1938, p. 116, 13 June
1938, p. 127, 22 Oct. 1938, p. 181, 5 Dec. 1937, p. 41; *Ciano Diaries, 1939–43,* entry
18 Aug. 1939, p. 123; Minister in Hungary (Erdmannsdorff) to Weizsäcker, 7
March 1938, *Documents Secrèts,* II, Doc. 8, pp. 33–36.

40. "Aufzeichnung über die Versorgungslage auf dem Betriebsstoffgebiet und
ihre Auswirkungen für die Wehrmacht," 9 March 1936, Doc. 1301-PS, in International Military Tribunal, *Trial of Major War Criminals Before the International
Military Tribunal, Nuremberg 14 November 1945–10 October 1946* (Nuremberg,
1948) (hereafter cited as *IMT*), XXVII, 129–30.

Southeastern Europe. Any large-scale refusal to trade with the Reich would have meant economic suicide since by 1938 Germany was not only the single largest supplier of the Balkans, but, even more important, their primary purchaser.[41]

The Western democracies did little to alert the Balkan nations against the German danger. France and Britain either refused to grasp or were unable to understand the political implications of the German economic drive in the Balkans. They certainly ignored the dangers before 1936,[42] and there are indications that as late as the spring of 1939 the British government had no particular objections to assigning to Germany all of the Balkans as an economic sphere of influence.[43] Western actions outside Southeastern Europe presented an equally discouraging spectacle. The Anschluss, which opened the door to the Balkans for Germany, was accomplished while France and Great Britain stood idly by.[44] The Munich settlement followed in October 1938; and in March 1939 the remainder of Czechoslovakia became a German protectorate. Again, the Western powers acquiesced, and the Southeastern European nations could only accommodate themselves to new realities.

In view of their own inadequate strength and the lack of effective support from the Western nations, at least some of the Southeastern European nations clung to the hope that Italy would safeguard them against the German danger.[45] Such a policy, however, involved a number of risks. While Italy had no illusions about Germany's political designs in the area,[46] and it was certainly in her interest to oppose any German attempts

41. For the increase in the German share of Balkan trade, see Germany, Statistisches Reichsamt, *Statistisches Jahrbuch für das Deutsche Reich 1938* (Berlin, 1938), pp. 127*–29* [sic].

42. Treue, "Balkan," p. 48.

43. For a contemporary comment on German conditions in the Balkans, see the editorial "Dr. Funk's Progress," *The Times* (London), 20 Oct. 1938, p. 15; for a postwar analysis of the British position, see Martin Gilbert and Richard Gott, *The Appeasers* (Boston, 1963) pp. 194–97, 213, 227.

44. Boris Celovsky, *Das Münchener Abkommen von 1938* (Stuttgart, 1958), p. 138.

45. Bullock, *Hitler*, p. 437.

46. *Ciano Diary, 1937–38*, entries 13 March and 13 June 1938, pp. 88, 127.

to obtain hegemony in Southeastern Europe, her own territorial ambitions in Yugoslavia and Albania made her a rather unsatisfactory protector of Balkan independence and integrity. Actually by the end of the decade, even the choice of Italy or Germany was largely illusionary. Mussolini had already decided to pursue his own narrowly nationalistic policy at the side of the Reich,[47] rather than risk Germany's wrath by protecting the integrity of the Balkans.

The beginning of the World War II, then, found the countries of Southeastern Europe in a political and economic straitjacket. Whatever sympathies they may have had with the cause of the Western powers,[48] political and economic realities made any significant opposition to German leadership an absurdity. The early victories of the German armies seemed to confirm the Reich's invincibility. After the German victory in Poland, and particularly after the defeat of France, the Balkan nations became increasingly convinced that Germany would indeed be the new master of the Continent, and that only a more active collaboration with the Third Reich would serve their national interests.[49]

Even more important for the history of the organization and the policies that are the subject of this study, however, was the effect which the German military victories had on the National Socialist elite itself. German confidence increased in direct proportion to the Reich's successes on the battlefield. In the very early days of World War II, Germany had been favorably inclined toward an Italian proposal for a neutral Danubian bloc

47. Cf. Ciano's statement that as long as there were 80 million Germans in the heart of Europe, "for Rome and Belgrade German friendship is a fatality, oppressive perhaps, but very real." *Ibid.*, entry 13 March 1938, p. 88.

48. The Germans themselves regarded the Balkan nations as very unreliable factors. See OKW to the Foreign Ministry, "Betr.: Ausfuhrgenehmigungen bezw. Verbote, OKW Nr. 66f 20/a Wstb. WW: VII, 39g," 22 July 1939. This is an enclosure to Wiehl, "Aufzeichnung über die Lieferung von Kriegsgerät," 22 July 1939, *ADAP*, D, VI, Doc. 703, p. 808.

49. Legation in Yugoslavia to Foreign Ministry, "Tel. No. 320 of April 30," 1 May 1940, *DGFP*, D, IX, Doc. 182, p. 258; Minister in Rumania to Foreign Ministry, "Tel. No. 808 of May 29, 1940," *ibid.*, Doc. 345, p. 466; Lukacz, *Eastern Europe*, p. 291.

under Italy's leadership.[50] Two months later, after the defeat
of Poland had been fully appreciated in Berlin, the Third Reich
had no further use for neutral blocs in the Balkans.[51] By then,
the time of Germany's alleged political disinterest in Southeastern Europe had passed.

German self-confidence reached new heights after the defeat
of France. Perhaps the German minister in Slovakia expressed
the new German attitude most clearly. He wrote, "the time has
now come to make it perfectly plain once again, particularly
with reference to the countries of Southeastern Europe that
Slovakia is in our *Lebensraum*, that is, that our wishes alone
count."[52] These statements are an accurate reflection of the confidence and consciousness of power which the Third Reich felt
after it had defeated its enemies on the Continent. Long-term
National Socialist control of Europe seemed a reality; plans for
the postwar hegemony could now be drawn up. In the midst
of this atmosphere of confidence in the ability of Germany to
create her New Order, the *Südosteuropa-Gesellschaft* began its
activities as an agency which was to play an important part
in establishing and administering the New Europe.

50. *Ciano Diaries, 1939–43*, entry 28 Sept. 1939, p. 152.
51. Minister in Rumania to Foreign Ministry, "Tel. No. 916 of Nov. 27,"
28 Nov. 1939, *DGFP*, D, VIII, Doc. 392, p. 457.
52. Memorandum by the Minister to Slovakia (Bernard), 25 June 1940, *ibid.*,
X, Doc. 17, p. 18.

2

A Case Study in Neo-Darwinism and Neofeudalism: The Organizational History and Structure of the SOEG

In February 1940 the Reich Ministry of Economics created a new agency, the *Südosteuropa-Gesellschaft* (SOEG, Southeastern Europe Society), with headquarters in Vienna. The formal jurisdictional relationship between the Society and its parent organization was always nebulous. Although it remained a political and financial subsidiary of the Economics Ministry throughout its four-and-one-half-year history, the SOEG quickly gained a largely autonomous position. It achieved its position of relative independence in association with the ministry, that is, its own development was an integral part of the growth and interaction of the entire National Socialist governmental and administrative structure. For this reason the SOEG's establishment, the development of its internal structure, and the growth of its functions can only be put into sharp focus when they are viewed against the larger

16

background of the consequences that resulted from the National Socialists' deliberate destruction of the traditional German bureaucratic and administrative system.

The modern *Rechtsstaat* (that is, a state based on law as opposed to an arbitrary regime), which Germany was before 1933, is characterized by a number of identifiable factors. In it a relatively sharp division exists between the state, as represented by the administrative bureaucracy, and the citizens of the country.[1] The state allows a citizen to structure a large part of his life; beyond insuring that his private activities do not infringe on the basic rights of his fellow residents, the state, particularly in a democratic Rechtsstaat, sharply limits its sphere of control or influence in the life or the citizen.

The Rechtsstaat is also characterized by a specific type of administrative apparatus, the bureaucracy. In the course of centuries, this institution has evolved to carry out those governmental functions that even in a Rechtsstaat cannot (or should not) be performed by the citizens themselves. Within the permanent bureaucracy, power is highly institutionalized and largely depersonalized; the degree of authority of individual chiefs and subchiefs in the apparatus is based primarily on legally defined functions, not on specific authority arbitrarily assigned to a forceful personality. A modern bureaucracy is also marked by a high degree of rationality:[2] jurisdictions within the system are, or should be, clearly established, and the purpose of administration is accomplished by rigidly specializing the tasks of the individual bureaucrat (or his office), and thus, for the permanent administrative staff, the special task becomes in effect the routine job.[3]

As in any institution controlled by humans, discrepancies between the ideal and the actual will appear in the work of bureau-

1. Franz Neumann, "Notes on the Theory of Dictatorship," in *The Democratic and the Authoritarian State: Essays in Political and Legal Theory,* ed. Herbert Marcuse (Glencoe, Ill., 1957), p. 244.

2. Max Weber, *The Theory of Social and Economic Organization,* ed. Talcott Parsons, tr. A. M. Henderson and Talcott Parsons (New York, 1947), pp. 320–21, 339.

3. Victor A. Thompson, *Modern Organization* (New York, 1961), p. 14.

cracies. To assure that such deviations do not go beyond tolerated and reasonable limits is precisely why a Rechtsstaat that
has assumed the form of a liberal democracy encourages free,
constant, and pungent criticism and surveillance of the state
administrative apparatus through the organs of public opinion
and representative parliamentary institutions.

The civil administration of the Weimar Republic adhered
rather faithfully to these basic principles of efficient and effective
administration. The post World War I German national administrative corps continued the Prussian and imperial traditions
of efficiency, honesty, and relative incorruptibility. The Weimar
Republic, at least theoretically, strengthened these foundations
of good administration by exposing the civil service to public
criticism and by balancing the widely prevalent narrow caste
feeling of the Prussian bureaucrat with a greater emphasis on
the citizens' individual and organizational rights. It is now obvious that the Republic never succeeded in breaking down the
antidemocratic caste feelings of its civil servants, but it is also
clear that the Republic possessed, insofar as administrative procedures can assure such qualities, a well-nigh ideal national bureaucracy: jurisdictions between governmental organs were well
defined, matters of procedure were adequately and uniformly
regulated—after 1926 there was even a joint procedural code
for all national ministries.[4]

The Weimar Rechtsstaat came to an end on January 30, 1933.
It was replaced by Hitler's regime, as typical an example of
the modern totalitarian state as its predecessor had been of a
liberal democracy. The National Socialist dictatorship began almost immediately to remold and restructure Germany and the
German civil service along totalitarian lines. It obliterated the
barrier between society and the state; the modern totalitarian
state does not permit its citizens to organize any substantial
part of their lives in the absence of state control or influence.[5]

4. Arnold Brecht and Comstock Glaser, *The Art and Technique of Administration in German Ministries* (Cambridge, Mass., 1940), pp. 7–9. For the German
interministerial code, see "General Code of Administrative Procedure in the
German Reich Ministries of September 2, 1926," in *ibid.*, pp. 45–167.

5. Neumann, *Democratic and Authoritarian State*, pp. 244–45.

Instead, the totalitarian state organizes all aspects of human life in a series of vast, bureaucratic, mass organizations, all controlled by the state or, what is the same under a totalitarian system, the single state party permitted by the regime.[6]

The totalitarian regime is not content to break down the walls that shield the private life of the citizen from state or party interference. It also remolds the structure and above all the behavioral norms of the governmental bureaucracy to conform structurally and behavioristically to the totalitarian state's prototype, the monolithic mass party. While the bureaucracy of a Rechtsstaat is ideally centered on administration and efficiency, the focal point of all institutionalized activities in the totalitarian state is power oriented. Consequently, traditions of administrative or political autonomy are deliberately destroyed since they block the path toward increased power for the central leadership.[7]

The administrative changes initiated by the National Socialist regime rapidly stifled or destroyed political life and individual freedom in Germany, and it is particularly ironic that they achieved this effect behind an impressive facade of apparently increased administrative rationality and efficiency. In the absence of public criticism, the barrage of paper plans by the Party-controlled press organs dazzled even educated contemporary observers.[8] Actually, public administration became far less rather than more rational and efficient. The dictator in such a regime craves personal power; the administrative procedures of a Rechtsstaat depersonalize power in order to prevent the possibility of abuses of personal power. It is thus clear that the modern totalitarian leader can have no interest in improving

6. *Ibid.;* William Kornhauser, *The Politics of Mass Society* (Glencoe, Ill., 1959), pp. 41, 62; Carl J. Friedrich and Zbigniew K. Brzezinski, *Totalitarian Dictatorship and Autocracy* (Cambridge, Mass., 1956), p. 19.

7. For a detailed analysis of the administrative "reforms" in the years 1933–34, see Karl Dietrich Bracher et al., *Die nationalsozialistische Machtergreifung* (Cologne, 1960), pp. 9, 12–13, 488–89, 509, 600, 602, 611–12, 612, n. 122.

8. See, for example, Albert Lepawsky, "The Nazis Reform the Reich," *American Political Science Review*, XXX (April 1936), 324–50; Roger H. Wells, "The Liquidation of the German Länder," *ibid.*, pp. 350–61.

the fabric of public administration; his goal of personal power can be realized only with the destruction of the administrative fabric of the Rechtsstaat. In the interest of increasing Hitler's personal power, the new masters of Germany blurred lines of division between the government and the mass party they led. Similarly, carefully established jurisdictional patterns within the state administration were destroyed, with the result that units within the bureaucracy were actually encouraged to battle one another for administrative powers. Lines of coordination and liaison, previously constructed with great care to expedite the smooth flow of administrative business, became muddled and interrupted.[9]

Perhaps the most striking characteristic of the National Socialist system was the repersonalization of administrative power. Hitler assigned bureaucratic power not to an office, but to an individual. The practice was equally prevalent among the various subleaders, so that the rational, impersonal aspects of bureaucratic administration—salient characteristics of all well-organized modern bureaucracies—were deliberately eliminated from the National Socialist system. In their place came the personal qualities and connections of individual officials. The primary key to organizational success in the Third Reich was not the formally delegated, institutionalized authority, but rather the personalities of the individual officials that headed the Party or state agency. Far from making the regime more monolithic, Hitler's administrative reforms placed the administration of the German totalitarian society into a normless environment. The immediate, intended result was the rebirth of personalized administration. The Third Reich actually occasioned the rebirth of a type of feudalism, in which the constant struggle for survival and expansion in the bureaucratic maze was punctuated by an equally constant series of formal and informal armistices and regroupings, such as *Personalunionen,* involving the joint creation of a third agency by two or more other offices, appeals by opposing officials for arbitration by a third agency, and the disintegration of a rival agency's defense by the infiltration of a

9. Bracher, *Machtergreifung,* pp. 11, 600, 611.

presumably subordinate representative. And these were only some of the forms that the perpetual struggle for power within the system assumed.[10] In the absence of institutionalized, depersonalized behavior norms, leaders and subleaders in National Socialist Germany turned to personal relations as the base of institutional and organizational interactions.

The consequences of this type of administrative regression were on the one hand administrative chaos: officials spent far more time fighting rival agencies than they devoted to the actual execution of policy. Despite its imposing facade of pseudorationality, the Hitlerian system very quickly reached a nadir in administrative efficiency perhaps matched only by another modern totalitarian state, the Soviet Union during the Stalin era.[11] On the other hand, it is equally true that along with the breakdown of the administrative patterns of the Rechtsstaat, bureaucratic chaos brought opportunities for power aggrandizement unknown in less feudalistic times. Since the influence and power of bureaucratic officials within the National Socialist system depended far more on such factors as ruthlessness, personal connections, and the financial or military resources at their disposal than it did on the formally assigned jurisdictions of the offices or organizations they headed, it was not impossible to find officials who would normally have been destined to a mundane life at the secondary or tertiary administrative level at the head of relatively large accumulations of power.

The SOEG was founded, grew, and declined in this neofeudal environment. Its development is the story of an agency that took advantage of opportunities to rise from a paper organization with no clearly defined powers to become one of the more important agencies concerned with the planning and execution of German policies in Southeastern Europe. Its organizational failures and

10. See Robert Koehl, "Feudal Aspects of National Socialism," *American Political Science Review,* LIV (Dec. 1960), 921–33.

11. See, Julian Towster, *Political Power in the USSR 1917–1947* (New York, 1948), pp. 402–04; Merle Fainsod, *How Russia is Ruled* (Cambridge, Mass., 1953), pp. 328–29.

successes are directly attributable to the personal abilities (or inclinations) and personal tactics of its chief officials. The tactlessness and vanity of some of its top leaders almost cost the Society its life in the early weeks of its existence. On the other hand, the later tactfulness, finesse, and shrewd use of personal friendships by other officials not only rescued the SOEG from oblivion but eventually enveloped it with prestige and influence.

The SOEG was legally established as a registered club (*eingetragener Verein*) on February 8, 1940, although the date marks little more than the beginning of the organization's formal existence. At its establishment, the Society was not really an institution, but the corporate name of three ambitious officials: its protector (*Schirmherr*), the Reich Minister of Economics, Walther Funk; its president, Josef Bürckel, then Reich Commissioner for the Reunification of Austria and the German Reich; and its executive secretary (*Hauptgeschäftsführer*), August Heinrichsbauer.[12] Together these three neofeudal barons attempted to establish a new organizational fief.

In terms of personalities, the group was a rather ill-matched trio. Formally, the most important partner was Funk, who was a latecomer to the National Socialist movement, not joining the NSDAP until 1930, when he was forty years old. Until then he had been a journalist; during the 1920's he edited the influential *Berliner Börsen-Zeitung*. However, even before he formally associated himself with Hitler's movement, his political and economic views were those of the extreme right in Germany. He was a conservative in his economic thinking, and antiparliamentary, antidemocratic, and nationalistic in his political philosophy. In 1930 Funk apparently felt that the National Socialists were the wave of the future, and in the summer of that year he joined the Party. Hitler assigned him the task of

---

12. Südosteuropa-Gesellschaft (Hans Fischböck, Walter Rafelsberger, Karl Wilhelm Lehr, August Heinrichsbauer, Oskar van Raay, Hubert Graf Hardegg), "Niederschrift über die am 8. Feber 1940 in Wien 62, Strasse der Julikämpfer 19, abgehaltene konostituierende Versammlung des Vereins Südosteuropa-Gesellschaft mit dem Sitze in Wien 110, Hockegasse 73/75," National Archives Microcopy No. T-71 (hereafter cited as T-71), roll 78, frames 579700–05.

persuading business leaders to make financial contributions to the NSDAP. After the National Socialists seized power, Funk was appointed state secretary of the Reich Ministry of Propaganda and Public Enlightenment under Joseph Goebbels. There he remained until 1938 when Hitler, who needed a pliant personality willing to take a back seat to Göring and his Four Year Plan, appointed him Minister of Economics. Funk never exhibited noteworthy leadership qualities, his capabilities in the actual administration of an economy were limited, and he remained content to stay in Göring's shadow throughout his ministerial career.[13]

If Funk's political career marks him with all the characteristics of a German upper middle class opportunist during the Weimar Republic and the Third Reich, the life of Josef Bürckel is that of a lower middle class official who was never engaged in the sociopolitical value system of the Republic and who found the only outlet for his frustrations in the violence and terror of far-right activist groups. Bürckel was born in 1895 in the town of Lingenfels in the Palatinate. He was active in far-right political circles during the later 1920's and became a NSDAP deputy in the Reichstag in 1930, although he continued to earn his living as a schoolteacher until 1934, when Hitler appointed him plenipotentiary for Saar affairs. After March 1, 1935, Bürckel became Reich Commissioner for the Saar. He apparently remained in Saarbrücken until March 1938, when Hitler found a new use for his "reunification" skills and appointed him to his Viennese post. Bürckel's personality was the opposite of Funk's. Funk was timid, careful, pathetically anxious not to offend the top National Socialist leaders on whose good will his presence in the circles of the mighty depended. Bürckel, by contrast, was a blusterer. Unused to and untrained for the major administrative posts that the Third Reich sent his way,

---

13. On Funk, see Paul Oestreich, *Walther Funk, ein Leben für die Wirtschaft* (Munich, 1940), pp. 10, 78, 86–87, 92; Gustave M. Gilbert, *Nuremberg Diary* (New York, 1947), p. 187; Great Britain Ministry of Economic Warfare, *Who's Who in Germany and Austria* (restricted) (London, 1945) (hereafter cited as *Who's Who in Germany*), Part II, p. 43.

he stood foursquare at his desk and attempted to shout down all extraregime and intraregime opposition that stood in his way.[14]

The SOEG was fortunate in having as the third member of the founding trio a far more balanced and able man. The career of Heinrichsbauer, who was to become the most important official within the SOEG, illustrates with particular poignancy the effect that political unreliability and personal connections had upon the rise and fall of responsible officials in the Third Reich. He was born in Bochum in 1890 and spent most of his professional career in the 1920's in various capacities with the Ruhr coal industry in Essen. Like many of his fellow industrialists, Heinrichsbauer was politically active during the postwar decade. He became a personal friend of Gregor Strasser, and while he never joined the NSDAP, his wife was an early member. Heinrichsbauer also became a friend of Funk and seems to have had some part in Funk's decision to join the Party ostensibly to keep it from embarking on an anticapitalist course. In the twenties, then, Heinrichsbauer shrewdly attempted to maintain cordial connections with both the more anticapitalist and the probusiness wings of the Party. After the National Socialists came to power, Heinrichsbauer had to pay a penalty for his association with Strasser. He lost his position with the Ruhr industry and had to support himself as best he could by running a retail coal outlet. He was not rescued until 1940 when Funk, who had not exposed himself in his political dealings, offered him the position as executive secretary in the SOEG.[15]

14. On Bürckel's biographical data, see German Reichstag, *Der Grossdeutsche Reichstag 1938 IV, Wahlperiode (nach dem 30. Januar 1933)*, ed. E. Kienast (Berlin, 1938) (hereafter cited as *Grossdeutscher Reichstag*), p. 175. The assessment of his personality is based upon readings of his speeches and internal documents and on additional biographical data supplied to the author by Dr. Heinrichsbauer in a conversation with him on August 7, 1961, in Bonn, Germany. This conversation is hereafter cited as Heinrichsbauer Interview.

15. For Heinrichsbauer's views during the 1920's, see the following of his writings: *Das Bergbaumonopol* (Essen, 1919); *Die Kohlennot, der Ruin Deutschlands* (Berlin-Zehlendorf, 1920); *Der Sozialismus im Endkampf um die Kommune, weitere Erfolge der Novemberwahlen* (Essen, 1929). Funk speaks of Heinrichsbauer's influence on his decision to join the NSDAP in "Statement Prepared

The actual establishment of the SOEG made no impact on organizational life in National Socialist Germany. In February 1940 the Society had nothing with which to begin actual operations except a name and some chief officers. It lacked clearly defined functions. It even lacked office space; Heinrichsbauer's apartment became the SOEG's first official address.[16] The question is thus posed as to why the SOEG's sponsor arranged the hurried founding session. An examination of the wider circumstances surrounding the actual charter meeting reveals that the establishment of the SOEG represented another phase of the continuing bureaucratic infighting in the Third Reich. In early 1940, the Minister of Economics saw an unclaimed administrative jurisdiction, that of the formulation and coordination of German-Balkan relations, and the SOEG became his "legal" stake in the as yet unclaimed territory. That the new agency had neither an office nor specific functions did not matter: the need of the moment was a formally existing agency that could officially claim control of a piece of loose administrative power.

The Economics Ministry was not the first agency in Nazi Germany to show more than ordinary interest in the jurisdictional area "Southeastern Europe." Alfred Rosenberg's Foreign Policy Office (*Aussenpolitisches Amt*) had toyed with—though not pursued—the idea of establishing an important Southeast institute in Vienna as early as 1938.[17] But it was not until the beginning of the war and the subsequent expectation of an early German victory in the spring of 1940 that the whole field of relations

---

by Walther Funk on the Relationship of German Industry to the Party and National Socialist Leadership of the State," Document EC-440, in *Nazi Conspirary and Aggression*, ed. Office of the United States Chief of the Prosecution of Axis Criminality (Washington, 1947) (hereafter cited as *NCA*), Supplement A, p. 1194. The name of Heinrichsbauer is incorrectly spelled Reinrichsbauer in this document. Most of the personal data was supplied by Dr. Heinrichsbauer himself—the Heinrichsbauer Interview.

16. SOEG, "Niederschrift über die . . . konstituierende Versammlung . . . ," T-71, roll 78, frames 579700, 579703–04.

17. See NSDAP, Aussenpolitisches Amt. Stabsleiter to Schmitt (of the *Völkischer Beobachter* in Vienna), "38051/38," 5 Aug. 1938 (personal), National Archives Microcopy No. T-454 (hereafter cited as T-454), roll 53, frame 00816.

between the Reich and its Continental neighbors became an acute and imminent issue. Germany's victory would usher in a new phase of dependency on the Reich for the countries of Southeastern Europe. They would cease to be independent foreign nations and become instead subservient units in a German-dominated Europe.[18] Among the Reich's bureaucratic jurisdictions, the new status of the Balkan nations would usher in a period of realigning old competencies: as foreign nations, they were clearly within the province of the Foreign Ministry, but as components in a European *Grossraum* (sphere of influence) this would no longer be true. Since the Economics Ministry supervised the development of economic life in Germany, should it not also—as a logical extension of its jurisdictional powers—control economic life in those parts of Europe that would in the future be subordinate partners in the German Grossraum? Moreover, since economic affairs are clearly interrelated with all other aspects of interpeople relations, should not the ministry, as the first German agency to concern itself seriously with the jurisdictional field of formulating and executing German policies in Southeastern Europe, control and coordinate the activities of other German agencies concerned with the Balkans as well? The SOEG was the organizational realization of such ministerial ambitions. It was intended as a camouflaged agency of the ministry, centralized in structure and endowed with broad powers of supervision and coordination—first for German Southeast agencies operating only in Vienna and Austria, but later also for those of the Reich as a whole.[19] In effect, the SOEG was the means through which the Ministry of Economics attempted to make

18. See Lothar Gruchmann, *Nationalsozialistische Grossraumordnung* (Stuttgart, 1962), pp. 105–09.

19. SOEG (Heinrichsbauer), "Tätigkeitsbericht der Südosteuropa-Gesellschaft (hereafter cited as "Tätigkeitsbericht Mai 1942") T-84, roll 196, frames 1562156–57; Heinrichsbauer to Funk, 2 June 1940, T-71, roll 52, frames 447539–40; SOEG, Hauptgeschäftsführer, "Tätigkeit und Aufbau der Südosteuropa-Gesellschaft" (hereafter cited as "Tätigkeit Juni 1941"), T-84, roll 196, frame 1562253; SOEG, "Arbeitsplan der Südosteuropa-Gesellschaft," 1940, *ibid.*, frame 1562262; Heinrichsbauer to Kratz (Berlin representative of the *Reichsstatthalter* in Vienna), 23 March 1940, T-71, roll 72, frame 572338.

the execution of German policy toward Southeastern Europe a fief of Funk's ministry.

Funk's decision to locate his new subsidiary in Vienna rather than Berlin, and to give it the form of a private club, may, in view of the prevailing bureaucratization and centralization in the Third Reich, seem surprising and naive. Yet some shrewd calculations lay behind these decisions as well. Funk apparently felt that the establishment of the SOEG in Vienna was in line with the thoughts of the most future-oriented among the National Socialist planners. At least some of the numerous Grossraum projects circulating in Germany in the spring and summer of 1940 envisioned a large degree of decentralization in the administration of postwar Europe. While Berlin would become the capital of Europe, much of the actual administrative work would be channeled through regional central offices. The regional offices would be located not in Berlin, but in cities that were geographically closer to the area of control. Among such subcapitals, Vienna was, of course, the logical seat of German agencies controlling the Balkans.[20]

Even if the plans for regional subcapitals were not put into effect, locating the SOEG in Vienna had some obvious advantages for the Economics Ministry. The SOEG's shy and easily discouraged protector had become Minister of Economics precisely because Göring regarded him as a pliable individual.[21] For such a man, the prospect of defending his creation against the inevitably ruthless and bitter attacks of Berlin officialdom could only be viewed with horror. Vienna, on the other hand, was removed—although as the SOEG discovered, not very far—from the center of at least the fiercest bureaucratic jousting.

20. Baldur von Schirach, "Wien und der Südostraum," in *Tagung der Südosteuropa-Gesellschaft und der Deutschen Gesellschaft der Wirtschaft in Böhmen und Mähren,* 18–21 Dec. 1941 (Prague, 1942) (hereafter cited as *Prag Tagung*), p. 25. See also the draft of SOEG, Gruppe Ernährung und Landwirtschaft (Rischka) to Reichsministerium für Ernährung und Landwirtschaft (Ministerialdirektor Dr. Moritz), 24 June 1941, T-71, roll 52, frame 448307; Adolf Hitler, *Hitler's Secret Conversations,* ed. Hugh R. Trevor-Roper (New York, 1953), entry 1–2 Nov. 1941, p. 86.
21. See Bullock, *Hitler,* p. 376.

While the minister was psychologically unable to protect the SOEG against open aggression by a stronger personality or agency, he did attempt to strengthen his creation through liberal financial support. It is not clear how the SOEG financed its operation in 1940 (presumably Viennese city and Party funds were advanced to it), but in March 1941 Funk allocated 1,000,000 Reichmarks (RM) to the SOEG. The same amount found its way to Vienna in October of the following year, and a final payment came from the minister in February 1944. The amount of the third payment is not known, but since Funk seems to have paid the SOEG round sums of RM 1,000,000, it can perhaps be assumed that the third tranfer also involved this amount. Assuming this to be true, the SOEG had in liquid financial assets a total of RM 3,000,000 at its disposal between April 1941 and about October 1944 (when the Society all but ceased to operate), or about RM 71,000 per month.[22] These amounts were more than sufficient for the Society's purposes and activities: the SOEG's 1942 budget (the only one for which figures are available) included total expenditures of RM 606,000, an average of RM 50,500 per month.[23]

The SOEG received all of its financial support from public funds;[24] it was a club without members or dues. The "club" aspect of the Society, however, was an essential part of its actual purpose; it was largely a propagandistic screen erected to hide the SOEG's true nature. As a club, the SOEG was planned as an institutionalization of the German conception of a British original. In the eyes of National Socialists the English club was a very useful organization: under the cloak of private social functions, the British government busily and effortlessly pursued its

22. Heinrichsbauer to Funk, 3 April 1941, T-71, roll 14, frame 404804; Heinrichsbauer to Kratz, 9 Oct. 1942, T-71, roll 52, frame 447687; Augenthaler (Heinrichsbauer's successor as executive secretary) to Funk, 23 Feb. 1944, T-71, roll 14, frame 404775.

23. Of the RM 606,000, RM 530,000 were to be spent on the SOEG's operations in Vienna; RM 71,000 and RM 5,000, respectively, covered the expenses of its branch establishments in Zagreb and Bratislava. See SOEG, "Aktion Gen. v. Unruh-Meldung Soeg, 25.5.1943," 25 May 1943, T-71, roll 65, frame 563775.

24. *Ibid.*

official aims and policies.[25] The choice of Vienna, aside from the other considerations, was also a part of the club facade. The old Habsburg capital was "Germany" in the minds of most Balkan business and cultural leaders, and the SOEG expected to capitalize on this association.[26]

Both its financial resources and its physical location were only aids in achieving the SOEG's foremost intrasystem goal: to control and to coordinate the activities of the German Balkan agencies in Austria and the Reich.[27] Here, the Society's first task was clearly to subordinate the Balkan agencies in Vienna to its control. In the early spring of 1940 this did not appear an unreasonable goal. After all, the SOEG had a broad jurisdictional mandate from a Reich ministry and its president, Bürckel, was the highest Party and state official in Austria. The Society confidently began its active operations with a frontal assault on the fields of competency of other Viennese agencies.[28] The initial attack was a complete and immediate failure. It may seem surprising that the SOEG, backed by the Ministry of Economics, was unable to overcome the opposition of local Viennese agencies, but the outcome of the initial battle is not startling when

25. See, for example, Kurt von Rischka, "Die mögliche Bedeutung der Südosteuropa-Gesselschaft als Organ der neuen europäischen Wirtschaftsgemeinschaft," 25 May 1943, T-71, roll 14, frame 404851.

26. Although the club side of the SOEG was never very important, neither was it wholly ignored. Not long after it was established, the Society negotiated the right to use Vienna's fashionable Rennclub for its public functions. See Heinrichsbauer to Hans Fischböck (at this time the SOEG's vice-president), 19 July 1940, T-71, roll 61, frame 559168–69, and Fischböck to Heinrichsbauer, 25 July 1940, *ibid,* frame 559167.

27. "Tätigkeitsbericht Mai 1942," T-84, roll 196, frames 1562156–57; Heinrichsbauer to Funk, 2 June 1940, T-71, roll 52, frames 447539–40; "Tätigkeit Juni 1941," T-84, roll 196, frame 1562253; SOEG, "Arbeitsplan der Südosteuropa-Gesellschaft," 1940, *ibid.,* frame 1562262; Heinrichsbauer to Kratz, 23 March 1940, T-71, roll 72, frame 572338.

28. This information is based upon remarks made by Professor Hermann Gross, in 1940 head of the I. G. Farben's Vienna branch office (*Volkswirtschaftliche Abteilung*) and now associated with the University of Munich, to the author during a conversation with him on July 6, 1961, in Kiel (the interview is hereafter cited as Gross Interview), and the Heinrichsbauer Interview. According to the latter, Bürckel was responsible for these early attempts. Heinrichsbauer claims that he saw the futility of this approach almost immediately.

it is viewed against the background of the overall breakdown of lines of administrative procedure and jurisdiction in National Socialist Germany. In the Weimar Rechtsstaat, a broad mandate from a Reich ministry was a decisive factor in jurisdictional quarrels at the local or regional level; in the Third Reich the degree of authority of various administrative agencies was by no means clearly established. In deliberately eroding the administrative foundations of the Rechtsstaat in the interest of increasing his own personal power, Hitler had intentionally blurred the previously established lines of jurisdictional demarcation.[29]

The power of Reich ministries under the Hitlerian system varied sharply. Generally speaking, a ministry's jurisdiction was unassailable only in fields of administration that fell clearly into its traditional spheres of authority. If a ministry (or other agency) intended to venture beyond these routinely assigned areas of competency it had to be prepared for a jurisdictional battle, unless the head of the agency had previously obtained a personal grant of power from Hitler extending his agency's sphere of authority to include the questionable area before he began his trespassing attempt. The SOEG's claims of authority fell into neither category. Hitler had not conferred special powers of control over German Balkan policies on Funk, and the ministry could hardly derive this authority from its previous supply of administrative power. The outcome of the battles between the SOEG and its Viennese opponents was thus a foregone conclusion: the SOEG might flourish a sweeping mandate, but since its grant of authority did not come from the only real source of power in the Third Reich—Hitler—the Viennese local agencies remained unassailable in their own more clearly and more authoritatively delineated spheres.[30]

Besides seriously misjudging the basis of jurisdictional power in National Socialist Germany, the SOEG was also beset with other difficulties in the early days of its existence. The concept of decentralizing the administration of the Reich was at best

29. Bracher, *Machtergreifung*, pp. 9, 11.
30. "Tätigkeitsbericht Mai 1942" T-84, roll 196, frame 1562156; Heinrichsbauer to Funk, 2 June 1940, T-71, roll 52, frame 447539.

rather premature. As yet, all major decisions were made in Berlin, and the Viennese offices of all Reich agencies were branches with very limited powers of decision. The SOEG soon found itself fighting rear guard actions, while the major battlefield remained in Berlin.[31] The SOEG's club character created a further problem. The private club facade may have been the proper one for the Society's planned social functions, but it was a serious handicap when the SOEG began its efforts to dominate other agencies. It was simply unreasonable to expect an already established government agency to subordinate itself and its prestige to an organization that was at least on the surface a private club.[32]

Most important, however, the Society suffered crippling personnel losses. Within the National Socialist neofeudalism, where personal relations were the primary vehicle of institutional interaction, the loss of major officials was a very serious calamity indeed. In the spring of 1940 Bürckel became Reich Plenipotentiary in Lorraine, thus leaving the Society without a president. Almost simultaneously the SOEG's vice-president, Hans Fischböck, assumed new duties in the occupied Netherlands. While Bürckel had hardly been an effective and successful president, he had at least provided the Society with a considerable amount of surface prestige. The loss of Fischböck was perhaps even more serious. Fischböck was an old-time Austrian National Socialist who had been a Viennese attorney during the 1920's and 1930's and who had personal connections with many of the Austrian and German Party leaders both before and after Hitler's seizure of power. After the Anschluss, he was one of the Austrian National Socialists who rose to immediate prominence. He became the first National Socialist Minister of Commerce and Transport in Seyss-Inquart's puppet government of Austria. However, in May 1940 he was transferred to the Netherlands as Commissioner General for Finance and Economics, and thus lost to the SOEG. His only legacy was the appointment of a Dr. Breza, about whom nothing else is known,

31. Heinrichsbauer to Funk, 2 June 1940, T-71, roll 52, frame 447540.
32. *Ibid.*

but who served as Heinrichsbauer's nominal deputy until his death in December 1942.[33] Finally, Reich Minister Funk, the SOEG's only support at the highest level, became gravely ill in the spring of 1940, and therefore his much needed assistance was lacking at a critical moment in the SOEG's history.[34] With a useless mandate of authority, a protector who was physically unable to protect, and a vacuum in the Viennese leadership, the *Südosteuropa-Gesellschaft* was soon floundering helplessly in a turbulent administrative sea. Other agencies in Vienna either ignored it (by March 1940, it still had no office space[35]) or, even worse, attempted to draw the SOEG into their own spheres of jurisdiction.[36]

The SOEG's executive secretary recognized quickly that the Society's first attempt to establish itself had failed. The SOEG, if it was not content to remain an inconsequential enterprise used and abused by other agencies, had to find another method of carving out its particular administrative fief. After he realized the futility of further frontal assaults, Heinrichsbauer first attempted to protect and entrench the SOEG's existence by obtaining a specific and incontestable area of jurisdiction for his Society.[37] Presumably, once its jurisdiction in a functional area under the firm control of the Ministry of Economics was established, the SOEG would have at least a solid base of power

33. On Fischböck, see *Who's Who In Germany*, Part II, p. 37; Germany, Reichstag, *Der Grossdeutsche Reichstag IV. Wahlperiode, Beginn am 10. April 1938 verlängert bis zum 30. Januar 1947*, ed. E. Kienast (new ed., Berlin, 1943) (hereafter cited as *Grossdeutscher Reichstag 1943*), p. 203; "Sonderauftrag für Fischböck," *Südost-Echo*, 31 May 1940, p. 1; the Heinrichsbauer Interview. Fischböck left the Netherlands in January 1942 to become Reich Commissioner for Price Supervision. For a comparative listing of the SOEG's "German" and "Austrian" officials see Appendix, below.

34. Breza to Siegert (head of the *Aussenhandelsstelle* for Berlin, Brandenburg, and Pommerania), 11 June 1941, T-71, roll 61, frame 559031.

35. Heinrichsbauer to Fischböck, 21 March 1940, *ibid.*, frames 559200–01.

36. For an example of this type of reaction, see NSDAP, Deutsche Arbeitsfront, Gauleitung Wien, Hauptarbeitsgebiet II, Abteilung für Berufserziehung und Betriebsführung to Leiter der Südoststelle, Pg. Heinrichsbauer [sic], "G2/B 6/St. Fr.," 18 April 1940, T-71, roll 60, frame 558240.

37. Heinrichsbauer to Schlotterer (*Ministerialrat* in the Ministry of Economics), 26 Aug. 1940, T-71, roll 14, frame 404813.

as a starting point for further expansion. Heinrichsbauer's proposal met with little enthusiasm in Berlin. The ministry promised that it "would keep his [Heinrichsbauer's] interests properly (*nach Gebühr*) in mind,"[38] but the specific authority the executive secretary had requested was not forthcoming. The frontal attacks of the SOEG had obviously alerted other agencies and ministries to protect their spheres of authority against the new challenger. The resultant furor in turn persuaded the unaggressive Minister of Economics to withdraw the SOEG as an open rival of existing agencies. The SOEG was not dissolved; its creator merely made it clear that, aside from financial support, it had to make its administrative way on its own.

Actually, the SOEG made no real headway in its battle for survival until the late summer of 1940, when its personnel power vacuum was filled. In August, Baldur von Schirach assumed his duties as the new *Gauleiter* (Party leader) of Vienna, and a month later he became the SOEG's new president. Schirach was born in 1907, and joined the NSDAP in 1925 while a student at the University of Munich. He rose quickly as a Party youth leader, becoming head of the National Socialist Student Association in 1927, and Reich Youth Leader and head of the Hitler Youth in 1932. In late summer of 1940, partly because he was becoming too old to function as a youth leader and apparently also because Hitler wished to have an artist as Gauleiter in Vienna (Schirach regarded himself as an artist and cultural leader), the former head of the Hitler Youth was appointed to the Viennese position. Personally vain and shallow, Schirach had a liking for useless displays of grandeur. Nevertheless, he was a decided improvement over his bullying predecessor. Schirach was a veteran of several jurisdictional jousts with various officials, and he had generally been victorious in his battles. At the beginning of 1933 Schirach had been the head of a youth group in a political party; when he retired as Reich Youth

38. Schlotterer to Heinrichsbauer as quoted in Heinrichsbauer to Fischböck, 13 July 1940, T-71, roll 61, frame 559171. The original Schlotterer letter seems to have been lost.

Leader in mid-1940 he had almost complete control of the education and training of German youth between the ages of ten and
eighteen. The transfer of such a personality to Vienna could
only be regarded as a major asset for the fledgling SOEG. In
addition, Schirach made it a point to interest himself in the
work of the SOEG without interfering with Heinrichsbauer's
day-to-day administration of the Society.[39]

However, Schirach's arrival in Vienna was not an unmixed
blessing. Like most National Socialist barons, the new Gauleiter
traveled from post to post with his personal band of retainers.
Schirach appointed one of these close associates, Günter Kaufmann, to the newly created post of the SOEG's vice-president
for cultural affairs, and Kaufmann quickly involved the Society
in a major feudal war with the Foreign Ministry. Among the
officials whom Schirach brought to Vienna, Kaufmann seems
to have been one of the most ambitious and least able. He liked
to collect titles and offices in a number of not very closely related
areas. In October 1940, he was already chief of the Reich Office
of Propaganda (*Reichspropagandaamt*) in Vienna, cultural
affairs officer (*Landeskulturwalter*) for the *Gau* (Nazi Party
district) of Vienna, Schirach's press secretary, and editor of the
Hitler Youth's ideological journal *Wille und Macht*.[40] The new
title as cultural vice-president appears to have stirred considerable ambitions in him, and he tried to realize his dreams with
the establishment of a Prince Eugene (of Savoy) Society
(*Prinz-Eugen-Gesellschaft*). Unfortunately for the SOEG,
Kaufmann (and Schirach as well)[41] had failed to consider the
jealousy of Joachim von Ribbentrop.

The Reich Foreign Minister, a man notorious for his jealous

39. On Schirach, see *Who's Who in Germany*, Part II, p. 142; Ulrich von
Hassell, *Vom andern Deutschland* (Zurich, 1947), entry 22 Sept. 1940, p. 163;
Henrietta von Schirach, *The Price of Glory*, tr. and adap. Willi Frischauer
(London, 1960), p. 173; cross-examination of Schirach by his defense attorney,
Dr. Sauter, 23 May 1946, *IMT*, XIV, 409–10; Heinrichsbauer Interview. Schirach
has recently been released from the Allied prison at Spandau.

40. See *Wille und Macht*, XII (Jan. and Feb. 1944), 40; Kraus to Heinrichsbauer, 19 Dec. 1941, T-71, roll 56, frame 452055.

41. However, according to the Heinrichsbauer Interview Kaufmann was the
more aggressive supporter of the project.

defense of what he regarded as his and his ministry's interests,[42] had from the beginning shown considerable apprehension over the establishment of the SOEG. Ribbentrop's first reaction to the Society had been guardedly sympathetic. He stipulated that the new organization "must not concern itself with matters of foreign, commercial, and cultural policy," but he did appoint Carl Clodius, the deputy chief of the Foreign Ministry's foreign economic policy department as his representative in the SOEG.[43] Cultural policy had not been excluded from the organization's initial plans,[44] and Ribbentrop's condition thus restricted the SOEG to a considerable extent, but the mere fact that Heinrichsbauer and the SOEG did not meet complete and immediate opposition must have been a hopeful sign in the trying days of early 1940. Moreover, personal discussions between Ribbentrop and Heinrichsbauer in May of that year helped to allay still further Ribbentrop's fears and suspicions about the SOEG.[45]

By early fall, then, the relationship between the SOEG and the Wilhelmsstrasse was correct; by the end of the year it was one of open hostility because Ribbentrop, in the meantime, had come to feel that the SOEG was threatening the very foundation of his sphere of decision-making authority in Southeastern Europe. The overt cause of Ribbentrop's anger was Schirach's and Kaufmann's plan for the establishment of a Prince Eugene Society. The planned society was a pure power play. Schirach and Kaufmann hoped to recast Vienna's traditionally close cultural ties with the Balkans into the mold of National Socialist propaganda and, once recast, to place all cultural propaganda efforts under their own auspices and control. The Prince Eugene Society was to have been the first step in the realization of this ambitious

42. See, for instance, Paul Seabury, *The Wilhelmsstrasse* (Berkeley, 1954), pp. 67, 124; Paul Schmidt, *Statist auf diplomatischer Bühne* (Bonn, 1952), pp. 548–49.

43. Minister for Foreign Affairs to Bürckel, "W I 1048," 27 March 1940, T-71, roll 78, frame 579699.

44. See SOEG, "Arbeitsplan der Südosteuropa-Gesellschaft, 1940," T-84, roll 196, frame 1562262; Heinrichsbauer to Rafelsberger, 21 Dec. 1940, T-71, roll 74, frame 575389.

45. See Heinrichsbauer to Bergemann (Official in the Reich Ministry of Economics), 1 June 1940, T-71, roll 68, frame 567358.

project.[46] It never got beyond the paper planning stage; Ribbentrop somehow heard about it, decided it was a threat to his fief, and refused to permit its establishment.[47] Without a specific power grant to counter Ribbentrop's objections, Schirach and his associate could only acquiesce and withdraw their plans.

Schirach had attempted to invade a rival's territory and had been repulsed; Ribbentrop was entitled to an appropriate victory prize. Merely shelving the plans for the Prince Eugene Society did not suffice to appease the Foreign Minister's wrath, since he was also determined to hinder the development of what in his eyes was the manipulating force behind the concept of the Prince Eugene Society, the SOEG.[48] As an initial, sacrificial offering, Schirach suggested that Ribbentrop join Funk as coprotector of the SOEG,[49] but the Foreign Minister rejected this offer as inadequate. Instead, he proposed a scheme that would have given him virtual control of the organization.[50] It was fortunate for the SOEG's future development that Ribbentrop's initial anger subsided rapidly. He did not press his demands for a great measure of control over it and, indeed, even lost interest in becoming its cosponsor. Nevertheless, the quarrel had serious effects on the SOEG's future; it excluded the organiza-

46. Heinrichsbauer to Rafelsberger, 15 Oct. 1940, T-71, roll 74, frame 575539; Felix Kraus to Heinrichsbauer, 11 Dec. 1940, T-71, roll 56, frame 452157.

47. Heinrichsbauer to Rafelsberger, 10 Dec. 1940, T-71, roll 74, frames 575434-35.

48. Actually, the relationship between the SOEG and the future Prince Eugene Society was never clarified, although Heinrichsbauer, for one, feared that the new organization would have become an independent companion agency of the SOEG or, perhaps, even its superior. See Heinrichsbauer to Rafelsberger, 21 Dec. 1940, T-71, roll 74, frames 575389-90.

49. Schirach to Reich Economics Minister, 18 Feb. 1941, T-71, roll 74, frame 575311. The final decision to invite Ribbentrop to become cosponsor of the SOEG was made in a conversation between Schirach and Funk on 25 February 1941. At this time the two officials also agreed that Schirach would become de jure president. Heinrichsbauer to Kurt von Rischka (Head of NSDAP, Gauleitung Wien, Amt für Agrarpolitik), 26 Feb. 1941, T-71, roll 131, frame 634976.

50. The plan involved two protectors, three vice-presidents and two executive secretaries, with one of the officials in each category named by the Foreign Minister. Heinrichsbauer to Bergemann, 27 March 1941, T-71, roll 68, frame 567312.

tion from any activities in the field of foreign cultural policy, and gave it yet another vigilant if passive enemy in Berlin.[51]

The SOEG's second new vice-president (for administrative affairs), Walter Rafelsberger, was no less ambitious than Kaufmann, but for the moment he had no vast plans to propose. If Heinrichsbauer typifies the political opportunist in the Third Reich, Rafelsberger is the totalitarian fanatic. He is one of the most interesting and least known personalities in the Society. At the time of the SOEG's establishment, Rafelsberger was about forty years of age. His specific connections with the National Socialists before 1938 are not clear, but it would appear that he was an ardent advocate of the movement long before the Anschluss. After March 1938, Rafelsberger was appointed the provincial economic expert of the National Socialist Party (*Gauwirtschaftsberater*) in Vienna, an *SS-Oberführer*, and head of the Vienna office for the Control of Jewish Property (*Vermögensverkehrsstelle*). He handled the reorganization of the industrial structure of Austria, that is, he was responsible for carrying out the aryanizations. The vice-president was one of the really convinced believers in the National Socialist myth of the innate superiority of Aryans among the chief officials of the SOEG. In April 1941, when even Schirach was beginning to have some doubts as to the wisdom and chances of success of Hitler's policies, Rafelsberger commented that the war aims for 1941 as set by the Führer would undoubtedly be accomplished: "the entire Balkans, Russia to the Caucasus, the Near East, and North Africa!" This sort of fanatical, amoral approach to politics and plans for the future of Europe pervaded all of Rafelsberger's thinking. Heinrichsbauer's personal secretary reports that on several occasions she "was afraid of him (*hatte Angst vor ihm*)."[52]

51. Heinrichsbauer to Hanns Blaschke (vice-mayor of Vienna), 4 April 1941, T-71, roll 61, frame 560743.

52. For biographical data, see *Who's Who in Germany,* Part II, p. 126. Rafelsberger's views on the war aims of 1941 are quoted in Hassell, entry April 7, 1941, p. 200; Heinrichsbauer's secretary's impression was given the author during an interview with Dr. Hanel in Vienna on August 19, 1961 (hereafter cited as Hanel Interview). For Rafelsberger's views on the control of economic

The Prince Eugene Society fiasco convinced the SOEG's leadership that its goal of becoming a centralized control agency was an unrealistic one for the foreseeable future. Therefore the Society put into effect far-reaching organizational changes, the net result of which made the SOEG far less Schirach's and Kaufmann's Society and far more Heinrichsbauer's and Rafelsberger's. The SOEG reversed itself and became an extremely decentralized coordinating agency, with no detailed functions or administrative procedures. This umbrella form of administrative organization, a *Dachgesellschaft,* was unique among governmental organization in the Third Reich. It was totally unbureaucratic (in the red-tape sense) and even unstructured. It had no place among the traditional Rechtsstaat administrative agencies, but this hardly mattered. Since the old norms and procedures were no longer applicable, the SOEG was free to improvise. The SOEG's improvisation met with astounding success; the Society began to adopt its new format in the late summer of 1940,[53] and by May 1941 the SOEG's executive secretary proudly noted that the SOEG "has . . . in the course of time succeeded in maintaining friendly contacts with most organizations interested in Southeastern Europe. The determining factor in this process has been the Society's adoption of the *Dachgesellschaft* structure. In this way, existing organizations could come within the SOEG framework (*Rahmen*), while their independence was not touched."[54]

The Dachgesellschaft concept of governmental administration originated with Heinrichsbauer. It was a successful attempt to utilize the aim and structure of the industrial holding company within the context of governmental organization and administration.[55] Under it, institutional growth was based to an unprece-

---

life in Austria, see Walter Rafelsberger et al., *Wirtschaftsbetreuung in der Ostmark* (Berlin, 1939). Nothing is known of Rafelsberger's postwar fate.

53. Heinrichsbauer to Kraus, 13 Dec. 1940, T-71, roll 56, frame 452150.

54. "Tätigkeitsbericht Mai 1942," T-84, roll 196, frames 1562156–57. See also Heinrichsbauer's description of the SOEG's relationship to the independent agencies affiliated with it in Heinrichsbauer to Würdinger, 12 July 1940, T-84, roll 197, frame 1563564.

55. Heinrichsbauer Interview.

dented extent on personal relations among agency heads. In its final form, the SOEG Dachgesellschaft was characterized by both decentralization and rigid centralization. A small but very centralized main office supervised and coordinated a wide variety of rather loose and even informal relationships with subordinates and affiliates of the parent organization. The basic aim of the SOEG in all of the agreements that it concluded with other agencies was to obtain the right to participate in and, if possible, control the activities relating to Southeastern Europe that the partner agency either performed or hoped to undertake. Since a large degree of flexibility was one of the major advantages of the Dachgesellschaft concept, the actual forms of cooperation between the SOEG and other organizations varied considerably. They ranged from the SOEG's virtual control of another agency to very loose working arrangements, but in most cases the formal agreement of cooperation involved a financial subsidy by the SOEG to the other agency, together with the development of administrative *Personalunionen* through a mutual exchange of administrative officials. The latter aspect of the relationship usually involved the appointment of the SOEG's executive secretary to a seat on the invaded agency's governing or administrative board, while, simultaneously, the official in charge of the agency's Balkan activities became in addition to his other duties the specialist (*Sachbearbeiter*) for his field of competency in the SOEG's main office. In his new position the official was directly subordinate to the SOEG's executive secretary. The Dachgesellschaft thus served to establish symbiotic relationships— other agencies, with the help of the SOEG's money, could enlarge the scope of their activities, while the SOEG slowly moved to gain control or influence in a larger number of policy areas. Instead of commanding obedience, the SOEG bought itself into fields of competency.

Since the effectiveness of the Dachgesellschaft was in large part dependent on the degree of control the SOEG's central office could exercise over the Society's affiliates, it is perhaps most appropriate to begin an analysis of the SOEG's administrative growth with a description of the head that controlled the many tentacles extending into other organizations. The administrative office (*Zentralbüro*) was organized along strictly centralized lines. Presiding over the entire apparatus was the actual mainspring of the SOEG, the executive secretary. Until February 1944, this post was filled by August Heinrichsbauer; during the last months of the SOEG's existence the Society was headed by Dr. Hans Augenthaler as executive secretary, and by Dr. Leonhard Oberascher as assistant executive secretary in charge of cultural affairs. Augenthaler initiated no new policies, but weakly carried on what Heinrichsbauer had begun. He was a colorless bureaucrat who had been in the Austrian civil service before 1938 and was taken over into the Reich bureaucracy as a department head (*Ministerialrat*) in the Reich Ministry of Economics after the Anschluss. Before coming to the SOEG he had been in charge of the Hungarian and Slovakian trade policy desk in the Economics Ministry.[56] Oberascher was considerably more energetic, but also far less realistic. Little is known of his early career, but he seems to have been an SS-affiliated journalist. In 1940 he served as an associate editor on the editorial board of the *Südost-Echo*, whose owner, van Raay, was one of the official founders of the SOEG. During the same year he also handled the resettlement of the Bessarabian Germans, and in 1944 he had to be released by the SS before he could take over his SOEG post. At some time before coming to the SOEG, Oberascher had also been editor of the German language *Donauzeitung* in Belgrade.[57]

Throughout the SOEG's years of operation, the most important unit of the central office on the level below executive secretary, the secretariat, was headed by Dr. Erika Hanel. She admirably complemented Heinrichsbauer's energy and inventiveness with feminine charms, youthful vivaciousness, and administrative skill. Dr. Hanel was born in 1916 and received her law

56. See, *Who's Who in Germany*, Part II, p.6. After the war Augenthaler continued his civil service career. In 1961 he was a section chief in the Austrian Ministry of Reconstruction.

57. See Joseph B. Schechtmann, *European Population Transfers, 1939–45* (New York, 1946), p.178; Heinrichsbauer to Stadler (President of the *Deutsches Wissenschaftliches Institut* in Zagreb), 24 Jan. 1944, T-71, roll 51, frame 446268.

degree in December 1939. She then joined the staff of the *Südost-Echo* in Sofia, but because of personal differences with the paper's owner, van Raay, she welcomed the opportunity to change her position and join the staff of the SOEG in February 1940.[58] The secretariat handled all of the SOEG's own correspondence and also received and filed carbon copies of all relevant letters sent or received by the SOEG's affiliates. In addition, the office was responsible for handling the technical and administrative details of the conferences, congresses, and other meetings the SOEG sponsored. The SOEG's office staff was quite small. Besides Heinrichsbauer and Hanel, the central office had only five other full-time employees.[59]

Almost all of the actual work performed by the SOEG was handled by Heinrichsbauer and his staff with little or no guidance or interference from the Society's theoretical superstructure. The protector, the president, and the members of the presidium (*Präsidium*) and the board of directors (*Beirat*) played a largely ceremonial role. Funk seldom interfered in the Society's affairs; Schirach pursued his own pet projects, but did not regard the presidency of the SOEG as one of his more important positions.[60] The appointment of members to the presidium or the board of directors was based largely on public relations considerations. The members of the presidium usually held positions of high intermediate rank in Reich ministries and other major Reich agencies. An appointment to one of the SOEG's governing bodies was meant to flatter them and thus render them and their agencies well disposed toward the SOEG and its aims. The membership of the board of directors was largely an amalgamation of Viennese academic, business, and Nazi Party leaders; the men who served on the board were the local

58. See Hanel to Kratz, 13 April 1940, T-71, roll 52, frame 572335; Hanel Interview.

59. SOEG, "Geschäftsordnung der Südosteuropa-Gesellschaft," n.d. (ca. Oct. 1942), T-84, roll 196, frames 1562265-66.

60. At his postwar trial in Nuremberg, he grouped it in the same category as his presidency of the German Bibliophile Society. See crossexamination of Schirach by his defense attorney, Dr. Sauter, 23 May 1946, *IMT*, XIV, 413.

counterparts of the men in the presidium.[61]

The degree of flexibility inherent in the concept of the Dach-gesellschaft and the lack of policy dictation by the SOEG's superstructure left Heinrichsbauer virtually free to negotiate almost any type of agreement between the SOEG and other Balkan agencies. Only the ever-present need to guard against offending a previously established and firmly entrenched jurisdiction inhibited his ingenuity in seeking new means of affiliating other Balkan agencies with the SOEG. In time, the SOEG evolved four basic categories of relationships between the parent organization and its affiliates: (1) organizations that were by order of a central agency virtually put at the disposal of the SOEG; (2) agencies that were newly created on the local (Viennese) level and then joined to the SOEG; (3) components that were the joint creation of the SOEG and another organization on the national level; and (4) informal and formal agreements of cooperation between the SOEG and another organization in which the SOEG made no formal attempt to actually control any part of the other agency's activities. Between the first and the last category lay a spectrum of administrative relationships stretching from virtual subordination to the SOEG to very loose agreements on general cooperation between the Society and other independent agencies, but in almost every case the degree of successful cooperation was very largely dependent upon the personal relations between Heinrichsbauer and his partners.

There is little point in detailing the administrative history of each of the more than twenty units that were affiliated with the SOEG. By no means all of these organizations are of any real importance for the history of either the SOEG or the Third Reich, and several, indeed, developed little beyond the paper-planning stage. It may be of some interest, however, to describe one or two of the important agencies in each category and to sketch their administrative growth. Together, these sketches will yield a composite picture of dynamic empire building and fief warfare that made an invisible mockery of the Third Reich's monolithic facade.

61. Heinrichsbauer to Kaufmann, 10 April 1941, T-71, roll 57, frame 453787. The *Beirat* was originally intended as a more functional local coordinating body, but these plans were never realized. See *ibid.*

The Vienna Institute for Economic Research (*Wiener Institut für Wirtschaftsforschung,* WIW) was the only affiliate of the SOEG that fell into the first category. Funk gave the SOEG full control of this institute in the spring of 1940, and it remained a subordinate of the SOEG until the fall of 1944.[62] The institute remained a category of one, since it became the SOEG's affiliate at a time when the Society was still expecting to conquer and subordinate other agencies. Despite its uniqueness, the relationship established between the SOEG and the institute gives a good indication of the extent of direct control that the SOEG originally intended to exercise over its subordinate agencies. If the frontal assault tactics had met with success, the administrative relationship between the SOEG and the Viennese institute would undoubtedly have provided a model for the Society's relations with other subordinates as well. As a visible symbol of the institute's new position of vassalage, Heinrichsbauer became chairman of its administrative committee (*Verwaltungsausschuss*). In this capacity he had the right to make or approve all basic policy decisions. These safeguards of the SOEG's control were embodied in a new set of bylaws, which could not be amended without Funk's approval. Only the day-to-day administration of the institute remained in the hands of a director appointed by the Berlin parent organization,[63] the German Institute for Economic Research (*Deutsches Institut für Wirtschaftsforschung*). Financially, the Viennese institute was completely dependent on the Society; the SOEG contributed more than 90 percent of its operating budget.[64]

It lay within the very nature of the SOEG as an agency whose

62. Wagemann (head of the *Institut für Konjunkturforschung*) to the Reich Economics Minister, 3 April 1940, T-71, roll 54, frame 450138. See also the draft of a letter of the Reichskommissar (für die Wiedervereinigung der Ostmark mit dem Deutschen Reich) to the Reich Economics Minister (ca. Feb. 1940), T-71, roll 71, frame 570756. The draft was prepared by the *Deutsches Institut für Wirtschaftsforschung (Institut für Konjunkturforschung).*

63. Wiener Institut für Wirtschaftsforschung, "Satzung des Wiener Instituts für Wirtschaftsforschung, e.V.," 27 Aug. 1940, T-71, roll 54, frames 450144–46.

64. "Ausgaben des Wiener Instituts für Wirtschaftsforschung für das Geschäftsjahr 1940/41," 5 Oct. 1940, T-71, roll 54, frame 450118; see also the untitled tabulations by Dr. Hanel, *ibid.,* frame 450116; Heinrichsbauer to Bauer (of the Deutsches Institut für Wirtschaftsforschung), 19 March 1943, T-71, roll 70, frame 570573.

future growth depended almost entirely on the growing importance of Vienna, that most of its affiliates would lie within the
second category, that is, subsidiaries and components newly created on the local level as a result of local Viennese initiative.
The Working Committee for Cultural Policy (*Kulturpolitischer
Arbeitskreis*) was a particular masterpiece of people-handling.
Basically the committee was an administrative ruse to enable
the Society to reenter the field of cultural policy after the Prince
Eugene Society fiasco. In returning to this arena, the SOEG took
great care to prevent a new flare-up of Ribbentrop's tempera-
ment.[65] The Society accomplished this feat by making use of
the bureaucratic *Personalunion*, or multiple office holding, a
widespread practice among National Socialist officialdom. Felix
Kraus, whom Heinrichsbauer and Rafelsberger had selected to
head the SOEG's cultural section, was an official of the Association for Germans Abroad (*Volksbund für das Deutschtum im
Ausland*). He also held a position in the SS-affiliate Liaison
Office for Ethnic Germans (*Volksdeutsche Mittelstelle*) and
later became head of a section in the Party's Vienna district
administration (*Gauamtsleiter*) for ethnic and border German
affairs (*volksdeutsche und grenzlanddeutsche Fragen*).[66] These
various positions had one factor in common: all three empowered Kraus to exhibit a legitimate concern for the German
minorities in Southeastern Europe, and none involved direct supervision of his work by the Foreign Ministry. On this narrow
but firm basis of concern with the affairs of ethnic Germans
in the Balkans, the SOEG began to reestablish its cultural affairs
section.

In 1941, both Heinrichsbauer and Kraus worked on organiza-

65. The later chairman of the Working Committee for Cultural Policy, Felix
Kraus, had worked out an elaborate scheme for a SOEG cultural affairs agency
(which was even to publish its own journal) in the fall of 1940. Because of
the Prince Eugene Society fiasco, the plans remained on paper. Kraus, however,
does not seem to have had a part in the Prince Eugene Society project. See
Kraus, "Ausbau der Südosteuropa-Gesellschaft," 11 Dec. 1940, T-71, roll 56,
frames 452153–56. Kraus' earlier scheme had the approval of Rafelsberger. Kraus
to Heinrichsbauer, 11 Dec. 1940, *ibid.*, frame 452158.

66. Heinrichsbauer to Heinz Gehrold (head of subdivision export in the Viennese Chamber of Economics), 25 Feb. 1941, T-71, roll 55, frame 450677.

tional drafts for the SOEG's new affiliate. Originally, the plans involved only a Viennese liaison office to handle matters of common concern for Reich Germans and the Balkan Volksdeutsche.[67] But, as these projects were wont to do, the original concept quickly grew to considerably increased proportions. In the summer, Kraus felt that the new agency, now renamed the SOEG Working Group for Ethnic Affairs (*Arbeitsgemeinschaft für Volkstumsfragen der SOEG*) should have not only a liaison function, but should also concern itself with foreign ethnic affairs "insofar as these are of interest from the German point of view."[68] In effect, the Working Committee for Cultural Policy had become at least on paper a remodeled form of the previously planned SOEG coordinating office for all German cultural propaganda originating in Vienna.[69]

While the Foreign Ministry was the SOEG's major obstacle on the road toward a cultural fief, the Society also took immense care to cultivate the goodwill of all other interested Reich and Viennese agencies and officials before it established the new affiliate. On the local level, the establishment of the Working Committee for Cultural Policy forced the SOEG to deal with the problems of Hanns Blaschke and Günter Kaufmann. Like Rafelsberger, Blaschke was an old guard Austrian National Socialist. He was born in 1896, and obtained a diploma from the Vienna Institute of Technology in 1915. After World War I he briefly headed an Executive Committee to Carry Out the

67. Felix Kraus, "Südosteuropa-Gesellschaft und volksdeutsche Arbeit," 14 April 1941, T-71, roll 56, frames 452133–35; [Heinrichsbauer?], "Entwurf [for an agreement with Kraus]," n.d., T-71, roll 55, frame 451496. These plans had Rafelsberger's approval, Kraus to Heinrichsbauer, 15 April 1941, T-71, roll 56, frame 452132.

68. SOEG, Arbeitsgemeinschaft für Volkstumsfragen (Kraus), "Aktenvermerk," 17 June 1941, T-71, roll 55, frame 451491.

69. *Ibid.*, frames 451491–94. The plans for the cultural group were not actually put into effect until 1942, i.e., when the SOEG had become firmly established and an influential organization. See Kraus, "Aktenvermerk über eine Besprechung Pg. Blaschke-Pg. Kraus am 27. Mai 1942," T-71, roll 52, frames 447736–37. For the Committee for Cultural Policy's detailed and involved organizational scheme, see SOEG, Kulturpolitischer Arbeitskreis (Kraus), "Niederschrift [concerning the first session of the Kulturpolitischer Arbeitskreis]," n.d., *ibid.*, frame 451463. For additional information on the work of the committee, see Chapter 3.

Anschluss to Germany, and launched into extreme right-wing
politics. He joined the Austrian National Socialists in 1932, and,
as he proudly noted in his biographical entry in the *Grossdeutscher Reichstag,* he participated actively in the July 1934
uprising. As a result, Blaschke was sentenced to life imprison-
ment in February 1935, but he served only until July of the
following year, when he was released on parole. After the
Anschluss, Blaschke was appointed vice-mayor of Vienna and
received the SS rank of brigade leader (*Brigadeführer*). In 1942
he was also the head of the cultural affairs department of the
city of Vienna and Schirach's personal expert (*Referent*) for
Southeastern Europe.[70] He was thus clearly one of the more
influential Viennese Party leaders. The SOEG took cognizance
of this and delicately appeased him by offering him the largely
titular chairmanship of the Working Committee for Cultural
Policy.

The matter of Kaufmann's place in the new committee posed
another potential difficulty. As the SOEG's vice-president for
cultural affairs (he still held the title in 1942), Kaufmann might
be expected to exert an influential voice in the SOEG's new
venture into cultural policy. But Kaufmann was one of those
NSDAP officials whose interest lay less in the actual exercise
of functions than in the random collecting of titles. Moreover,
by late 1941 he foresaw an even more hopeful cultural future
for himself—he had hopes of becoming the director of a large
film company associated with the Propaganda Ministry, so that
he was actively interested only in his positions as Schirach's
press secretary and Southeast expert, and the editorship of *Wille
und Macht.* (He did not relinquish the latter until early 1944).
At any rate he was quite content to retain only his title. At
his own request, he took no part in the work of the policy committee—he did not even care to be informed of its activities.[71]

70. See *Who's Who in Germany,* Part II, p. 14; *Grossdeutscher Reichstag
1943,* p. 161. With the change in the SOEG's administrative hierarchy in February
1944, Blaschke was appointed vice-president of the Society as well as mayor
of Vienna.

71. Reichsstatthalter in Wien (*Obergebietsführer* Müller) to Blaschke, 12 April
1942, T-71, roll 55, frame 451474; Kraus, "Aktenvermerk—Besprechung mit Pg.
Blaschke," 30 April 1942, *ibid.*, frame 451472.

It must be explained that while the SOEG was quite liberal in the dispensing of titles, it went to some length to avoid relinquishing the substance of administrative control. Kraus, who was named executive secretary of the committee, also became the SOEG's deputy executive secretary for cultural affairs. In this capacity he was directly subordinate to Heinrichsbauer, not to Blaschke.[72]

The plans for the establishment of the Nutrition and Agriculture Group (*Gruppe Ernährung und Landwirtschaft*), eventually one of the most important of the SOEG's affiliates, owed their inception to the frustrated ambitions for power of two Viennese officials. Sometime near the end of 1940, Kurt von Rischka, head of the provincial Party office for agricultural policy (*Gauamtsleiter für Agrarpolitik*), and Karl Mayerzedt, president of the provincial farmer's association (*Landesbauernführer*) approached the SOEG's executive secretary with a proposal for mutual cooperation. The ambitious duo noted that they wanted to concern themselves with matters involving agricultural cooperatives in Southeastern Europe, but that their specific administrative competencies did not permit them to show any official interest in these fields. Since Heinrichsbauer found it rather difficult to understand what prevented the two major agricultural officials in the Party hierarchy of Vienna from having an official interest in Balkan agricultural cooperatives, these professed motives did not appear very credible to him. His lack of enthusiasm in turn persuaded Rischka and Mayerzedt to end the masquerade and reveal their actual motives. The two intended to expand their administrative niches by adding the control of agricultural exports and imports in Vienna to their jurisdictions.[73] Within the National Socialist system, this was the legitimate concern of the local office of the Economic Group for Wholesale Commerce, Imports, and Exports (*Wirtschaftsgruppe Gross-, Ein- und Ausfuhrhandel*) or the *Reichsstellen*.[74]

72. Heinrichsbauer to Rafelsberger, 20 March 1942, T-71, roll 55, frame 451475.
73. Heinrichsbauer to Rafelsberger, 3 and 10 Dec. 1940, T-71, roll 74, frames 575452, 575437.
74. The *Reichsstellen* were agencies under the supervision of the Reich Ministry of Agriculture charged with determining import quotas for foodstuffs and with administering food surpluses that might develop within the Reich. The

Rischka and Mayerzedt intended to utilize the SOEG in order
to expand their official spheres into jurisdictional areas where
their presence was based on what was at best rather dubious
authorization. Heinrichsbauer, once Rischka and Mayerzedt had
made their confession, was not unwilling to enter into the partnership. On January 1, 1941, Rischka became, along with his
other posts, a member of the SOEG's administrative staff and
nine days later Heinrichsbauer gave him the task of establishing
the "Department (*Abteilung*) of Agriculture, Nutritional Economy, and Market Analysis (*Marktordnung*) of the SOEG."[75]

What considerations pursuaded Heinrichsbauer and Rafelsberger (who had to approve the arrangements) to agree to Rischka's
and Mayerzedt's scarcely veiled project for power aggrandizement? Rafelsberger had civic and personal motives. As head
of the Party's district office for economic affairs (*Gauwirtschaftsberater*) in Vienna, he had a vital interest in the economic prosperity and importance of his region. Any organization that
helped to improve Vienna's economic position without detracting
from the importance and powers of his own office would, from
his point of view, be a welcome addition to Viennese officialdom.
In addition, Rafelsberger, Rischka, and Mayerzedt all held Party
offices, but the object of the agricultural officials' invasion attempt were state agencies. Since all Party officials had a common
interest in reducing the administrative power of state agencies,
Rischka and Mayerzedt found a willing collaborator in Rafelsberger. Heinrichsbauer, for his part, was fully aware that the
future influence of the SOEG rose and fell with the importance
of Vienna as the Reich's Southeastern capital. In 1940 and 1941,
however, Vienna was little more than an important provincial
center.[76] It had no political importance, and the city's economic
life was seriously hampered by discriminatory regulations which

---

import quota allocations were determined on a geographical basis, using the
1937 imports into that area of the Reich as a base for calculation.

75. Heinrichsbauer to Rischka, 10 Jan. 1941, T-71, roll 131, frame 634993;
Heinrichsbauer to Rischka, 28 Jan. 1941, *ibid.*, frame 634984.

76. Bullock, *Hitler,* p. 398.

favored *Altreich* firms even in the importation of products from Southeastern Europe into Germany.[77]

The Nutrition and Agriculture Group could boast the most ambitious program and the most involved organizational structure among the SOEG's affiliates. As was true of the SOEG itself, the Group had long and short-term objectives. Its eventual goal was to make Vienna the most important marketing center (*Umschlagplatz*) for agricultural imports from the Balkans, and the hub of agricultural industry for that area of Europe. Vienna was to become "an example for the development of a European economy."[78] More immediately, the Group was concerned with increasing the volume of agricultural imports from the Balkans to Germany, and with channeling more of these imports into the Reich via Austria and Vienna.[79] To accomplish its immediate goal, that of removing the discriminatory import quotas established in Berlin, Rischka tried two approaches. The Group originally hoped that the volume of imports could be measurably improved by vigorously protesting the unfair discrimination against Viennese firms at the appropriate office in Berlin.[80] Since this approach was appeal without power, it failed completely. The Group then turned to local Viennese resources. By the middle of 1943, Rischka had created a number of committees, each covering a specific group of agricultural products generally

77. Rischka to Straubinger (a *Ministerialdirektor* in the Reich Ministry of Agriculture), "Betrifft: Verlegung einer Oelmühle von Hamburg nach Wien," 23 April 1942, T-71, roll 131, frames 634668–69; Hermann Reischle and Wilhelm Saure, *Der Reichsnährstand, Aufbau, Aufgaben und Bedeutung* (Berlin, 1940), p. 240.

78. SOEG, Gruppe Ernährung und Landwirtschaft, *Geschäftsbericht der Gruppe "Ernährung und Landwirtschaft" der Südosteuropa-Gesellschaft. Wien 1. Dezember 1942* (confidential; for official use only), T-84, roll 202, frame 1568706.

79. See *ibid.*, Getreideausschuss, "Satzungen des Ausschusses für Getreide und andere landwirtschaftliche Produkte der Gruppe 'Ernährung und Landwirtschaft' der Südosteuropa-Gesellschaft, T-71, roll 131, frame 634521; SOEG (Gruppe Ernährung und Landwirtschaft, Rischka et al.), "Protokoll [der] Besprechung im Gauhaus, Amt für Agrarpolitik . . . 20.8.1942, 17 Uhr," *ibid.*, frame 634518.

80. For an example of the protests reaching Berlin from Vienna, see Rischka to Straubinger, "Betrifft: Verlegung einer Oelmühle von Hamburg nach Wien," 23 April 1942, T-71, roll 131, frames 634668–69.

corresponding to the topical division of the *Reichsstellen.* Membership of the committees consisted almost entirely of representatives from leading Viennese agricultural import and processing firms.[81] Simultaneously, the Group used its committee network as a catalytic agent to effect a series of mergers among Viennese import firms. Beginning in December 1941, the SOEG's agricultural affiliate began to establish a number of import syndicates (*Gemeinschaftsfirmen*). These were trusts in which a number of Viennese firms agreed to pool their procurement offices in the Balkans and put them at the disposal of the new company. The development of the new firms meant the cartelization of the Viennese agricultural import business. Rischka's reasoning in establishing the new units was frank and pragmatic. He argued that as individual enterprises the relatively small and impotent Viennese firms would never be able to compete with the more formidable Altreich companies. Organized into cartels and at least linked to an agency of the Reich Economics Ministry, Viennese firms might well become competitive and thus be able to convince the allocation agencies of the efficiency and initiative of Viennese enterprises.[82]

One of the most interesting cases of National Socialist gamesmanship and exploitation of personal relationships was Rischka's and Mayerzedt's establishment of the Black Sea Trading and Industrial Company, Inc. (*Schwarzmeer Handels- und Industriegesellschaft m.b.H.*). This organization was incorporated in the summer of 1942 with some individual Viennese import firms and the previously established import syndicates as charter subscribers.[83] The Black Sea Company would have had the same functions in the Crimea and the occupied Russian territories

81. SOEG, Gruppe Ernährung und Landwirtschaft, Kanzlei to L. et al., "2/42 Dir P/S," 16 Dec. 1942, *ibid.,* frame 634393; SOEG, Gruppe Ernährung und Landwirtschaft (Rischka), "Aktennotiz über die erste Dienstbesprechung der Gruppe 'Ernährung und Landwirtschaft' der Südosteuropa-Gesellschaft am Dienstag, den 12. Jänner 1943, im Gauhaus, Amt für das Landvolk," n.d., *ibid.,* frames 634341–44.

82. Rischka to Heinrichsbauer, "Betrifft: Gemeinschaftsfirmen für den Einsatz im Südosten," 13 Dec. 1941, *ibid.,* frame 634767.

83. SOEG, Gruppe Ernährung und Landwirtschaft, "Aktenvermerk—Betrifft: Besprechung über die Gründung einer Schwarzmeer Handels-und Industriegesellschaft," n.d., *ibid.,* frame 634581.

as the previously formed syndicates performed in the Balkans. Thus the organization was clearly the starting point of what the SOEG hoped would become its important role in the German exploitation and control of the newly conquered Russian territories. To be sure, the SOEG was in no position to claim a jurisdictional concern with Crimean economic affairs, but what it lacked in organizational authority it made up with personal friendships. The proposed venture into the Soviet Union under the sponsorship of an organization constitutionally limited to a concern with Balkan affairs was possible only because of the active support of the project by the Gauleiter-designate of the Crimea, Alfred Eduard Frauenfeld, an old Viennese National Socialist. The SOEG could anticipate playing an important part in the future economic life of the Crimea merely because the territory's anticipated governor assumed the right to favor personal friends—regardless of their jurisdictional competencies. Here, surely, is an excellent illustration of the extent of bureaucratic chaos and arbitrariness in the Third Reich.

The extension of the administrative tentacles of the Nutrition and Agriculture Group into Viennese agricultural concerns, as well as some in the Soviet Union, provided Rischka's and Mayerzedt's organization with an administrative structure that was more complicated and involved than that of the current SOEG. As a result, the growth of the Group also revealed one of the inherent structural weaknesses of the Dachgesellschaft form of organization—the danger of an affiliate outgrowing the protection and control of the parent organization. Under Rischka, this potential danger became an acute possibility for the SOEG. The executive secretary of the Group forgot (or chose to ignore) his obligation to operate his organization as a unit of the SOEG dependent on Heinrichsbauer's continued supervision of basic policy decisions. In theory, Heinrichsbauer retained his usual controlling powers. He approved the Group's bylaws, appointed its chairman, had the right to veto committee chairmen appointments, and maintained a seat on the board of directors.[84] In practice, however, Rischka proved an at times extremely unco-

84. Heinrichsbauer to Rischka, 6 Oct. 1941, *ibid.*, frame 634841; Rischka to Heinrichsbauer, 27 Feb. 1941, *ibid.*, frame 634975.

operative and independent subordinate. He attended important meetings as the representative of the SOEG and spoke in the name of the Society on such occasions, but apparently frequently neglected to inform Heinrichsbauer of either the action taken at these meetings or of his own statements. Similarly, Rischka spent some SOEG funds without obtaining the required prior approval of Heinrichsbauer.[85] It is true that the misunderstanding never reached the point of open conflict, but this was not the result of Rischka's willingness to restrain his own ambitions. Rather, by the time the Group's elaborate structure had been finally established, the days of the Third Reich were clearly numbered, and the opportunities for economic exploitation in the Balkans markedly fewer.

In spite of an elaborate administrative structure, the Nutrition and Agriculture Group could deal effectively only with the practical problems of increasing Vienna's agricultural imports. As its entry in the field of agricultural research activities in Southeastern Europe, the SOEG created yet another subsidiary, the Corn Committee (*Maisausschuss*). Like most agencies in the Third Reich, the Corn Committee served both to further the Reich's general aims and the specific goals of its founding agencies. Corn and soybeans always held an immense fascination for the Party's agrarian planners. Vastly expanded acreage of both crops would be needed to help German-dominated Europe achieve economic autarky, since once they were available in sufficient quantity, soybeans could fill the need for fat, while corn would serve as animal fodder and perhaps supplement human diets in the Balkans as well.[86] The Balkan countries offered excellent climatic and soil conditions for the growth of corn and soybeans, and ever since the Wohltat Pact in March 1939,[87] German

85. On these various complaints, see the blistering letter of Heinrichsbauer to Rischka, 2 July 1942, *ibid.*, frame 634578.

86. See Sawa Ulmansky, "Bericht für die 1. Tagung des Maisausschusses am 27.9.1943—zu Punkt 1 der Tagesordnung" Sept. 1943, T-71, roll 73, frames 574219–20.

87. See Wohltat, "Report on the Conversations of February 13 to 22, 1939, with the Rumanian Government in Bucharest," 27 Feb. 1939, *DGFP*, D, V, Doc. 306, p. 405; "Treaty for the Promotion of Economic Relations Between

agricultural experts had urged the nations of Southeastern Europe to devote a greater share of their acreage to oleaginous plants. The German victory over France seemed to bring considerably closer the day when Germany would dominate all agricultural planning in Southeastern Europe, and the SOEG was anxious to secure a generous slice of what promised to become a very large administrative pie.

As before the question was "how," or rather "who." In this case it was Professor Sawa Ulmansky, an agricultural expert living in Zagreb, though he apparently held German citizenship. Ulmansky had hoped to join the staff of the SOEG as early as the spring of 1941 but, presumably for reasons involving German-Croatian political relations, he was not appointed consultant to the Society in agricultural matters until January 1942.[88] By the end of the year Ulmansky had found an administrative partner who was willing to support the SOEG's venture into sponsorship of agricultural research, and he proposed the establishment of a central corn committee. Operating under the direction of the SOEG, this agency would coordinate all German research activities on the growth and utilization of the corn plant in the Balkans. As a suitable fellow charter-founder of the new venture, Ulmansky suggested the Reich Office for Economic Development (*Reichsamt für Wirtschaftsausbau*).[89] Heinrichsbauer agreed.

The Corn Committee was thus the result of a symbiotic compromise between the SOEG and an agency on the national level. Thus the new affiliate exemplified units in the third category of SOEG components, affiliates jointly established by the Society

---

the German Reich and the Kingdom of Rumania," 23 March 1939, *ibid.*, VI, Doc. 78, pp. 91–92. On the significance of the Wohltat Pact, see also below, pp. 101–02.

88. Ulmansky to Heinrichsbauer, 20 Aug. 1940 and 10 May 1941, T-71, roll 64, frames 562935, 562883–84; Heinrichsbauer to Schubert (the SOEG's representative in Zagreb), 31 Jan. 1942, T-84, roll 87, frame 1377712.

89. Sawa Ulmansky, "Vorschlag betreffend Vereinheitlichung der Führung einer Aktion zur Rationalisierung der Maisnutzung in den Südoststaaten" Dec. 1942, T-71, roll 64, frames 562770–73.

and another Reich-level organization. The Reich Office for Economic Development was an agency of the Economics Ministry headed by Dr. Carl Krauch, an executive of I. G. Farben, who was also head of the Office of the Plenipotentiary General for Special Questions of Chemical Production in the Four Year Plan. The Office of Economic Development had been created in 1936 soon after the inception of the Four Year Plan and originally had the task of encouraging and promoting within Germany all new inventions and methods that might enable the Reich to reduce its imports of raw materials or foodstuffs.[90] While Krauch's office in the Four Year Plan apparently handled only construction material allocations for new chemical plants during the later war years,[91] the functions of the Office of Economic Development grew not only territorially to include the entire German sphere of control in Europe, but also changed topically so that the office interested itself in methods that might increase the volume of exports to Germany from the rest of Europe, instead of attempting to reduce them.

It is clear from even a brief glance at the administrative history of the office that, like many other German agencies, it had vastly expanded its original jurisdictional niche by assuming a number of functions not originally assigned to it. Much of this abrogation of authority was informal and extralegal, and the Office of Economic Development was understandably interested in any administrative device that legalized its previous jurisdictional expansion. Indeed, the office welcomed the SOEG's and Ulmansky's overtures with a great deal of enthusiasm, and a conference between the partners was quickly arranged in late January 1943. The Office of Economic Development agreed to become the SOEG's partner in the establishment of the Corn

90. "Extracts from the Testimony of Defendant Krauch—Direct Examination (by his defense counsel Dr. Boettcher)" (hereafter cited as Krauch Testimony), in Nuernberg Military Tribunals, *Trial of War Criminals before the Nuernberg Military Tribunals Under Control Council Law No. 10—Case 6, The United States against Carl Krauch et al.* (hereafter cited as *Nuernberg Military Tribunals: The Farben Case*), VII (Washington, 1953), pp. 996–98, 1022.

91. "Interrogation of Albert Speer by Dr. Charmatz (of the Prosecution) [sic] on 12 March 1947, from 10.00 to 12.00 Hours," *ibid.*, p. 986.

Committee,[92] subject only to a later stipulation that no other
Reich agencies be involved—a provision in which the SOEG
fully concurred.[93] Two months later, Ulmansky drafted a work
program for the new agency and submitted it to Heinrichsbauer.
The tasks of the Corn Committee, in line with its eventual goal,
were phrased very broadly to include the study of all matters
pertaining to the production and processing of corn.[94]

The organizational structure of the committee followed the
SOEG's usual pattern. A prominent Viennese official, in this
case Rafelsberger, became chairman of the new agency. Other
committee members included Heinrichsbauer and Baron Häusler,
a man who had invented a new technique for utilizing corn
flour. The Corn Committee hoped to promote the general
adoption of Häusler's process in Germany and Southeastern
Europe. Ulmansky became the group's administrative secretary.
Financial control of the committee's operations remained with
the parent organization; Heinrichsbauer had the right to veto
all expenditures. The particularly close relationship that existed
between the new agency and the Office of Economic Development was formally expressed through the insertion of a provision
in the committee's bylaws "that the committee will work together with all relevant Reich offices, particularly the Reich
Office for Economic Development."[95]

In many respects the fourth category of affiliates, that of
formal and informal agreements between the SOEG as a whole

92. Ulmansky, "Aktenvermerk—bezüglich Konferenz im Reichsamt für Wirtschaftsausbau bei Prof. Bauer am 21.1.1943," 25 Jan. 1943, T-71, roll 70, frame
570369.

93. Ulmansky, "Aktenvermerk über Absprache mit Direktor Dr. Bauer, Reichsamt für Wirtschaftsausbau, am 15.3.43 in Wien," n.d., T-71, roll 73, frames
573944–45.

94. Ulmansky, "Aktenvermerk—betreffend die Errichtung eines Maisausschusses der Südosteuropa-Gesellschaft," 23. March 1943, T-71, roll 73, frame 573938.
See also SOEG, Maisausschuss, "Geschäftsordnung des Ausschusses für Fragen
der Rationalisierung der Maisnutzung in den Südoststaaten in der Südosteuropa-
Gesellschaft ('Maisausschuss der SOEG')" [ca. May 1943], *ibid.*, frame 573910.

95. SOEG, Maisausschuss, "Geschäftsordnung . . . ," T-71, roll 73, frames
573910–13.

and another agency of "equal" status, is the most interesting and important. In this relationship the SOEG entered the mainstream of National Socialist bureaucratic infighting; here the Society moved from its provincial base to establish bilateral contact with important Reich-level agencies. It is at first glance surprising to find the respected and venerable German Academy (*Deutsche Akademie,* DAM) in Munich among the SOEG's equal partners. The German Academy had been established in 1925 to propagandize the use and instruction of the German language and culture beyond the borders of the Reich. It was thus a firmly established institution by the time the SOEG began its operations. Moreover, since November 1941, the academy's authority was based on a *Führererlass,* at least in theory the most unencroachable type of authorization obtainable in the Third Reich. By a decree of November 15, 1941, Hitler established the DAM as an institution of public law (*Körperschaft des öffentlichen Rechts*), that is as a quasi-official agency. Its president, previously elected by the DAM senate, was now named directly by Hitler. The Führer specified that the DAM's specific functions were to be the cultivation of the German language in the Reich and the teaching of German abroad. In these fields the DAM was given a jurisdictional monopoly; Hitler expressly empowered its president to forbid other agencies to compete with the DAM, and, if necessary, the president was authorized to request that a rival organization be dissolved. The Ministry of Propaganda (for the DAM's work within the Reich) and the Foreign Ministry (for the activities abroad) had only general supervisory powers over the DAM.[96]

In contrast, the SOEG had been seriously rebuffed when it attempted to establish itself in the area of cultural policy, and, although it had gained considerably in status since its inauspicious beginnings in 1940, it always remained an organization of secondary importance among Reich agencies. It is unlikely,

96. "Erlass des Führers über die Deutsche Akademie vom 15. November 1941," in Germany Reichsministerium des Innern, *Reichsgesetzblatt* (Berlin, 1941) (hereafter cited as *RGBl.*), I, 717–18.

for example, that Hitler ever knew of its existence. Thus, the benefits for the SOEG from an agreement with the DAM are obvious; not so, however, what motivated the DAM to agree to the partnership.

The union between the two unlikely partners came about because by mid-1942, when the contacts between the SOEG and the DAM resulted in more formal agreements for mutual cooperation, the Munich institute was beset by a serious problem. Goebbels' Propaganda Ministry, dissatisfied that it exercised only general supervision over the academy's activities, had begun a campaign of subversion against the DAM, undermining its independent status and usurping its tasks.[97] Goebbels' ultimate aim was clearly to incorporate the DAM completely into the Propaganda Ministry. To guard against this fate the German Academy needed any additional support it could obtain, and a working agreement with the SOEG, by 1942 a well-known and influential agency, provided a significant rampart in the DAM's defense against the Reich Minister of Propaganda.[98]

Within the framework of a general agreement on mutual cooperation, the SOEG and the DAM joined forces to establish three new organizations: the Society of Friends of the German Academy in Vienna (*Gesellschaft der Freunde der Deutschen Akademie in Wien*), the Southeast Seminar (*Südost-Seminar*), and a planned but never formally organized Prince Eugene Institute.[99] The impetus for the Society of Friends undoubtedly came

97. See [Heinrich] Hä[rtle] (assistant to the head of the Office of Academic Affairs in Rosenberg's office for the control of Party ideology), "Aktennotiz für den Reichsleiter [i.e. Rosenberg]—Betrifft: Amt Wissenschaft und NS-Dozentenbund," 2 April 1941, National Archives Microcopy No. T-81 (hereafter cited as T-81), roll 52, frame 55001; Heinrichsbauer to Kraus, 7 June 1943, T-71, roll 55, frame 451658; and particularly Heinrichsbauer to Schirach (report on a trip to Berlin 2–4 Dec. 1942), 5 Dec. 1942, T-71, roll 53, frame 448849.

98. Kratz to Heinrichsbauer, "Betr.: Deustche Akademie," 10 March 1942, *ibid.*, frame 558444.

99. There was no connection between this project and the earlier Prince Eugene Society. Aside from these specific organizations, the DAM and the SOEG also planned (but never fully carried out) a general bilateral title exchange, in a manner very reminiscent of the regimental uniform exchanges common among

from Schirach, whose ambitions to appear publicly as a cultural leader in Vienna could not be satisfied by the behind-the-scenes coordinating work of the Working Committee for Cultural Policy. Kratz, the Vienna Party representative in Berlin made contact with the DAM in March 1942, and by the end of the year an agreement had been reached on the specific functions of the Society of Friends. The Society of Friends sponsored the DAM's language courses in Vienna, while the Working Committee for Cultural Policy and the DAM's Goethe Institute undertook jointly to organize a series of lectures (*Volksbildungswerk*) in Vienna. On the propagandistic side, the new agency would appear as the sponsor of various cultural meetings, lectures, and exhibitions.[100]

The organizational structure of the Society of Friends of the German Academy in Vienna reflected the relative power position of the partners. Schirach became its president; Kraus along with his other tasks, executive secretary; Heinrichsbauer, an adminis-

---

European royalty before World War I. The exchange was to involve the following officials and titles:

Name	SOEG Position	Proposed DAM Title
Schirach	president	senator
Rafelsberger	vice-president	member of the economic council
Kratz	Berlin representative	⎰members of the committee on
Heinrichsbauer	executive secretary	⎱ German Balkan relations

Name	DAM Position	Proposed SOEG Title
Siebert	president	vice-president
von Strauss	vice-president	members of the *Beirat*
Dölger	vice-president	members of the *Beirat*
Heitzer	vice-president	members of the *Beirat*
Druschky	vice-president	members of the *Beirat*

See Gnauk (of the Berlin office of the DAM), "Bericht über eine Besprechung in Wien am 30.6.1942 zwischen Herrn Heinrichsbauer, Herrn Felix Kraus, Herrn Professor Dölger, Herrn Heitzer, Herrn Druschky und Herrn Gnauk über die Aufgaben der Gesellschaft der Freunde der Deutschen Akademie in Wien und über die Zusammenarbeit zwischen der Südosteuropa-Gesellschaft und der Deutschen Akademie," 4 July 1942, T-71, roll 60, frame 558431.

100. Gnauk, "Bericht . . . ," 4 July 1942, T-71, roll 60, frame 558430; Kraus, "Aktenvermerk—Betrifft: Gesellschaft der Freunde der Deutschen Akademie in Wien," 10 Nov. 1942 [?], *ibid.*, frames 558397–98; SOEG, Gesellschaft der Freunde der Deutschen Akademie in Wien [Kraus?], "Satzung," ca. Nov. 1942, paragraph 1, *ibid.*, frame 558407.

trative presidium member (*geschäftsführendes Präsidialmitglied*); and the SOEG's own treasurer, Buzzi, performed the same service for the Society of Friends.[101] The SOEG's means of control over this new affiliate were, however, rather limited. Not only did the DAM retain control over all basic policy decisions, but, aside from the salary of Kraus and his office staff, the SOEG provided no financial support for the organization. The Society of Friends financed itself partly from the members' regular contributions,[102] but primarily by the well-established NSDAP practice of forced contributions from prominent firms and individuals.[103]

The Southeast Seminar was of Austrian origin. It had long been recognized in Viennese National Socialist educational and academic circles that the city's claim to preeminence as the Reich's Southeast City was to a considerable extent dependent on the quality of its educational facilities for training Balkan and German students for work in the Balkan countries. Blaschke, as head of the city's office for cultural affairs, became particularly concerned with the lack of adequate language training facilities, and in mid-1942 he suggested to Kraus that the SOEG sponsor a Southeast Seminar. This agency in turn would organize language courses for the German and Balkan languages.[104] These plans, which envisioned a new and independent facility for language instruction, met with the determined opposition of the DAM. During the discussions in July 1942, which led to the agreement between the SOEG and the DAM, the DAM representatives apparently reminded Heinrichsbauer and

101. Schirach to Kraus, 31 March 1943, T-71, roll 61, frame 559416; Schirach to Buzzi, 3 May 1942, *ibid.*, frame 559361.

102. Heinrichsbauer and Kraus agreed that the total number of members of the Society of Friends should be between 80 and 100. See Kraus to Heinrichsbauer, 29 July 1942, T-71, roll 56, frame 451983.

103. "DAM Satzung," paragraphs 2, 4, 6, T-71, roll 60, frames 558407–08; Kraus, "Aktenvermerk—Betrifft: Gesellschaft der Freunde der Deutschen Akademie in Wien," Nov. 1942, *ibid.*, frame 558400; Heinrichsbauer to Kraus, 20 Nov. 1942, T-71, roll 56, frame 451867; Kraus to Buzzi, 1 Sept. 1943, T-71, roll 55, frame 451613; Heinrichsbauer to Kraus, "Betrifft: Finanzplan des Wiener Freundeskreises der D.A.," 4 Sept. 1943, *ibid.*, frame 451608.

104. Kraus, "Aktenvermerk," 22 June 1942, T-71, roll 56, frames 452009–10.

his associates of the *Führererlass,* according to which the DAM
alone was entitled to promote the use and knowledge of the
German language abroad. The DAM did not, however, insist
on sole control of the Southeast Seminar. Instead, it offered a
compromise proposal that indicated its great interest in arriving
at a satisfactory working agreement with the SOEG. The DAM
became the SOEG's partner in founding and administering the
Southeast Seminar.[105]

When it was formally organized, the Southeast Seminar was
governed by a working committee (*Arbeitskreis*), consisting of
various academic and Party personalities, to whom the director
was responsible. The SOEG's central office maintained complete
organizational and administrative control over the seminar.[106] Financially, the SOEG's influence was limited; it contributed only
a third of the seminar's operating budget, with the DAM and
the city of Vienna paying the remainder.[107]

Despite their agreements and joint projects, the relationship
between the SOEG and the DAM was permeated by mutual
vigilance and distrust. The DAM resented its position of weakness, and the SOEG hoped to bring the older organization's activities in Southeastern Europe under its control. The strange
nature of this marriage of convenience is vividly reflected in
the negotiations over the establishment of the abortive Prince
Eugene Institute. Plans for this organization were first discussed
in April 1943. The institute was apparently the brainchild of
Felix Kraus. The executive secretary of the SOEG's Committee

105. Kraus, "Aktenvermerk—Besprechung mit Direktor Heitzer von der
Deutschen Akademie," 16 Sept. 1942, *ibid.,* frame 451962; Gnauk, "Bericht . . . ,"
4 July 1942, T-71, roll 60, frame 558430; Kraus [?], "Niederschrift über die
gründende Besprechung eines Arbeitskreises für das Südost-Seminar-der Südosteuropa-Gesellschaft und der Deutschen Akademie am 4.9.1942, 9 Uhr 30," 3
Sept. 1942, [sic], T-71, roll 56, frames 451968–69. The DAM exercised its partial
control through its Viennese affiliate, the *Freundeskreis.*

106. Kraus, "Entwurf für ein Schreiben der SOEG an die D.A. München,"
22 Oct. 1942, *ibid.,* frame 451908. When eventually constituted, the following
organizations were represented in the *Arbeitskreis:* SOEG, DAM, *Reichspropagandaamt,* the rectors of the University of Vienna and the *Hochschule für
Welthandel,* the *Volksbildungswerk* of the *Deutsche Arbeitsfront,* and the
Fachschaft für Dolmetscherwesen. See *ibid.*

107. Kraus, "Aktenvermerk—Besprechung mit Direktor Heitzer von der
Deutschen Akademie," 16 Sept. 1942, *ibid.,* frame 451963.

for Cultural Policy hoped to establish the Prince Eugene Institute as a coordinating office to handle propaganda and public relations activities for all joint DAM–SOEG projects.[108] Quite probably, Kraus intended to use the new office to broaden his own field of activity to include public cultural affairs, while at the same time maintaining the Committee for Cultural Policy for its behind-the-scenes coordinating and controlling functions. The new institute was definitely not intended as a replacement for the earlier organization.[109] The DAM opposed Kraus's plans because it claimed that to subordinate its cultural work in Vienna to a new Dachgesellschaft was incompatible with the DAM's status and prestige. The DAM favored a loose working agreement, not a new, formally established agency.[110] The battle remained stalemated (the issue was still hotly contested in February 1944),[111] and the institute was never established, but the brief episode does illuminate the true nature of the relations between the DAM and the SOEG: an established, tradition-laden agency fighting a determined but losing battle against a large and more powerful opponent allies itself momentarily with a third organization—new, ruthless, dynamic, but of second-rate status—thereby aiding the ally in its climb upward and simultaneously arresting the established office's own downfall. To obtain at least an approximate picture of the history of public administration in the Third Reich, this process must be multiplied countless times.

In accordance with the unwritten laws governing National Socialist bureaucratic struggles, defeat resulted in the subordination of one's own agency to the victorious office; victory brought the right to annex or subordinate the defeated agency. Working agreements and compromises represented momentary armistices between equals. Such a truce could either take the form of a specific joint undertaking, as was the case in the DAM–SOEG

108. Kraus [?], "Entwurf—Abkommen zwischen Stadt Wien, Deutscher Akademie und Südosteuropa-Gesellschaft," 27 Oct. 1943, T-71, roll 60, frames 558487–88.

109. Kraus to Heitzer, 27 April 1943, *ibid.*, frames 558495–97; Kraus to Heitzer, 12 Oct. 1943, *ibid.*, frame 558490.

110. Heitzer to Kraus, 2 July 1943, *ibid.*, frames 558492–93.

111. See Kraus, "Aktenvermerk," 10 Feb. 1944, T-71, roll 60, frames 558485–86.

agreements, or it could result in more general accords of cooperation. The SOEG's relation with the Central Association of Industry in Bohemia and Moravia (*Zentralverband der Industrie in
Böhmen und Mähren*) falls into the latter category. The place
of the Czech Protectorate in the Greater German Reich was
in some ways similar to that of Austria. In comparison with
the Altreich, both were rather neglected stepchildren located
on the geographic fringes of the Third Reich. Like the SOEG,
the industrial association was an agency whose own administrative expansion was to a very large degree dependent upon the
development and prosperity of its geographic area. A desire for
mutual cooperation was thus a natural one for the two
organizations.

The SOEG and the association approached each other warily.
A first agreement between the two agencies was concluded in
May 1940. It represented the SOEG's formal recognition of the
Zentralverband's fief. The SOEG and the association merely recognized the need for constant study of the relations between
the Balkans and the Czech Protectorate. The two organizations
agreed that the supervision of such studies should be left in
the hands of the German business interests in the former Czech
territory as represented by the Association of German Businessmen in Bohemia and Moravia (*Deutsche Gesellschaft der
Wirtschaft in Böhmen und Mähren*), the compulsory corporative
organization encompassing all German business firms in the
protectorate.[112]

This first agreement was followed by a period that marked
the SOEG's own rapid growth and development. At the same
time the Viennese organization assiduously cultivated the goodwill and friendship of the Prague agencies.[113] The *Zentralverband*
was receptive, and in December 1941 the two organizations held

112. SOEG (Breza) to Zentralverband der Industrie in Böhmen und Mähren
(Adolf) (head of the *Zentralverband* and chairman of the presidium of the
Deutsche Gesellschaft der Wirtschaft in Böhmen und Mähren), 7 May 1940,
T-71, roll 57, frame 454868. The *Deutsche Gesellschaft* represented the *Zentraver-
band's* own administrative expansion within the Protectorate. When it was fully
established, the Deutsche Gesellschaft superceded the earlier *Zentralverband*.

113. See, for instance, Heinrichsbauer to Adolf, 12 Nov. 1941, *ibid.*, frame
453926.

a joint congress in Prague to demonstrate publicly their mutual interests. The meeting, which was attended by such high-ranking personages as Funk and Reinhard Heydrich (then deputy protector) was an immensely successful affair.[114] Eleven months later, the two organizations signed a formal treaty.

This document is of considerable interest, not only because it illustrates that the SOEG, in contrast to its position in May 1940, had now become the senior and more powerful partner of the two, but also because the treaty undoubtedly exemplified the type of relationship the SOEG hoped to establish with other equals. The pact was the blueprint for the intended future position of the SOEG among other Balkan agencies.[115] Each organization agreed to consult the other in regard to matters affecting the other's field of competence and to establish a close working relationship (*Arbeitsverhältnis*). The heart of the pact, however, was contained in the following passage:

The German Economic Association in Bohemia and Moravia looks upon the SOEG primarily as that organization which is to coordinate the wishes of the Reich territories interested in exports to the Balkans among each other, and to bring them into conformity with the needs of the entire Greater German *Raum*. . . . Economic plans for all those districts of the Reich interested in Southeastern markets are to be drafted within the framework of the SOEG.[116]

In its relations with the economic interests of the Czech Protectorate, the SOEG had achieved its ultimate ambition—it had

114. For a description of the convention, see below, pp. 79–81.

115. Heinrichsbauer to Deutsche Gesellschaft der Wirtschaft in Böhmen und Mähren, 24 Nov. 1942, T-71, roll 57, frame 453887. The treaty character of the document was underscored by the fact that it was signed on the occasion of a state visit by the state secretary of the Protectorate, Karl H. Frank, to Vienna. See "Besuch Staatessekretär Frank, Prag, in Wien am 23./24.11.1942 —Allgemeines," Nov. 1942, T-84, roll 197, frames 1562722–23.

116. SOEG and Deutsche Gesellschaft . . . , "Abkommen," 24 Nov. 1942, T-71, roll 57, frame 453888. The German original is as follows: "Die Deutsche Gesellschaft . . . sieht in der Südosteuropa-Gesellschaft insbesondere das Instrument die Belange der am Südostexport interessierten Reichsgebiete untereinander abzustimmen und mit den Erfordernissen des gesamten Grossdeutschen Raumes in Übereinstimmung zu bringen. . . . Im Rahmen der Südosteuropa-Gesellschaft soll die Wirtschaftsplanung für alle jene Bezirke des Reiches vorgenommen werden, die am Südostmarkt interessiert sind."

been fully recognized as the controlling and decisive German Balkan agency.[117]

The first need of the SOEG was undoubtedly to expand its number of affiliates and agreements. Only in this manner could the Society demonstrate its dynamic nature and attract the support and cooperation of Reich and Viennese agencies. But the SOEG, and in particular Heinrichsbauer, also had to realize that expansion without cooperation could quickly result in administrative chaos at the center and institutional autonomy for the affiliates. Moreover, the administrative flexibility and informality of the Dachgesellschaft structure made the task of effective intra-SOEG coordination both more pressing and more difficult.

The SOEG could solve its problem in two ways. On the one hand, the Society's presidium and board of directors could become institutions that were representative of the various affiliates and empowered to reach basic policy decisions. Such a development, however, would have required a membership in the SOEG's governing bodies that was chosen on a basis other than propaganda and public relations. This the SOEG, in view of its precarious position within the maze of Reich agencies, could not afford to do. In addition, such a decision-making body would have severely affected the pivotal power position of the SOEG's executive secretary, a development in which Heinrichsbauer could not be expected to acquiesce. Instead, intra-SOEG coordination was achieved by placing the major administrative officers of the SOEG in important administrative positions in the affiliates, and by reciprocally appointing the leading affiliate officers to posts on the governing boards of other affiliates. Heinrichsbauer, it will be recalled, made it a guiding principle of his administration to be appointed a member of the governing body of all SOEG affiliates. The same is true to some extent

117. The agreement did not contain any specific benefits or advantages to the *Deutsche Gesellschaft* as it did for the SOEG. Apparently, the *Deutsche Gesellschaft* was convinced that the SOEG was indeed *the* German Balkan agency of the future, and therefore regarded the provision in the agreement that the SOEG would consult the *Deutsche Gesellschaft* on all matters affecting the Protectorate as sufficient payment for its recognition of the SOEG's dominant position. See "Abkommen."

of Rafelsberger who, as vice-president of the SOEG, was also head of the Corn Committee and the Industrial Planning Committee (*Ausschuss für Wirtschaftswissenschaftliche Planung*),[118] and a presidial member of the Society of Friends of the DAM. Buzzi, the SOEG's treasurer, held the same post with the Society of Friends.

The agricultural affiliates of the Society were particularly effective in integrating their personnel. Both Mayerzedt and Rischka added important positions in the SOEG's Southeast Cooperative Institute (*Südostgenossenschaftsinstitut*) to their leadership of the Nutrition and Agriculture Group.[119] Only the Corn Committee represented an exception to this picture of close integration. Ulmansky held no SOEG position except that of administrative secretary of this committee. This situation must undoubtedly be attributed to Rischka's opposition to the establishment of the Corn Committee, and in itself testifies to the influence of his Party office within the other agricultural units of the SOEG.

The same pattern was to a lesser extent repeated in the cultural polity category of SOEG affiliates. Hanns Blaschke, head of the Committee for Cultural Policy, was also a member of the governing bodies of the Society of Friends and the Southeast Seminar.

The Dachgesellschaft form of organization was undoubtedly the decisive factor in the SOEG's rise to respected power in the Third Reich. The Society's development was completely stifled when it attempted to establish itself as a centralized control organ; as a Dachgesellschaft it rapidly attained a position of influence and prestige.[120] By 1944 the SOEG had established itself as a direct, recognized, and influential participant in almost all fields of German Balkan activities—from academic research and cultural propaganda to economic planning and aid to German private enterprise.

118. The work and structure of this committee, in many respects the most important of the SOEG's affiliates, is discussed in some detail in Chapter 4.

119. The work of the *Südostgenossenschaftsinstitut* is discussed below, pages 168–69.

120. Gerhard Misch (the SOEG's representative in Budapest) to Heinrichsbauer, 12 Dec. 1942, T-84, roll 137, frame 1439875.

It may not be an exaggeration to suggest that the Dachgesell-schaft succeeded precisely because as a decentralized, loosely connected but well-run organization, it stood out as a refreshing novelty in a system that by and large knew only cumbersome centralism, overbearing bureaucratism, and—not infrequently— appalling incompetence. The SOEG's success was also a personal triumph for August Heinrichsbauer. Not only did he originate the Dachgesellschaft concept and manage to administer his so-ciety with fewer than ten full-time employees, but the respect, goodwill, and financial support that the Society enjoyed was in large measure a direct result of his tactful and effective ad-ministrative techniques.

3 | The Harmless Display Case: The SOEG's Public Image

THE SOEG's administrative growth was largely a behind-the-scenes development. The agreements that created new affiliates or moved the Society into new areas of policy execution were confidential documents that never reached the public eye. Yet the SOEG took great pains to structure an imposing and favorable public image for itself. Not only was the Society always conscious of its eventual representational role, its leaders also never forgot that the public image of an agency in the Third Reich was an important factor in the institution's total compendium of power. The history of the SOEG provides voluminous evidence that the give-and-take of political interaction does not cease in a totalitarian system; the rules and goals of the political game are merely redefined to avoid disturbing the system's monolithic facade. Instead of political parties competing for public favor, power

67

groups and agencies vie for favorable attention of the uncontested central leadership. All political life thus takes place
within the system, but far from being insignificant, the public
relations and image of a National Socialist agency actually
acquired significance beyond that found in plural–democratic
political societies. Thus, while the public facade of an organization in the Third Reich was inevitably structured so as to become
an integral part of the overall propaganda image desired by the
center, fulfilling this indispensable prerequisite still left the
organization a great deal of freedom to use its public image as
an element of strength in its intrasystem struggles. An impressive public image could do a great deal toward propelling an
agency to regional or national prominence and perhaps even
attract the favorable attention of the center itself.

Since its uniqueness among German agencies lay precisely in
combining within its framework the functions of a governmental
executive organ and those of an ostensibly private group, the
establishment of a public image was for the SOEG a predetermined necessity.[1] However, while the need for the creation of
an effective public image was never in question, the SOEG had
no ready-made patterns for the construction of an effective public
image available. Like its administrative structure, its public
facade had to be built on an ad hoc basis in full view of its
political rivals and victims.

The formation of the SOEG's public image falls into two
broad chronological dimensions: the first spans the months from
the founding of the Society to about June 1942; the second
from mid-1942 to late in 1944.

At the outset, the SOEG's public image program had the immediate task of documenting the insignificant Society's existence
to the widest possible circle of agencies and personalities. This

1. The dual nature of the SOEG has been completely neglected in the postwar
descriptions of the Society's functions. Schirach, understandably, mentioned only
its public and scientific purposes, while Balkan authors, also understandably,
have seen only the exploitative nature of the SOEG. See examination of Schirach
by his defense attorney, Dr. Sauter, on May 23, 1946, in *IMT*, XIV, 413;
and Berend and Ranki, "Expansion," p. 320. Schirach apparently felt that his
post as president of the SOEG was a material point in his defense. See, *IMT*,
XIV, 413.

first goal could be achieved most effectively by staging presentations and arranging contacts that had an intrasystem impact (that is, they should impress but not alienate other Nazi agencies), while simultaneously aiding the overall German propaganda effort vis-à-vis the Balkan nations. To begin with, the SOEG could offer little more than promises of future significance, though it made the best of these. Van Raay, one of its nominal founders, was the owner of the *Südost-Echo*, an important regional newspaper, and the Society obtained early publicity through this media. Rafelsberger, too, appeared in print to underscore the Society's future importance.[2]

By late spring of 1940, the SOEG realized that the rapid development of a nationwide public image was an impossible goal,[3] and the Society shifted its primary attention to the creation of a position of local importance. The SOEG lacked influence,[4] but even in 1940 it did not lack money; it used its abundant financial resources to establish its public image in Vienna. In late April the SOEG began to sponsor a series of lectures on Southeastern European economic problems. The talks began with an address by Karoly Ereky, a former minister in the Hungarian government. Two weeks later Kerge Kalendjeff, director of the Cereal Export Corporation in Sofia, spoke on "The Bulgarian Economy and Its Relations with the Economy of the German Reich," and on May 21, the Slovakian economist (and later the director of the Slovak National Bank) Karvas chose the title "Slovakia as an Economic Unit" for his lecture. The series closed with a lecture by Mihail Manoilescu, a former Rumanian minister. The SOEG bore all costs of the series—honorariums, travel, dinners, hotel accommodations.[5]

2. "Wien—Südosten, die Gründung der Südosteuropa-Gesellschaft," *Südost-Echo*, 5 April 1940, p. 2; Rafelsberger, "Wirtschaftsplanung," p. 378.

3. See above, pp. 30–33.

4. This was the time of the Prince Eugene Society fiasco. See above, pp. 34–37.

5. A list of the lectures, including the speaker, the subjects, and the dates, appears as an enclosure to SOEG to Aussenhandelsstelle Wien, 18 Dec., 1940, T-71, roll 53, frame 453070. The SOEG also attempted to broaden the impact of the lecture series by publishing several of the talks in the newly established Schriften series. See, for example, SOEG, *Südosteuropa-Probleme* (Vienna, 1940); SOEG, *Agrarpolitische Vorträge der Südosteuropa-Gesellschaft* (Vienna, 1940).

Important as it was, the lecture series could have little immediate significance beyond the Viennese area. To widen the
SOEG's appeal in the Balkans and in the Reich, Heinrichsbauer
in the spring of 1940 set out to become an agency-to-agency
salesman. His first trip took him to five Southeastern capitals,
Budapest, Bucharest, Sofia, Athens, and Belgrade. The purpose
of the journey was patently promotional; in a whirlwind tour
of the five cities he managed to speak to various officials (including the minister and commercial attachés) in the German lega-
tions, the correspondents of the leading German newspapers,
officers of the German-Balkan chambers of commerce, branch
managers of important German firms in the Balkans, as well
as high-ranking officials of the Southeastern European economics
and commerce ministries and the officers of leading Balkan banks
and business firms—all within some three weeks.[6] In the fall,
the executive secretary travelled north to the Reich capital.
Again, he attempted to establish satisfactory relations with, or
at least allay the fears of, a large number of governmental and
corporative agencies. Heinrichsbauer's success was limited. While
the various agencies usually provided at least a noncommittal
promise of cooperation, they rarely gave him specific and formal
assurances of support.

Heinrichsbauer's journeys were nevertheless an important
facet of the SOEG's campaign to develop an impressive public
image. No Nazi official was more poignantly aware than August
Heinrichsbauer that in the context of the debureaucratized,
neofeudal Nazi governmental system purely institutional dealings
were always less satisfactory foundations for effective interagency
cooperation than personal relations.[7] In the trying days of 1940
the SOEG had few friends, and while Heinrichsbauer sought
to enlarge their number, the Society also made astute use of
those it did possess. For example Carl Clodius, deputy chief of

6. See the enclosure in Heinrichsbauer to Fischböck, 29 April 1940, T-41,
roll 61, frame 559194; the untitled list of names and addresses, *ibid.*, frames
559182–86. Heinrichsbauer's general impressions of the trip were published in
the Schriften series. See *Eindrücke von einer Balkanreise im April/Mai 1940*
(Vienna, 1940).

7. Heinrichsbauer to Rafelsberger, 5 Oct. 1940, T-71, roll 74, frames 575561–68.

the economic policy department of the German Foreign Ministry, gave an after-dinner talk under the auspices of the SOEG.
The audience consisted of some forty specifically invited Viennese businessmen and government officials; the atmosphere was
deliberately intimate. In view of the highly select audience,
Clodius was able to speak quite informally and to touch upon
matters of a semiconfidential nature unsuitable for the general
public.[8] The guests were presumably flattered by their own presence at the occasion and, the SOEG hoped, would recall that
the Society had provided the opportunity for the confidential
talk.

At the end of 1940, the SOEG could look back on its advertising campaign as only a partial success. Heinrichsbauer was
pleased with the results of the Balkan trip,[9] but in many other
areas the Society's position was by no means firmly established.
Funk did not see fit to mention his creation in his opening address at the 1940 Vienna Fall Fair,[10] and a book published in
1940 cited one of the lectures given before the Society in June
of that year, but made no mention of the SOEG itself.[11] Heinrichsbauer realized that in the new year, too, the SOEG needed
to continue its efforts to arouse interest.[12]

As was true of so many other facets of the SOEG's organizational development, a significant change in the SOEG's image-
creating tactics occurred with the Society's adoption of the umbrella (*Dachgesellschaft*) form of administrative organization.

8. Heinrichsbauer to Hudeczek (of the Foreign Ministry), 4 Jan. 1941, T-71,
roll 51, frame 447204. Clodius was one major official who had supported the
SOEG and its aims from the very beginning. See Breza, "Bericht über ein
Gespräch mit Gesandten Clodius gelegentlich eines von ihm veranstalteten Mit-
tagessens im Hotel Imperial zu Ehren der ungarischen Handelsdelegation am
16.11.1940," T-71, roll 69, frame 568382; Heinrichsbauer to Rafelsberger, 21 Nov.
1940, T-71, roll 74, frame 575478.
9. Heinrichsbauer to Bergemann, 30 April 1940, T-71, roll 68, frame 567361.
10. [Walther Funk], "Rede des Reichswirtschaftsministers Funk über den or-
ganischen Wirtschaftsaufbau in Europa bei der Eröffnung der 38. Wiener
Herbstmesse im Festsaal des Konzerthauses zu Wien vom 1. September 1940,"
in *Dokumente der Deutschen Politik*, ed. Franz A. Six, (Berlin, 1943) VIII,
Part 2, pp. 692–701.
11. Leibrock, *Südosten*, p. 156.
12. Heinrichsbauer to Rafelsberger, 18 Jan. 1941, T-71, roll 74, frame 575344.

Late in 1940 or during the first part of 1941 the SOEG, while
not abandoning its attempts to establish an impressive facade,[13]
began to shift the focal point of its public activities to service
functions. The Society neglected a far-ranging program of public
functions in favor of specific services and aids directed to the
German business community, and particularly to its Viennese
segment. The SOEG began to play an active role in the Vienna
Fairs, deliberately assisting the Fair management without attempting to supersede it. During the 1940 Fall Fair, the Society
sponsored a series of lectures on Balkan transportation problems
in which such prominent officials as Rudolf Töpfer, the head
of the Reich railroads administration in Vienna, Dilg, a director of the German firm *Donaudampfschiffahrtsgesellschaft,* and
Phillipp von Schoeller, the head of the Viennese chamber of
commerce, spoke.[14] In the following year the SOEG, as usual
financially well situated, treated foreign delegations to breakfasts, opera visits, and other peacetime amities.[15]

Perhaps the most important of the services the SOEG provided under its new policy was the publication of the *Vertrauliche Wirtschaftsnachrichten der Südosteuropa-Gesellschaft*
(VWN), a newsletter offering confidential economic news. This
news service apparently met a distinct need among German businessmen. To conduct their affairs effectively, they needed a great
deal of information on foreign economic and political developments. The German mass media provided only the most cursory
(and hence useless) generalities, and all confidential reports from
the Balkans normally went only to high-level Reich offices.[16]
In May 1941, the SOEG's *VWN* began to fill this void. The

13. In September 1940, Schirach was attempting to secure the former winter
palace of Prince Eugene for use by the SOEG, but Heinrichsbauer feared even
it would be inadequate in view of Schirach's plans for the Society. See Heinrichsbauer to Kratz, 24 Sept. 1940, T-71, roll 72, frame 572244.
14. Enclosure in SOEG to Aussenhandelsstelle Wien, 18 Dec. 1940, T-71, roll
53, frame 453071. The talks were also published. See SOEG, *Verkehrspolitische
Vorträge der Südosteuropa-Gesellschaft* (Vienna, 1940).
15. See "Wiener Herbstmesse 21. bis 28. September 1941," T-84, roll 197, frames
1563107–18.
16. The need for a sort of German Kiplinger letter had been apparent as
early as 1939. See Edmund Fürholzer (an official of the Transocean News Service

reports appeared continuously in both a daily (five times a week) and a weekly edition from May 12, 1941 to about July 1944, with the exception of some two months in 1942 when its continued publication was under review by the Propaganda Ministry. The weekly reports appeared in an edition of about twenty pages; the daily reviews contained from five to eight pages. The *VWN* had a security classification of confidential, sufficiently low to enable about 220 interested firms and agencies to receive the SOEG's newssheet.[17] The editor of the service was Franz Ronneberger, who also headed the Viennese press office of the Foreign Ministry, and edited the *Völkischer Beobachter*'s Viennese edition.[18]

The *VWN* reported on all aspects of economic development in the Balkans. The daily editions focused on brief bulletin-type items of current interest to the practical businessman, and the weekly summaries carried longer articles analyzing general trends and large-scale aspects of the overall economic conditions in the Balkan countries. Throughout its years of publication, the *VWN* was marked by a high degree of objectivity. Particularly the earlier editions carried numerous reports from Swiss newspapers. The newsletter did not attempt to ignore German shortcomings. The issues carried articles acknowledging the German clearing debts to the Southeast European nations and the existing overvaluation of the Reichsmark in the Balkans. With the issues of July 1941, the contents of the *VWN* became quite

---

and I. G. Farben), "Wirtschaftsverlag und Presse," ca. March, 1939, T-81, roll 189, frame 0339639. The report was submitted at the request of the *Werberat der Deutschen Wirtschaft*.

17. Subscribers included not only well-known businessmen and firms but also prominent government and military offices. See, for example, OKW, Wehrwirtschafts- und Rüstungsamt to SOEG, "Betrifft: Vertrauliche Wirtschafts-Nachrichten, Az 37e Wi VIII a," 6 June 1941, T-71, roll 51, frame 446658.

18. Ronneberger was a prolific publicist, who expressed his views on a variety of current topics and in a number of periodicals. For examples of his output, see "Die Stunde der Entscheidung," *Wille und Macht*, VII (15 Dec. 1940), 16–19; "Der politische Südosteuropabegriff," *Reich, Volksordnung, Lebensraum*, VI (1943), 53–107; "Fünf Jahre Slowakischer Staat," *Zeitschrift für Politik*, XXXIV (March–April 1944), 95–100.

sophisticated; it began to carry fewer Swiss and other newspaper
stories, and instead relied more on its own correspondents.[19] The
SOEG also frequently reprinted edited versions of reports it received from its own field offices and confidential representatives.[20]

The development of the *VWN*'s editorial policies paralleled
German overall economic policy aims in the Balkans. In 1941
the reports concentrated on short-term business and commercial
opportunities for German firms, and the only noticeable political
tendency was a definite anti-Italian bias. Beginning in 1942,
in line with the German policies in the Balkans during that
year, the newsletter devoted more space to opportunities for
German investments. Toward the end of 1942 the *VWN*'s depth
and quality of coverage declined markedly, and by 1943 the
SOEG was faced with a definite lack of suitable material. This
is hardly surprising. The opportunities for German private business ventures in the Balkans were in a state of decline. Space
began to be filled with obvious filler material, such as lists of
Balkan companies engaged in a particular branch of industry,
and articles depicting the activities of the SOEG's affiliates and
institutes. Stories of the latter variety are particularly indicative
of a lack of meaningful material since until that time the Society
had kept the SOEG and its functions scrupulously out of the
newsletter.[21]

The *VWN* met with favorable reactions from prominent businessmen all over the Reich,[22] and it was clearly a major step

19. See, for example, "Die Lage in der ungarischen Filmindustrie," *VWN*,
I (Wochenbericht 5–12 May 1941), 6–7; and "Banken und Währung in Serbein,"
ibid., I (Wochenbericht 11 July 1941), 4. There is no list of correspondents
for the *VWN* available, but most appear to have served the SOEG's publication
along with another paper or periodical. The SOEG had no full-time reporters.

20. The articles "Nachkriegspläne der ungarischen Industrie," *VWN*, III
(Wochenberichte 19 and 26 November, 1943), 1–3, 3–5, were edited versions
of Misch's reports to Heinrichsbauer. The functions of the SOEG's field offices
are listed below, pp. 142–43, 154.

21. The account of the *VWN*'s characteristics is a composite impression gained
from a perusal of the publication's entire run. For this reason, it has been
felt that specific article citations would be superfluous as well as inadequate.
A complete file of the *VWN* is available in the Österreichische Nationalbibliothek in Vienna, and the Institut für Weltwirtschaft in Kiel.

22. See Morgenstern (of the Deutsche Bank) to Verschuer (an official of
the Propaganda Ministry?), 11 Nov. 1941, T-71, roll 47, frame 441496.

in clothing the SOEG with the reputation of a service-conscious organization. The image was reinforced by the Society's selfless services in other areas. Fully aware that the Prince Eugene Society fiasco precluded any active role of the SOEG itself in the field of cultural affairs,[23] the Society was content with the indirect benefits that goodwill and personal connections could bring. There was no lack of service opportunities, and other agencies readily welcomed the SOEG's administrative talents and its full coffers. In February 1941, for example, the SOEG sponsored (that is, paid the expenses for) an evening of Rumanian chamber music. The concert was an affair of the Reich Office of Propaganda and it commissioned the SOEG to organize the technical details of the concert.[24]

Through such underground, unheralded activities, the SOEG slowly established a solid foundation of goodwill and trust among other German agencies. It is true that its activities gave it a facade of prestige and influence that had no relation to the reality of its power, but this did not matter. In the Third Reich, with its breakdown of old norms of behavior, activity could easily be mistaken for influence. Indeed, should this appearance or facade be accepted as reality by agencies that were indeed influential, such acceptance could in turn become part of a real foundation for further growth. By the end of 1941, the SOEG had succeeded in weaving together appearances and realities to form a foundation that invited not only inspection but also association by high-level Reich agencies.[25]

23. Even Felix Kraus, who was by no means without grandiose ambitions in this area, realized that at least in 1940 and 1941 it was inopportune to place the SOEG in a cultural limelight. See Kraus, "Ausbau der Südosteuropa Gesellschaft," 11 Dec. 1940, T-71, roll 56, frames 452153–54; Kraus to Karl Haushofer, 5 Dec. 1940, T-253, roll 59, frame 1516241. Kraus knew Haushofer through his activities in the VDA.

24. SOEG to Reichspropagandaamt Vienna, 15 March 1941, T-71, roll 47, frame 441878; "Kosten des Rumänischen Kammermusikabends 17.11.41," T-84, roll 197, frame 1563122. The performance cost the SOEG RM 897.09. At the same time, the Society scrupulously refrained from advertising its cultural activities. The SOEG was not even mentioned in Schirach's speech of April 6, 1941, in which he gave a general review of the Viennese cultural program and agencies. See Schirach, *Das Wiener Kulturprogramm* (Vienna [1941]).

25. The SOEG's new policy of service to the business community was very effective in establishing the SOEG's place in this sector of economic life. By

Perhaps the most significant, tangible by-product of the SOEG's growing stature was Funk's renewed interest in his ward. In the summer of 1940 the Reich Minister of Economics had quickly abandoned the Society to its own devices. However, after the SOEG had rescued itself by Heinrichsbauer's astute diplomacy and tact and had received substantial recognition as a German Balkan agency both among government officials and in private business circles, Funk was more than willing to increase its luster by gracing an important public function of the SOEG with his ministerial presence and a major speech. On June 12, 1941, Funk presided over the installation of the SOEG's presidium and board of directors. Since neither body ever performed any actual work, the ceremony served no other purpose than to put the SOEG's physical presence before the eyes of the public and the press. As a step in the development of the SOEG's public image the ceremony was quite important, for although Funk's public recognition of the SOEG did not establish the Society's status but rather resulted from the influence it had established on its own, the speech and presence of a Reich minister did serve to increase still further the SOEG's status in the eyes of agencies who had not yet come to respect the SOEG's new stature.

The SOEG recognized the propagandistic possibilities of the occasion, and staged the entire event to obtain maximum press coverage and propaganda value from the ceremonies. The SOEG's purpose in staging the meeting was never in doubt. Schirach struck the keynote in introducing Funk. He noted that the minister had been the originator of the SOEG, thereby establishing that despite the lack of any earlier public ties between the SOEG and the minister, the connection between the two

---

the end of 1941, the SOEG's facade was so impressive that the German business sector both in Vienna and in the Reich as a whole regarded the Society as an effective and potent force whose voice carried considerable weight in the councils of Berlin government agencies. See Morgenstern to Heinrichsbauer, 30 Sept. 1941, T-71, roll 47, frame 441504; Hanf-, Jute-, und Textil- Industrie AG to Reich Ministry of Economics, "Betr.: Arisierung der Firma . . . ," 10 Dec. 1941, *ibid.*, frame 564233.

was not a new development.[26] Funk responded with lavish praise for the SOEG and its officials. He singled out Schirach and Heinrichsbauer for specific mention and, perhaps most important of all, he established the SOEG's role as the executive organ for the creation of the New Order in the Balkans in both the governmental and the private German sphere.[27] The substantive content of Funk's address was little more than a reiteration of the public Nazi plans for the New Order and since this presented nothing new to the audience, the center of attention was not the speech but the glittering array of personalities that sat before the Reich minister. All members of the presidium and board of directors were present; in addition to Clodius, Funk addressed such luminaries as Erich Neumann, the State Secretary of the Four Year Plan, Karl Hanke, the Gauleiter of Silesia, Franz Hayler, the head of the Import-Export Group, Werner Lorenz, the president of the Liaison Office for Ethnic Germans, and Alfred Pietzsch, the president of the Reich Chamber of Commerce.

The overall impact of the Vienna meeting was most gratifying to the SOEG. Its own publications, the *VWN*, issued a special edition to commemorate Funk's speech,[28] but such self-praise was hardly necessary. Actually, the Society succeeded in obtaining broad press coverage in several mass-circulation organs.[29]

Despite its grandeur, the June affair was soon overshadowed by a new effort in the SOEG's 1941 saturation campaign to establish an impressive public image, a still more imposing gathering in Prague in December. The two affairs together, and particularly the Prague congress, firmly established the SOEG for Austria, the Czech Protectorate, and even the Reich as the most

26. For Schirach's introduction, see Funk, *Wirtschaftsordnung im Neuen Europa* p. 5. The address was published as part of the Schriften series.
27. *Ibid.*, pp. 9–10. For an analysis of this new order, see below, Chapter 4.
28. "Sonderbericht: zur Rede des Schirmherrn der Südosteuropa-Gesellschaft, Reichsminister Funk, im Rahmen einer Veranstaltung der Gesellschaft am 12.6.1941," *VWN*, I (Wochenbericht 14 June 1941), 1.
29. R[udolf] F[ischer] "Europas erstes Jahr—zur Rede Funks auf der Tagung der Südosteuropa-Gesellschaft," *Südost-Echo*, 13 June 1941, pp. 1–2; "Das Portrait des Tages, Reichsminister Funk—Schirmherr der Südosteuropa-Gesellschaft," *Donauzeitung*, 15 July 1941, p. 3. See also Ulbrich, "Europas Wirtschaftskraft," *Völkischer Beobachter* (North German ed.), 14 June 1941, p. 2.

promising German Balkan agency in the peacetime future. The
Vienna-based SOEG and the German economic interests of
the Czech Protectorate had a common interest in the economic
future of the Balkans since both Austria and Czechoslavakia
had always had extensive commercial and cultural relations with
the Southeast European states. Moreover, as noted before, under
the National Socialists the prestige and influence in the Balkans
of both areas had been overshadowed by the more favored economic interests from the Altreich. It will be recalled that these
reasons had led to the establishment of cordial relations between
the SOEG and the economic interests of the protectorate at
an early date.[30] A joint convention of the two organizations to
underscore their cooperation on Balkan matters was an almost
natural continuation of these relations, particularly after the
SOEG became fully respectable in June 1941. The immediate
impulse for the Prague meeting, however, seems to have come
from Schirach. Since June, Schirach had been the president of
a respected and influential organization, but he still lacked the
prestige of having officially represented the organization at some
function outside his own Gau. He (or his aides) therefore devised
the plan of a state visit to Prague. This would establish the
SOEG's status outside Vienna and simultaneously increase
Schirach's own importance. Heinrichsbauer enthusiastically supported the plan, feeling that it would be as important for the
development of the SOEG as Funk's visit to Vienna had been.[31]

For some reason the idea of a state visit mushroomed into
a full-fledged joint convention of the SOEG and the Association
of German Businessmen in Bohemia and Moravia (*Deutsche
Gesellschaft der Wirtschaft in Böhmen and Mähren*), with about
700 delegates in attendance.[32] It is not difficult to surmise possi-

30. See above, p. 62.

32. The SOEG's records do not give the exact attendance figures, but the
number of German delegates can be estimated from the list of recipients of
a small book reprinting the speeches. The publication was sent as a memento
(*Erinnerungsbuch*) for the delegates. From these lists it would appear that
about 620 German delegates attended. See "Anschriften für den Versand des
Prager Buches der Südosteuropa-Gesellschaft durch Dr. Husty," n.d., T-84, roll

ble reasons for the changed plans. Funk may have shown an interest in a journey to Prague and another speech, and for this the format of the Schirach visit was inadequate. Moreover, the president of the business association, Dr. Bernhard Adolf, a rather pompous and vainglorious individual,[33] may have hoped to increase his own status with a convention in which he would play a prominent part. The new deputy protector of Bohemia and Moravia, Reinhard Heydrich, who had just assumed his post, may have wanted to increase the influence of the SS in the SOEG and the *Deutsche Gesellschaft*. But in all likelihood, the primary motivating factor was a crassly materialistic one: meetings of this sort were a favorite National Socialist pastime and the protectorate was a particularly desired convention site, since conferences there always provided a splendid opportunity for a great number of Party and state officials to travel and be fed at someone else's expense.

In Prague the delegates were no more expected to do actual work than they had been in Vienna. The meeting was held on December 17, 18, and 19, 1941, and it was by far the most elaborate event the SOEG ever sponsored.[34] Such notables as Heydrich, Frank, Funk, and the leading officials of the SOEG and the *Deutsche Gesellschaft* spoke; and high-ranking government, military, and Party officials from the Gaue of Sudetenland, Upper and Lower Silesia, Thuringia, Bayrische Ostmark, Lower and Upper Danube, as well as from the *Generalgouvernement* (Nazi government of Poland), made their appearance in Prague. Even a Czech delegation led by President Hácha sat through the sessions. The agenda for the conference was a model of Third

---

197, frames 1563052–77. The SOEG's draft programs also included plans for the attendance of 50 to 60 Czech officials at the public functions. See "Teilnehmer an der Tagung am 24./26. Oktober in Prag," *ibid.*, frame 1562985. The meeting was originally scheduled for October.

33. Hanel reports that he made a grand entrance to one of the receptions during the Prague meeting wearing a large silk scarf in addition to his suit, and accompanied by two large dogs—one on either side of him. Hanel Interview.

34. "Prager Tagung vom 17. bis 19. Dezember 1941—Teilnehmer an der Tagung am 24./26. Oktober," T-84, roll 197, frame 1562985. The invitation lists for the meeting are on *ibid.*, frames 1562987–1563004.

Reich play-acting, complete with ceremonial visits, receptions, attendance at the theater, and, lodged between the ceremonies, some pseudowork sessions. On December 17, at 4:00 P.M., Funk and Schirach accompanied by Rafelsberger, Heinrichsbauer, Adolf, and Husty (the executive secretary of the business association) called on Heydrich at the Hradčany. Two hours later the convention was formally opened with a program that began with the tones of "solemn music" performed by the Sudeten German Philharmonic Orchestra, included speeches by Heydrich, Funk, and Adolf, and concluded with a pledge of loyalty to the Führer (*Führerehrung*).[35] At 8:00 P.M. Heydrich held a reception for some sixty leading delegates, while the others attended various theaters and other functions in Prague. The morning program of the following day was devoted to working sessions and additional speeches by Funk, Rafelsberger, Adolf, and Hayler. The "work" was soon over. During the afternoon the delegates had an opportunity to visit the Prague city hall and to go sightseeing. In the evening Schirach gave a supper for sixty persons. The delegates spent the third day equally pleasantly. The only planned item was a visit by the delegates to Karlstein Castle and a breakfast that Funk gave.[36]

The various speeches reflected the propagandistic character of the meetings. Heydrich emphasized that the protectorate was by all rights a part of the Reich, but that it had many interests in the Balkans, which in turn led to manifold connections between it and Vienna and the SOEG, "of which you, dear Comrade Schirach, are head, and which is the liaison agency between the

35. In view of the presence of Czech guests, the SOEG had some doubt as to the appropriateness of a *Führerehrung*, but it was held nevertheless, apparently at Heydrich's insistence.

36. "Veranstaltungsfolge der Tagung der Südosteuropa-Gesellschaft Wien und der Deutschen Gesellschaft der Wirtschaft in Böhmen und Mähren, Prag am 17.18. und 19. Dezember 1941" (draft III), 2 Dec. 1941, T-84, roll 197, frames 1563012-13. Despite its appearance, the loose schedule with few formal working sessions had a purpose. Since the meeting was primarily a propaganda and public relations affair, it gave Heinrichsbauer and other SOEG officials long periods of time to meet other important delegates and discuss the SOEG and its stature at length. In the meantime, the delegates of no significance went sight-seeing and hence would not feel left out.

Reich and Southeastern Europe in the realms of economic and cultural policy."[37] Schirach gave a review of the Society's overall (public) aims and briefly described the work of its various units. Funk delivered his usual review of the economic aspects of the New Order, and Rafelsberger in turn lauded the Reich Minister of Economics and the SOEG's president for their interest in the Society. He also touched on the public aspects of the industrial planning project (*Industrieplanung*), and concluded his talk with a note of high praise for Heinrichsbauer. Finally, Adolf emphasized the close cooperation between his organization and the SOEG.[38]

The meetings in Prague added considerable new luster to the SOEG's public image. Simply the presence of a large number of notable Nazi officials would have greatly increased the SOEG's prestige. The fact that these "highest Reich agencies"[39] had proclaimed the SOEG's leading role in the area of economic relations between Germany and the Southeast European states made the Prague meetings a very significant milestone in the SOEG's road to national prominence.[40] One quite tangible result was the SOEG's sudden desirability as a conference partner and organizer. Although it was never held, the Reich Commerce

37. Heydrich, "Die Wirtschaft als massgeblicher Faktor in der staatlichen und politischen Neuordnung Böhmens und Mährens im Reich," *Prag Tagung*, p. 19.

38. Schirach, "Wien und der Südostraum," pp. 21–32; Funk, "Die Aufgabenstellung der Wirtschaft Grossdeutschlands," pp. 33–43; Rafelsberger, "Die Aufgaben Wiens im Rahmen der Wirtschaftsbeziehungen des Reiches," pp. 46–47, 51–54; Adolf, "Die Wirtschaft des Protektorats Böhmen und Mähren und ihre Beziehungen zum Südosten," pp. 98–99. All in *Prag Tagung*.

39. The phrase was used by Gutknecht, head of the *Wehrwirtschaftliche Nachrichtengruppe* (military and economic intelligence section) of the *Wehrwirtschafts- und Rüstungsamt* (Office for War Materiel) in announcing a visit to the SOEG in order to inform himself firsthand what the city and the SOEG had done to carry out their broad mandate. See Gutknecht to Heinrichsbauer, 15 April 1942, T-71, roll 51, frame 446652.

40. The Prague convention received extensive national press coverage. An issue of the periodical *Böhmen und Mähren* (III [Jan. 1942]) was devoted entirely to it. See also "Südostaufgaben des Protektorats," *Donauzeitung*, 8 Jan. 1942, p. 5; "Böhmen und Mähren im europäischen Wirtschaftsraum," *Völkischer Beobachter* (North German ed.), 20 Dec. 1941, T-41, roll 47, frame 441485.

Group planned a large-scale joint convention with the SOEG in the spring of 1942.[41] Clodius and Hayler were to speak, and the various regional committees of the Reich Commerce Group were to hold meetings on Balkan problems.[42] Even the Foreign Ministry found some use for the SOEG. During his stays in Vienna on a journey to and from Berlin, the Croatian Minister of Commerce, Toth, was a guest of the SOEG. The Society's services were requested by the German legation in Zagreb.[43]

In June 1942 the SOEG had another major opportunity to display its organizational talents. The Workshop of the Association of Institutes for Research on Eastern and Southeastern Europe (*Arbeitstagung der Arbeitsgemeinschaft wissenschaftlicher Ost- und Südostinstitute*) was held in Vienna under the auspices of the SOEG and the Balkan Committee of the Vienna Institutes of Higher Learning (*Südostgemeinschaft Wiener Hochschulen*) from June 24 to 28. There is little point in reiterating the individual events, since essentially they duplicated those in Prague. Like the earlier meeting, it was a distinct triumph for the SOEG. Reich Minister of Education Rust attended this meeting in preference to a similar affair sponsored by Rosenberg's Ministry for Occupied Eastern Territories in Berlin.[44] The usual pattern of visits, breakfasts, and a solemn opening address was repeated. It is true that the conference scheduled some actual work sessions, but practical results of the meetings were negligible. The conference had originally been scheduled to coordinate the academic research work of the German economists with the aims and activities of the SOEG's In-

41. See Janowsky (executive secretary of the *Wirtschaftsgruppe Gross-, Ein- und Ausfuhrhandel*) to Heinrichsbauer, 12 March 1942, T-84, roll 88, frame 1378726.

42. Hanel, "Südosttagung der Reichsgruppe Handel und der Südosteuropa-Gesellschaft" (draft), 6 March 1942, T-84, roll 197, frame 1562914. The galley proofs of the official program are on *ibid.*, frame 1562917.

43. "Besuch Minister Dr. Toth, Agram (Betreuung durch die SOEG auf Veranlassung der Deutschen Gesandschaft Agram im Auftrage des Auswärtigen Amtes—Programm für den Wiener Aufenthalt von Herrn Minister Dr. Toth)," 7 Feb. 1942, *ibid.*, frames 1562975-77; "Aufenthalt auf der Rückreise von Berlin nach Agram in Wien 12. u. 13.2.," *ibid.*, frame 1562978.

44. Kratz to Rafelsberger, 27 March 1942, T-71, roll 52, frame 447701.

dustrial Planning Committee,[45] but by June 1942 the nature of that committee's plans and projects had undergone such drastic revisions that it was no longer possible to communicate them to the large number of economists and law professors attending the sessions. The lack of substantive results did not, however, detract from the conference's propagandistic success; for the first time even the *Krakauer Zeitung* commented on one of the SOEG's activities.[46] Heinrichsbauer's conventioneering at Prague had obviously borne ample fruit.

After mid-1942, the nature of the SOEG's public functions and the scope of its ambitions changed substantially. The SOEG was now a firmly established agency; it had no further need for mere attention-attracting programs. On the contrary, the Society sought to divert public attention from its top secret industrial planning project, and attempted instead to focus the public spotlight on more harmless items in its display window.[47] Schirach and his associates were able to indulge in their passion for cultural affairs,[48] and the SOEG even unearthed plans for a businessmen's club, which had not been seriously considered since 1940.

The Southeast Club (*Südost-Klub*) was one of the SOEG's earliest business promotion schemes. Heinrichsbauer and his as-

45. For an analysis of this committee's functions and organization, see below pp. 102ff. and 115ff.

46. "Die Ost- und Südosteuropa-Institute—Arbeitstagung in Wien," *Krakauer Zeitung* (Reich ed.), 30 June 1942.

47. One of the effects of the SOEG's preoccupation with industrial planning was a decided decline in the quality of the *VWN*, since the SOEG's Balkan representatives were now used primarily to supply background material for various reports connected with the Society's project. See Kratz to Breza, "Betr.: Vertrauliche Wirtschaftsnachrichten der SOEG," 27 July 1942, T–84, roll 86, frame 1376609; Oberascher to Margl (the *VWN* correspondent in Bucharest), 17 June 1944, T-71, roll 67, frame 567016.

48. Heinrichsbauer to Hudeczek, 19 Dec. 1942, T-71, roll 51, frames 447370, 447373; [Hanel], "Aufenthalt in Ungarn der Südosteuropa-Gesellschaft auf Einladung der Kulturpolitischen Abteilung des Ungarischen Aussenministeriums [24–30 Jan. 1943]—Programm," n.d., T-71, roll 53, frames 448786–88; [Hanel], "Aktenvermerk—Betrifft: Besprechung der Teilnehmer der Ungarnreise der Südosteuropa-Gesellschaft am Samstag, den 23.1.1943 . . . im Hotel Bristol," 3 Feb. 1943, *ibid.*, frame 448790.

sociates hoped to create the elegant and tasteful surroundings of an English gentlemen's club in Vienna, and then use the setting as a place of informal meetings for German and Balkan businessmen. Like most of the SOEG's early plans, the project proved completely unworkable in its original form. As the SOEG struggled to preserve its very existence in the summer and fall of 1940, the plan was soon forgotten, and all that remained of the early dreams was a stillborn agreement enabling the Society to use the fashionable Rennclub's facilities as an eventual setting for the Southeast Club.[49] Two years later the Society had acquired a posture that enabled it to resume its interest in the club plans, though yet another year passed before the club idea became even a rudimentary reality. In May of 1943 Hans Fischböck, then Reich Price Commissioner, delivered the first (and last) address in the most elegant of decorative and culinary surroundings to inaugurate what was intended as the first of a series of club functions. The war situation prevented the continuation of the planned series.[50]

Perhaps the most eloquent testimony to the SOEG's position of influence and prestige after mid-1942 was the sureness and openness with which it now entered the area of cultural affairs and policy. By mid-1942, the Foreign Ministry had apparently forgiven the SOEG the Prince Eugene Society affair, and the ministry agreed that the SOEG could intensify its cultural activities.[51] In response, the SOEG lost no time in launching a number of publications dealing with cultural affairs. A planned

49. See "Tätigkeit, Juni 1941," T-84, roll 196, frame 1562253; Heinrichsbauer to Hans Fischböck (at this time the SOEG's vice-president), 19 July 1940, T-71, roll 61, frames 559168–69; Fischböck to Heinrichsbauer, 25 July 1940, *ibid.,* frame 559167.

50. Heinrichsbauer to Würdinger, 31 May 1943, T-84, roll 197, frame 1563241. For information on the technical arrangements, see Südosteuropa-Gesellschaft, "Vortrag am 21. Mai 1943: Reichskommissar für die Preisbildung Minister a.D. Fischböck," T-71, roll 53, frames 448597–632.

51. Böhm (of the Foreign Ministry) to Kraus, 14 Aug. 1942, T-71, roll 52, frames 447444–45. The ministry later went as far as to suggest that the SOEG become a "clearing agency for cultural relations (*Kulturvermittlung*)" in the Balkans. See Oberascher, "Aktenvermerk-Anregungen des Herrn Dr. Böhm zur Gesamtarbeit der SOEG," 3 Aug. 1944, T-71, roll 51, frame 446911.

quarterly Balkan bibliography was never published, but the SOEG's cultural affiliate did collaborate in issuing a special Balkan supplement to the prestigious *NS-Bibliographie*.[52] No less impressive was the Committee for Cultural Policy's own publishing venture, the *Wiener Brief*. To be sure, in itself the weekly periodical was a modest effort of two and later three pages. It published short articles on Viennese cultural life, announced German editions of Balkan authors, and on occasion printed short, critical reviews of Viennese theatrical productions.[53] Far more important in terms of the SOEG's status among Nazi agencies was the very act of not only publishing a regular journal for cultural affairs under its own sponsorship, but also printing it in German, Slovakian, Croatian, Bulgarian, Rumanian, and Hungarian language editions, since this involved the SOEG directly in German cultural activities in the Balkans, a field in which the Foreign Ministry had previously claimed a monopoly.[54]

The Committee for Cultural Policy did not hold regular sessions until the summer of 1942, but it met on a regular monthly basis after that date. The sessions had an impact on the National Socialist cultural propaganda effort in the Southeast. The meetings always followed the same pattern. Ronneberger, as the group's press officer, gave a decription of cultural conditions in the Balkans (*Kulturpolitischer Lagebericht*), presumably an assessment of the success of German propaganda efforts in the area. The group's major activity, however, was its role as clearing house and directing agency for Viennese cultural propaganda efforts in Southeastern Europe. Each month committee members

52. See "Neues Südosteuropa—eine Sonderbibliographie," *Nationalsozialistische Bibliographie,* VIII (Sept.–Dec. 1943), 1–25.

53. Kraus, "Aktenvermerk über eine Besprechung bei Pg. Blaschke, Rathaus, mit Chefredakteur F. W. Kaiser und Herrn Bojiloff vom UTA-Press-Dienst," 1 June 1942, T-71, roll 56, frames 452012–13; Kraus, "Aktenvermerk—Betrifft: 'Wiener Brief'-UTA-Press," 8 Oct. 1942, *ibid.,* frames 451933–34. The description of the *Wiener Brief*'s contents is necessarily rather scant, since it is based upon an examination of the only issue still extant, that of *Wiener Brief,* III (No. 4, 1944), T-71, roll 60, frames 460401, 460403.

54. Kraus, "Aktenvermerk über eine Besprechung . . . ," 1 June 1942, T-71, roll 56, frame 452013.

representing the major Viennese cultural institutions and agencies submitted their plans to the committee.[55] The Committee in turn was to discuss and coordinate a massive indirect propaganda effort. Perhaps as a consequence of earlier prohibition on independent Viennese initiative, the Committee members seem to have had few actual projects to report during 1942.[56] However, with the blindness to the fortunes of war typical of almost all organizations in the Third Reich regime, the Committee did arrange a full program of Balkan cultural activities for the following season. The famous Burgtheater, the Vienna Philharmonic Orchestra, and the Theater in der Josephsstadt were all scheduled for road trips in the Balkans during that year. At the same time, various Balkan personalities were to give lectures in Vienna.[57] The work of the committee aided both the Reich's propaganda effort and furthered the SOEG's more parochial interests: the Viennese road trips presumably helped to mold and animate Balkan public opinion with pro-German feelings, while the SOEG, through the work of the committee was one step further toward its goal of controlling all Balkan activities in Vienna and the Reich.[58]

The SOEG's growing stature in the cultural affairs field also enabled Schirach to resume his quest for public recognition of his role as Viennese cultural leader. The behind-the-scenes work of the Cultural Committee was ill-suited to his ambitions, but his position as president of the newly created Society of Friends of the German Academy (DAM) in Vienna provided a natural

55. As examples of protocols of the committee's meetings, see Kraus, "2. Arbeitsbesprechung des Kulturpolitischen Arbeitskreises am 2. September 1942, 18 Uhr," n.d., T-71, roll 56, frame 451974; Kraus, "Niederschrift zur Arbeitbesprechung des Kulturpolitischen Arbeitskreises der SOEG vom 4. November 1942," 7 Nov. 1942, *ibid.*, frames 451877–79; Kraus, "Arbeitsbesprechung des Kulturpolitischen Arbeitskreises d. Südosteuropa-Gesellschaft am. 4. September 1944, 18 Uhr," 6 Sept. 1944, *ibid.*, frames 446711–12.

56. See Kraus, "2. Arbeitsbesprechung . . . ," T-71, roll 56, frame 451974; and Kraus, "Niederschrift . . . ," 7 Nov. 1942, *ibid.*, frames 451877–79.

57. Kraus, "Arbeitsbesprechung des Kulturpolitischen Arbeitskreises der Südosteuropa-Gesellschaft am 13. Januar 1943. Beginn 18 Uhr 30," 1 Feb. 1943, *ibid.*, frame 451783.

58. Heinrichsbauer to Kraus, 3 June 1944, T-71, roll 51, frame 446836.

forum for the Gauleiter to appear as a public cultural leader. The Viennese branch of the DAM was established in late June 1942. The president of the DAM, Ludwig Siebert, came to Vienna for the occasion. He paid the usual courtesy call on Schirach, attended the opera, and then—framed by the music of Handel and Bach—installed the Society of Friends and its president with an address on "The Greater German Mission of the German Academy," in the Ceremonial Room of the former imperial Hofburg in Vienna.[59] The technical arrangements for the meeting were handled partly by the SOEG's central office and partly by Kraus, who became the new Society of Friends' administrative secretary. The SOEG again used its ready supply of funds to make the inaugural occasion more impressive: it paid the RM 2,800 fee for a group of musicians from the Vienna Philharmonic Orchestra who played during the formal opening ceremonies.[60]

With eighty-three members, twelve sponsors, and one charter member by 1944, the Society of Friends became an important Viennese institution that did its best to fulfill the promise of the pompous opening ceremonies. As part of the inaugural festivities, Schirach and Siebert formally opened an exhibition of photographs entitled "German Art in the East and Southeast." The SOEG again negotiated the technical details with the DAM, and bore the costs of the showing as well.[61] Thereafter, its major activity was a series of regularly scheduled poetry recitals and lectures in the course of which some of the more prominent National Socialist writers and scholars appeared in Vienna.

59. "Programm—Gründung der Gesellschaft der Freunde der Deutschen Akademie in Wien, 28.–30. Juni 1942," T-84, roll 197, frames 1562772–76. See also "Die Grossdeutsche Sendung der Deutschen Akademie," *Völkischer Beobachter* (North German ed.), 30 June 1942, p. 6.

60. "Ablage Veranstaltungen—Gründung der Gesellschaft der Freunde der Deutschen Akademie in Wien," n.d., T-84, roll 197, frame 1562835.

61. Heinrichsbauer to Frauenfeld (of the RPA), "Betrifft-Gründung der Gesellschaft der Freunde der Deutschen Akademie in Wien/Ausstellung 'Deutsche Kunst im Osten und Südosten,'" 9 May 1942, T-71, roll 47, frames 441891–93. For a list of pictures in the exhibition, see "Bilder der Ausstellung 'Deutsche Kunst im Osten und Südosten,'" n.d., T-84, roll 197, frames 1562805–14.

These sessions of pseudoculture were quite well attended, the average being around 120.[62]

By mid-1942, the SOEG also found that its affiliates could acquire public images of their own by basking in the reflected prestige of the now well-known parent organization. The SOEG's components appeared with increasing frequency as the sponsors of their own periodical publications or as co-sponsors of established publication series, the latter cases no doubt again consequences of the SOEG's free-flowing financial support. Beginning in 1942, the Balkan Committee of the Vienna Institute for Higher Learning became a co-publisher of the *Südosteuropäische Arbeiten* and the *Südost-Forschungen* of the Southeast Institute (*Südostinstitut*) in Munich. Franz Würdinger, the head of the SOEG's legal institute, became an associate editor of the *Zeitschrift für osteuropäisches Recht*, and even the SOEG's in all other respects abortive Southeast Institute for Wood and Forest Research (*Südostinstitut für Wald- und Holzforschung*) in 1944 issued the first (and last) book in its planned *Schriftenreihe*.[63]

Other activities of the SOEG's affiliates similarly underscored the Society's attempt to establish itself publicly as the main German coordinating agency for a wide variety of Balkan affairs. A confidential newssheet, the *Südost-Dienst der Deutschen Wis-*

62. Kraus to Dienstelle Berlin der Deutschen Akademie, 3 July 1944, T-71, roll 51, frame 446727. There were apparently no public functions in 1942 after the installation ceremonies, but on February 15, 1943, the *Stadtkommissar* of Strasbourg, *SS-Standartenführer* Ernst, spoke on "German Alsace within the Greater German Reich," and a week later Dr. Scurla, an *Oberregierungsrat* in the Reich Ministry of Education, gave a lecture on the "Mission Idea [*Sendungsgedanke*] of European Peoples as a Factor in Their Foreign Cultural Policy." Other functions sponsored by the Society of Friends in 1943 and 1944 included a poetry recital by Hans Friedrich Blunck, a favorite Nazi poet (October 4, 1943), and a lecture by the noted Byzantine scholar Franz Dölger on November 23, 1943.

63. See the title pages of *Südost-Forschungen*, VIII (1942, No. 1/2), and *Südosteuropäische Arbeiten*, VIII (1942, No. 1/2); Hermann Schultze von Lassaulx, "Die Rechtsabteilung," in *Jahrbuch des Osteuropa-Instituts zu Breslau 1942*, ed., Hans-Jürgen Seraphim (Breslau, 1943), p. 85; Käte Kriege, *Schrifttumsnachweis über die Serbische Forstwirtschaft und deren Grundlagen* (Vienna, 1944).

senschaft, was scheduled to appear late in 1942. It was designed to keep German Balkan scholars abreast of developments within their field through the publication of dissertation topics, annotated bibliographies of recent publications, and short articles on the practical (that is, political) application of theoretical research. The *Südost-Genossenschaftliche Nachrichten,* a newsletter about cooperatives in Southeast Europe, had similar informative purposes. It appeared first in the fall of 1943, and ceased publication in September of the following year. Here, too, the SOEG provided the link between the Balkans and Germany, since the publication kept interested German circles informed on current developments within the cooperative movement in the Balkan countries.[64] Indeed, the SOEG's name had now acquired such luster in the Third Reich that quite important officials could be engaged as speakers at functions sponsored solely by an affiliate rather than by the Society as a whole. In the fall of 1942, the SOEG's Nutrition and Agriculture Group staged an elaborate convention. During the two-day affair all committees of the Group, as well as the board of directors of the Black Sea Trading and Industrial Company held separate meetings. Several important agricultural officials, led by Dr. Alex Walter, a division chief in the Reich Ministry of Agriculture, and including various high-ranking officials from the Reichsstellen, spoke during the sessions. Walter gave the keynote address for the convention, not surprisingly entitled "Agricultural Cooperation in the European Co-Prosperity Sphere."[65]

The extent to which the appearance of power and influence in the Third Reich became actual power and influence can

64. See "Südost-Dienst der Deutschen Wissenschaft—Mitteilungsblatt für die Deutsche Wissenschaftliche Südostarbeit," T-84, roll 198, frames 1564617–19. It is not clear if the newsletter was ever actually published. Only three issues of the *Nachrichten* are available in the filmed records of the SOEG; No. 3 (1 Dec. 1943), No. 4 (15 April 1944), and No. 6 (Sept., 1944), T-71, roll 76, frames 577571–93, 577535–62, 577501–26. '

65. [Rischka], "Zweite Tagung der Südosteuropa-Gesellschaft, Gruppe 'Ernährung und Landwirtschaft'—Tagungsfolge" (draft), 30 Oct. 1942, T-71, roll 131, frames 634466–67; "Zweite Tagung der Gruppe 'Ernährung und Landwirtschaft' der Südosteuropa-Gesellschaft, 30. Nov. bis 1. Dezember 1942—Veranstaltungsfolge," T-84, roll 197, frames 1562660–63, 1562665–83.

be readily seen by the greatly increased press coverage the
SOEG and its affiliates received in the latter half of the SOEG's
existence. Before 1942, the affiliates were virtually never mentioned in the press except as part of the coverage which the
SOEG itself received for its large conventions. But the meetings
in Vienna and Prague clothed the SOEG with the appearance
of influence that soon made even the activities of the Society's
subsidiaries newsworthy, and this in turn added to the accumu-
lated store of image-building factors and hence added even more
artificial luster to the SOEG. The SOEG's central office sent
press communiques about the fall meeting of the Nutrition
Group not only to all Viennese papers but also to such leading
Reich German newspapers and periodicals as the *National-
zeitung* of Essen, the *Deutscher Volkswirt,* the *Donauzeitung,*
the *Kölnische Zeitung,* and the *Frankfurter Zeitung.*[66] The communiques did not go unnoticed. The *Donauzeitung,* for instance,
carried a story on the meetings of the Nutrition Group in two
separate editions of the paper.[67] The creation of new affiliates
for the SOEG was also a newsworthy event in the second half
of the SOEG's operations. The establishment of the actually
quite unimportant Southeast Institute for Wood and Forest Research was commented upon at some length in the *Donauzeitung,*[68] and several papers noted the establishment of, and later
the first anniversary of, the Southeast Cooperative Institute.[69]
   It may have been precisely this aura of importance and pres-

66. "Zweite Tagung der Gruppe 'Ernährung und Landwirtschaft' der Südosteuropa-Gesellschaft, 30. Nov.–1. Dezember 1942—Presse," n.d., T-84, roll 197,
frames 1562687–88.
   67. "Fischreicher Donauraum-Gute Aussichten für die Zukunft–Tagung der
Südosteuropa-Gesellschaft in Wien," *Donauzeitung,* 16 Dec. 1942, p. 5; Landwirtschaftliche Zusammenarbeit," *Donauzeitung,* 19 Dec. p. 3.
   68. "Südostinstitut für Holzforschung," *Donauzeitung,* 19 Dec. 1942, p. 5.
   69. See, for instance, Anselm Lippisch, "Südosteuropas Bauern arbeiten mit-
Ein Jahr Genossenschaftsinstitut der Südosteuropa-Gesellschaft, Wien," *Donauzeitung.* 29/30 April 1944, p. 7; "Genossenschaftliche Beziehungen zu
Südosteuropa," *Hamburger Fremdenblatt,* 12 Feb. 1944; "Ein Jahr Südost-
Genossenschaftsinstitut, Wien," *Hamburger Fremdenblatt,* 26 May 1944. It is true
that German papers may have carried more articles about the SOEG for lack of
other printable National Socialist successes, but so far as the SOEG's public
image within the system is concerned, this possibility does not alter the basic
picture of the SOEG's growing intrasystem prestige.

tige[70] that led the new administrative staff assuming office in 1944 to labor and plan in an increasingly unreal atmosphere. It is as though the SOEG resolutely regarded the development of the Society's public image and its continued growth as entirely divorced from the reality of the war. Far from integrating all its administrative energies into the overall German effort to increase the Balkans' contribution to the Reich's war effort, top officials of the Society as late as June 1944 were busy drawing up plans for the establishment of the SOEG's permanent art gallery.[71]

Not all public activities of the SOEG during its last months of operation were quite as theoretical in content, but the aim of the SOEG's concern with Albania was hardly less unrealistic. After the Italian armistice, the National Socialists suddenly discovered that Albania had suffered grievously under Italian domination. Selflessly, the Reich stepped in to aid the Albanians on their road to political independence and economic prosperity. Part of the sudden German campaign of aid and friendship for Albania involved an invitation to some Albanian students to continue their studies in Germany. The Germans saw the presence of these youths in the Reich as an opportunity "for [us] to move into the positions of academic leadership vacated by the Italians."[72]

70. In the last months of the SOEG's existence even the creation of subdivisions within the affiliates was newsworthy. See "Saatgutaustausch im Südosten— eine Gründung im Rahmen der Südosteuropa-Gesellschaft," *Donauzeitung*, 31 March 1944, p. 5. The article commented on the creation of the *Saatgutausschuss*, another committee within the Nutrition and Agriculture Group.

71. Oberascher to Blaschke, "Betr.: Vorschlag einer ständigen Ausstellung der SOEG," 22 June 1944, T-71, roll 62, frames 560647–51. Oberascher was the major SOEG official concerned with cultural affairs in 1944. Kraus had left late in 1943 to join the staff of the Gauleiter of Styria. See Heinrichsbauer, "Aktenvermerk," 22 Dec. 1943, T-71, roll 55, frame 451506.

72. Böhm to Kraus, "Kul Pol. Fü St L V" (confidential), 14 Feb. 1944, T-71, roll 51, frame 447941. The SOEG's role in this scheme to bind the future political leaders of Albania to the Third Reich consisted of assisting in the administration of a dormitory set up for the Albanian students, and in generally aiding the university authorities in Vienna in handling the affairs of the students. See [Lt. Klein (the head of the dormitory)], "Protokoll über die Gründende Sitzung des Beirates des Albanerhauses am 8.6.44 . . . in den Gästeräumen der Gaustudentenführung Wien" (confidential), n.d., T-71, roll 52, frames 447613–16.

Albanian affairs loomed rather large on the SOEG's agenda in 1944. Not only were the students to be cared for, but since the Germans had shown no previous interest in the country, the SOEG also arranged a lecture by Gstöttenbauer, the German representative in Albania, to discuss the country and Germany's plans for its future. He spoke on May 22, 1944, in the presence of high Albanian collaborators, and pronounced that Kossovo would be annexed to Albania after the war, and that Germany, unlike Italy, would aid, not exploit, the country's economic development.[73]

Despite these last months of languid existence and concern with unrealistic projects, the SOEG's public triumphs actually came to an end, as they had begun, with a visit to Vienna by Funk. In March 1944, the Reich Minister of Economics addressed the SOEG again and formally installed Augenthaler as the new executive secretary. Again, the guests of honor were numerous, and included the Hungarian minister in Berlin, Döme Sztojay, and Clodius. Again, Schirach introduced Funk and the minister responded, but the prevailing atmosphere was different from that of Funk's first visit in June 1941. At that time the SOEG was attempting to establish its place among the German Balkan agencies; in 1944, both Schirach and Funk looked back with pride upon the Society's past accomplishments. The SOEG stood on a firm foundation and occupied a place of considerable honor and prestige in the maze of German organizations. The Viennese Gauleiter noted that the SOEG "had, despite the difficulties of the war situation, done everything [possible] to prepare the future peacetime cooperation between the Greater German Reich and the Southeastern European states . . . [and that it] had fulfilled all expectations."[74] Funk answered in the same spirit, particularly thanking Schirach for his work, and summing up the SOEG's activities with the sentence, "I can confirm that the SOEG has done its duty, and that it has fostered economic as well as cultural relations with the Southeastern European

73. [Oberascher?], "Vermerk," n.d., T-71, roll 52, frame 447636.
74. Funk, *Länder des Südostens,* pp. 6–7.

states with the greatest of success."[75] These thoughts were the keynote of the meeting. The SOEG's leaders, either unaware, or not daring to admit in public, the near and total German defeat, saw a rosy future both for Germany and for the SOEG. The Society would indeed become the Reich's executive organ for German Balkan policies and the visible, public manifestation of the Reich's interest in and control of the Balkans.

The SOEG had established its public image in a long and difficult struggle; that it could never fully exercise its potential power and influence was not its fault, but a result of the collapse of its foundation of power, the Third Reich.

75. *Ibid.*, p. 9. For the press coverage of the meeting, see "Hohe deutsche Exportleistung—der Reichswirtschaftsminister in Wien vor der Südosteuropa-Gesellschaft," *Donauzeitung,* 12 March 1944, p. 5; "Das Beispiel der europäischen Wirtschaftszukunft," *Völkischer Beobachter* (North German ed.), 12 March 1944, p. 2.

4 | Blueprints for a Frightening Utopia: German Plans for the Postwar New Order in the Balkans

THE SOEG's impressive intrasystem public structure was achieved by the end of 1944; but the Society's successes were never meant as more than stepping-stones to postwar greatness. In accepting neofeudal and neo-Darwinian struggle as the behavioral norm of the National Socialist regime, agencies in the Third Reich also accepted a constant need to be dynamic and future-oriented. In the same sense that the regime itself could never stop its military and political conquests, institutions in the system could never stop expanding their fields of power. Cessation of expansion marked the beginning of decline.

Since by 1940 all human activity in Germany itself was already largely subject to totalitarian controls, the focal point of administrative infighting in the Third Reich during the war shifted to the field of postwar control of all Europe. After the

94

beginning of the war all expanding German agencies projected plans for postwar National Socialist control of the European Continent and, equally important, their own place in effecting that control. Consequently, the historian who sets out to write a study of the National Socialist New Order plans for the Balkans will not be embarrassed by a lack of documentary material; a vast array of articles, books, memoranda, and conference minutes attest to the interest in postwar planning of virtually every major component of the National Socialist power structure.[1] He soon discovers, however, that the very abundance of historical raw material presents him with pressing methodological problems. The documentary evidence abounds with internal inconsistencies and incompatibilities that reflect the constant friction and infighting of the offices and agencies that produced it.

It is impossible to write a meaningful history of the National Socialist plans for the postwar future of Europe without imposing some firm standards of selection and categorization on the mass of distorted and contradictory material. The question then becomes, "which test of success is meaningful?" Intrasystem classification is not suitable: it is quite possible to find two diametrically opposed draft policies, submitted by two rival offices but both classified top secret. Even published materials show no clear policy directives, since Reich censors allowed both moderate, sensible exposés and the power-mad, surprisingly frank ravings of SS-racists to appear in print.[2] Nor is it possible to

1. No full-scale study of the Nazi planning effort in the Balkans has yet appeared, although a number of postwar publications have discussed the more general aspects of Germany's postwar intentions. See, for example, Clifton J. Child, "The Concept of the New Order," in *Survey of International Affairs, 1939–1946: Hitler's Europe,* ed. Arnold and Veronica M. Toynbee (London, 1954), pp. 47–73; Institut für Zeitgeschichte (Paul Kluke) ed., *Das Dritte Reich und Europa. Bericht über die Tagung des Instituts für Zeitgeschichte* in *Tutzing/Mai 1956* (Munich, 1957); Paul Kluke, "Nationalsozialistische Europaideologie," *Vierteljahrshefte für Zeitgeschichte,* III (July 1955), 240–75.

2. Cf., for example, the Mitteleuropäischer Wirtschaftstag's, *Vorschläge für eine neue deutsche Kapitalpolitik* (Berlin, 1940), with such publications as Karl Richard Ganzer, *Das Reich als europäische Ordnungsmacht* (3rd ed., Hamburg, 1941/42[sic]); Reinhold Brenneisen, "Grossraum—Grosswirtschaftsraum—Grossraumwirtschaft," *Nationalsozialistische Wirtschaftspolitik,* n. vol. (10 Sept. 1943), 269–73; Ernst Rudolf Huber, "Bau und Gefüge des Reiches," in *Idee und*

resolve all such internal conflicts by citing the apex of the Third Reich decision-making process, Hitler himself.[3] The Führer was neither a systematic nor a consistent thinker. His judgments of man and events—always categorically expressed—could change radically over relatively short periods of time.[4]

Nevertheless, Hitler's concepts and control of the entire system always remained the keystone of organizational and planning success. While Hitler was not consistent in all of his ideas, it is equally true that he had a number of striking ideas that served as an unshakable central framework into which he integrated all other perceptions and decisions.[5] And, since no office intended to challenge Hitler's position, it is unthinkable that a policy proposal that lay outside the boundaries of Hitler's ideological principles would have become Reich policy. Moreover, since the intrasystem struggles of the thirties had clearly left some institutional victors and losers, the fate of a draft policy for the postwar New Order could not be divorced from the fate of its agential author in the power struggles of the Third Reich. Finally, if various competing components actually agreed on a draft policy, its success was almost assured—provided it corresponded to one of Hitler's *idées fixes*. In the discussion that follows, then, the following guidelines have been used to separate National Socialist plans that would in all likelihood have become policy directives from those that would have remained ambitious but stillborn memoranda:

Ordnung des Reiches, ed. E. R. Huber (Hamburg, 1941), I, Part 1; Suthoff-Gross, "Deutsche Grossraumlehre- und Politik," *Deutsches Recht,* XIII (5 and 12 June 1942), 625–28; "Wirtschaftsraum ersetzt nicht Lebensraum," *Wirtschaftspolitische Parole,* V (5 Aug. 1940), 572–73.

3. In addition to *Mein Kampf* and the more recently published *Hitlers Zweites Buch,* ed. Gerhard L. Weinberg (Stuttgart, 1961), Hitler's more candid opinions are revealed in three major "thought-collections": Hermann Rauschning, *Gespräche mit Hitler* (New York, 1940); *Hitler's Secret Conversations;* and *The Goebbels Diaries, 1942–43,* ed. Louis P. Lochner (New York, 1948).

4. Note, for example, Hitler's changing evaluation of King Boris of Bulgaria in Hitler, *Secret Conversations,* entries 2 and 4 April, 16 Aug. 1942, pp. 315–16, 321, 512. On the problem of Hitler's shifting opinions, see also Gerhard L. Weinberg, "Hitler's Image of the United States," *American Historical Review,* LXIX (July 1964), 1009–10, 1020.

5. See Hugh R. Trevor-Roper, "Hitlers Kriegsziele," *Vierteljahrshefte für Zeitgeschichte,* VIII (April 1960), 121–33, for the history of one such idée fixe.

1. Plans that incorporated concrete expressions of persistent Hitlerian ideas. Such plans would have had an even higher probability of success if they had already received organizational realization in terms of a decree, the establishment of a study committee, and so forth.

2. Policy drafts that emerged from (or had been drawn up in consultation with) one of the ascending components of the National Socialist power structure—for example, the SS, the Four Year Plan, the Party, certain segments of the Foreign Ministry. Plans that owed their existence solely to a descending component (for example, the army or the government bureaucracy) would have had a correspondingly lower probability of success.[6]

3. Intrasystem compromises, that is, plans already agreed upon by major, conflicting segments of the Third Reich power structure.[7]

4. Finally, postwar plans that had already been partially realized through consistent German prewar and wartime policies and had clearly left the theoretical stage and become permanent policy directives.[8]

While components of the National Socialist power structure at every level of influence and importance felt a call to help plan the New Order, the degree of involvement and breadth

6. Thus, while the propagandistic and pseudoscholarly output of Werner Daitz' *Gesellschaft für europäische Wirtschaftsplanung und Grossraumwirtschaft e.V.* (Society for European Economic Planning and Grossraumwirtschaft) was impressive, its actual influence on the shaping of permanent Nazi plans, in view of a sharp reprimand from Bormann, would in all likelihood have been minimal. Bormann's reprimand is in Deputy Führer, Stabsleiter to Daitz, 18 Nov. 1940, T-71, roll 60, frames 558384–85; and the cover letter to this document, Deputy Führer, Stabsleiter to all Gauleiter and Gauwirtschaftsberater, "Rundschreiben" (confidential), 27 Nov. 1940, *ibid.*, frame 558383.

7. For a specific instance of such a compromise and a discussion of what this meant for the probable permanence of the policy, see Hans Ulrich Wehler, " 'Reichsfestung Belgrad'—Nationalsozialistische 'Raumordnung' in Südosteuropa," *Vierteljahrshefte für Zeitgeschichte,* XI (Jan. 1963), 72–84, esp. 80.

8. Wartime policies as guide posts for postwar plans have often been overlooked. For example, the otherwise very detailed analysis by Karl Brandt et al., *Management of Agriculture and Food in the German-Occupied and other Areas of Fortress Europe* (Stanford, Cal., 1953), pp. 156–57, 159–60, 162ff., 192–93, 206–08, and 221–27, completely ignores the long-range German goals, although these are often clearly apparent in the policies discussed.

of effort varied considerably. Thus, the Party as a whole did
not undertake the creation of a systematic planning apparatus,
but some important segments, for example, the *Auslandsorganisation* (the Nazi Party office responsible for members living
outside of the German borders), or Martin Bormann and the
Party chancellery, were by no means willing to leave postwar
planning to other factors in the system. Virtually all offices of
the SS hydra were vitally interested in the structure of Germany's future control of Europe. And the SS brought a number
of inherited advantages to the planning tasks. Not only was
it the generally accepted elite segment of the Nazi system, but
in the area of New Order planning it also derived additional
authority from its control of ethnic German affairs. Beginning
in 1939 with Himmler's appointment as Reich Commissioner
for the Strengthening of Germandon (*Reichskommissar für die
Festigung des deutschen Volkstums*, RKFDV),[9] the SS steadily
expanded its control over the Volksdeutsche until virtually all
matters connected with ethnic Germans were subject to Himmler and the SS.[10]

Among the state and private agencies, the Foreign Ministry
and the economic and business community were the most active
planners. Since the New Order had to deal with foreign states
and peoples, planning activities in this area touched the legitimate interests of the ministry. Moreover, a great deal of the
planning work in the Foreign Ministry was performed by officials
of the Domestic Affairs Department (*Inland*),[11] an office staffed

9. On this aspect of Himmler's activities, see Robert L. Koehl, *RKFDV:
German Resettlement and Population Policy, 1939–1945* (Cambridge, Mass.,
1957).

10. At the end of 1943 even scholarly research institutes concerned with the
Volksdeutsche were placed under the jurisdiction of the Reich Security Main
Office. See Reich Ministry of Interior to Publikationsstelle Berlin-Dahlem et al.,
"I (113/43)/5290" [sic] (secret), 29 Dec. 1943, National Archives Microcopy
T-120 (hereafter cited as T-120), cont. 1536, frame D653434. The microfilms
in record group T-120 are termed *containers*, rather than *rolls*.

11. The office at some time or other actually worked out plans, now unfortunately lost, for a New Order in Southeastern Europe. See Triska, "Verzeichnis
über die im Panzerschrank 177 befindlichen Vorgänge—D VIII 642g," 11 Dec.
1942, T-120, cont. 1536, frame D653096.

by some of the more fanatic National Socialists in the foreign service. This was particularly true of the department head, Hans Luther, a man whose political beliefs were radical enough to enable him to maintain excellent relations with the Party and the SS. The institutional spokesmen of the economic interests ranged from the corporate organizations to the Reich Ministry of Economics, though of course ultimate hope of obtaining a New Order structured along lines agreeable to their wishes rested on the authority of the Four Year Plan and Göring's fate as the Reich's economic czar.

National Socialist planning for the postwar period began in earnest in mid-1940, and followed a curious pattern. After the defeat of France, final military victory was thought to be a matter of weeks or months, and an array of officials in government and Party offices was confidently ready to draft the necessary plans to exploit Germany's hegemony on the Continent when the time came. None of the subplanners presumed to make the basic, highest level policy decisions (these were expected to come momentarily from Hitler's headquarters), but the lesser officials were more than eager to present their schemes for the implementation and execution of Hitler's expected broad policy outlines. The heady atmosphere of near victory even produced a spirit of cooperation among the various New Order planners; a seemingly endless series of interministerial and other high-level conferences occupied National Socialist officials in 1940 and the first half of 1941.

The planners soon realized that they were working in a vacuum. Victory did not come, Hitler was silent, and without him the subordinate agencies felt that they could only perform guesswork. After mid-1941 the spirit of cooperation broke down,[12] and each power segment retreated into its own realm, often hid-

---

12. Before June 1941, Colonel Drews, liaison officer for the *Wehrwirtschaft-und Rüstungsamt,* with the Reich Ministry of Economics and the Reichsbank, included some quite detailed descriptions of the New Order planning activities in the economic sphere in his regular reports to the *WiRü Amt.* After that date, such activities were apparently no longer reported to him, and he is silent on the subject. He was in his post until October 1943. See "Berichte VO z. R. Wi. Min. Obstlt. Drews," T-77, roll 679, frames 1886007–1887460.

ing from other components in the National Socialist system even
the fact that it continued to draft quite extensive New Order
plans.[13]

The SOEG entered the planning field in the train of the Reich
Minister of Economics. In July 1940, Funk received a specific
and quite far-reaching authorization from Göring as head of
the Four Year Plan: Funk was to direct the formulation of the
preliminary plans necessary to integrate the economies of the
occupied areas into the German economy and to establish a Con-
tinent-wide economic system under German leadership—the
Grossraumwirtschaft. All other government and Party agencies
were asked to subordinate themselves to Funk in this effort.[14]
Funk in turn selected Gustav Schlotterer, a high-ranking permanent official in the ministry, as his chief assistant.

The minister wasted no time. At this point the spirit of cooperation still prevailed, and a full-scale interministerial conference began the vast task of coordinating the various wishes of
the interested agencies. Nor was this effort entirely unsuccessful;
while the conference could not produce firm guidelines, it did
at least agree on a priority listing of the problems.[15]

Hitler's silence led to an abrupt curtailment of the project's
interministerial phase, but the Ministry of Economics continued
on its own to chart the blueprints for the economic future of
Europe. For Southeastern Europe, Hitler's refusal to specify his
wishes was not a serious obstacle to further planning, since the
Wohltat Pact of 1939 gave an effective set of guidelines to the

13. In establishing a "Europe Committee" within the Foreign Ministry in
the spring of 1943, Ribbentrop expressly reserved to himself the right to determine when other Reich agencies should be informed of the group's existence.
See Ribbentrop, "Verfügung—zu Pers. gen. 344/44g" (secret), 5 April 1943,
T-120, cont. 3155, frame E518688/1.

14. Körner to Deputy Führer, Reich Ministry of Agriculture et al., "V. P.
11088/1," 3 July 1940, T-120, cont. 3155, frames E518695-96. The letter is also
reprinted in *DGFP,* D, X, Doc. 103, p. 115.

15. See Janke (of the RWM), "Vermerk über die am 22. Juli 1940 unter
Vorsitz des Reichsministers Funk im Reichswirtschaftsministerium abgehaltene
Chefbesprechung" (secret), n.d., *IMT,* Doc. EC-121; Funk to Deputy Führer
et al., "Betrifft: Vorbereitung der Arbeiten für den wirtschaftlichen Wiederauf-
bau nach dem Kriege, Min.-B. 151g," 15 July 1940, T-120, cont. 3155, frame
E518701; Lammers' untitled memorandum of 22 July 1940, *ibid.,* frame E518702.

eager planners. This pact between the Reich and Rumania had been negotiated by an official whom Alfred Rosenberg described as one of those who really understood National Socialist economic principles,[16] and, as it was an international treaty, it had obviously received Hitler's prior approval. The treaty gave formal expression not only to the German economic goals in Rumania, but also to the preferred means of achieving the goals. To begin with, the pact postulated the long-term establishment of a German-Rumanian economic developmental partnership. Within this relationship the Reich would play the dominant role insofar as the further development of the Rumanian economy would be restricted to segments in whose expansion Germany had a direct interest. The areas and the type of development were spelled out in considerable detail in the treaty and the confidential Protocol of Signature that accompanied it. Thus, Germany agreed to underwrite the intensification of all aspects of Rumanian agriculture, though the focal points of development would be in the areas of industrial and oleaginous plants. The Reich also promised capital and technical aid for the exploitation of Rumania's mineral and timber resources and the buildup of some agricultural processing industries. While the German agreements meant considerable aid for Rumania's economic development, the treaty, by omission, also clarified the segments in whose further development Germany was not interested. Clearly, Rumania was not to develop into a major manufacturing country. On the contrary, gearing her primary and semiprocessed goods to the import market of the Reich, Rumania would also be dependent upon Germany for most of her manufactured and production good. In effect, Rumania would become an economic satellite of the Reich.

The 1939 pact also revealed the means of control the Reich would employ to insure that Rumania's economy would develop along approved lines. Overall planning was entrusted to bilateral industrial committees while specific projects would be handled

16. Alfred Rosenberg, *Das politische Tagebuch Alfred Rosenbergs aus den Jahren 1934/35 und 1939/40,* ed. Hans Günther Seraphim (Göttingen, 1956), entry for mid-May 1939, p. 68.

by joint Rumanian-German companies; that is, corporations in which Germany would be financially dominant.[17] Rumanian enthusiasm for the treaty declined as the Reich's military power grew, and the bilateral planning sessions envisioned by the Wohltat Pact were not very fruitful in 1939 and 1940.[18] However, the Reich was convinced that Germany's new status of political-military hegemony on the Continent would remove further Balkan resistance. Schlotterer therefore decided in the fall of 1940 that long-range planning for the economic future of Southeastern Europe should begin in earnest. As a first step he suggested that the SOEG and the Reich Industry Group should jointly establish a Planning Institute for the Southeast (*Planungsinstitut Südost*). The new agency would attempt to coordinate the wishes of the various German industrial and economic agencies. The institute was to function under the auspices of the SOEG.[19] Schlotterer met with considerable opposition from certain segments of German private industry,[20] but by

17. For the text of the Wohltat treaty and the confidential protocol, see "Vertrag über die Förderung der wirtschaftlichen Beziehungen zwischen dem Deutschen Reich und dem Königreich Rumänien," in *ADAP,* D, VI, Doc. 78, pp. 76–77; "Zeichnungsprotokoll zu dem Vertrag über die Förderung der wirtschaftlichen Beziehungen zwischen dem Deutschen Reich und dem Königreich Rumänien," *ibid.,* p. 78–80. For Wohltat's own public description of the treaty and its implications, see Helmuth Wohltat, "Der neue deutsch-rumänische Wirtschaftsvertrag," *Vierjahresplan,* III (20 April 1939), 560–63.

18. See below, pp. 144–46.

19. Kratz to Heinrichsbauer, 2 Nov. 1940, T-71, roll 72, frames 572166–67; Rafelsberger to Schirach, 9 Dec. 1940, T-71, roll 71, frame 571512; "I. Entwurf: Satzung des Südostplanungsinstitutes e.V.," 9 Dec. 1940, *ibid.,* frames 571524–26.

20. The major opponents were the powerful *Mitteleuropäischer Wirtschaftstag* (MWT) and, at least in the early stages of the conflict, the head of the Reich Industry Group, Wilhelm Zangen. The MWT had been founded in Vienna in 1924, and was originally a nonpolitical organization which attempted to promote better business relations between Central and Southeastern Europe. By 1940, however, it had come under the direct influence of the I. G. Farben concern, which was represented on the MWT's board of directors by a very aggressive and dynamic industrialist, Dr. Max Ilgner. Ilgner and Zangen opposed the establishment of the *Planungsinstitut Südost,* partly for reasons involving their personal prestige, but also because they feared a drift toward centralized state planning if Schlotterer's plans for the SOEG should come to fruition. See Heinrichsbauer to Rafelsberger, 11 Dec. 1940, T-71, roll 74, frame 575427; Heinrichsbauer to Rafelsberger, "[Bericht über eine Reise nach Berlin]," 13 Jan. 1941,

August of 1941 Funk had decided the matter in favor of the SOEG.[21]

Once armed with specific ministerial authority, the SOEG quickly expanded the original scope of the new agency. The Planning Institute for the Southeast became a Committee on Economic Planning (*Ausschuss für wirtschaftswissenschaftliche Planung*),[22] and it acquired an impressive membership headed by Rafelsberger as chairman.[23] Toward the end of 1941 the group began to compile the postwar wishes of the German economic community. Once completed, the committee anticipated that the results of this inquiry would then be analyzed, compared, computed, and cast into the form of specific recommendations to Funk and eventually to Göring.[24]

The approach proved totally unworkable. To be effective it

---

ibid., frame 575359; Heinrichsbauer to Rafelsberger, 16 May 1941, *ibid.*, frame 575229.

21. Kratz to Heinrichsbauer, 25 Aug. 1941, T-71, roll 48, frame 442988; Heinrichsbauer to Funk, 26 Aug. 1941, T-71, roll 14, frame 404789. Hassel had already commented on the MWT's loss of influence in May, 1941. See Hassel, *Vom andern Deutschland,* entry 18 May 1941, p. 208.

22. Local and regional activities in Austria paralleled the SOEG's national competence. See Arbeitskreis für wirtschaftliche Forschung, Planung und Wirtschaftsauflau im Reichsgau Niederdonau to Heinrichsbauer, "Betrifft: Zusammenarbeit Südosteuropa-Gesellschaft—AWUP [sic], MK/KL/4291-269/40," 1 Oct. 1940, T-71, roll 74, frame 575556; and Hirzel (*Baureferent* of the *Zentralbüro* of the Vienna Gau) to Müller (chief of the *Zentralbüro*), 15 April 1942, T-71, roll 65, frames 564349-50.

23. Heinrichsbauer's draft of a letter from Rafelsberger to Wagemann, 24 Sept. 1942, T-71, roll 71, frame 570633; Rafelsberger, "Niederschrift über die Besprechung mit dem Staatssekretär Landfried am 12. September 1942," 18 Sept. 1942, T-71, roll 58, frame 555745. The membership list included representatives from the corporate business associations, the Ministries of Economics, Agriculture, and Transport, as well as the SOEG. See "Aktion Gen. v. Unruh–Meldung Soeg," 25 May 1943, Fragebogen IV, T-71, roll 65, frame 563790.

24. Breza, "Terminkalender für die Arbeiten des Planungsausschusses," Dec. 1941, T-71, roll 71, frames 571413-14; Breza, "Aufzeichnung über die Mitwirkung der Wirtschaftsgruppen der Reichsgruppe Industrie bei den Arbeiten des wirtschaftswissenschaftlichen Planungsausschusses der Südosteuropa-Ges.," 10 Jan. 1942, T-71, roll 14, frames 405620-21; Reichsgruppe Industrie to members of the Aussenhandelsausschuss and the Sonderausschüsse für Devisenfragen, the Südostausschuss, the Länderausschüsse, and the Industrieabteilungen der Wirtschaftskammern, "Betr.: Sitzung des Aussenhandels-Ausschusses am 8.11.1941, IV G 12090/41," n.d., T-71, roll 52, frames 448258-59.

required the cooperation of individual business concerns and their regional organizations as well as guidance and direction from the Reich-level agencies. Both were lacking. Individual firms had neither the time nor the inclination to describe their future plans to their corporate organizations,[25] and much less to the SOEG. Ministries and other high-level agencies, while deeply interested in the economic future of the Balkans, frequently felt unable to overcome the silence at the center and issue the type of definite, though limited, objective policy statements that the SOEG expected. On the contrary, they expected the Society to issue them basic directives.[26] As an agency that owed its significance in large part to skillful exploitation of jurisdictional power vacuums, the SOEG was not to be stymied by lack of direction from the center. Since there were apparently no plans to coordinate, the SOEG began to construct its own. The Committee on Economic Planning transformed itself into a plan-shaping institution,[27] and assumed the authority to draft a full-scale, theoretical model of the economic aspects of the New Order in the Balkans.

From the viewpoint of the historian it is unfortunate that the committee's self-transformation was not completed until the spring of 1942. Since at the end of the year the focal point of its activities was shifted again to conform with the post-Stalingrad reorientation of German policies, the committee had only a few months during which it could devote its full efforts to

25. On the attitude of the *Wirtschaftsgruppen* toward the SOEG's project, see Breza, "Wirtschaftswissenschaftlicher Planungsausschuss der Südosteuropa-Gesellschaft—Fühlungsnahme mit den Wirtschaftsgruppen der Reichsgruppe Industrie" (Beilage 2), T-71, roll 14, frames 405562–74; "Bericht über die Besprechung in Berlin vom. 9.-12.3.1942," n.d., *ibid.*, frames 405601, 405603.

26. Rafelsberger to Wagemann, 25 Sept. 1942, T-84, roll 196, frame 1561819.

27. SOEG to Walter Hoffmann (of the staff of the *Institut für Weltwirtschaft* in Kiel) (draft), 11 June 1942, T-71, roll 54, frames 449992–93; Rafelsberger to Kratz, 25 Sept. 1942, T-84, roll 86, frames 1376441–42; Breza, "Der Arbeitsbereich des Ausschusses für wirtschaftswissenschaftliche Planung" (Vienna, 1942), T-84, roll 198, frames 1564676–721. The planned scope of the SOEG's activities may be surmised from the secret "Themenplan," which is attached to Bauer's (of the WIW) letter to Rafelsberger, 26 Nov. 1942, T-71, roll 71, frames 571154–61.

long-range New Order planning.[28] As a result, the potentially most significant period of the committee's existence has left the least systematic body of documentation of its work. There were only two plenary sessions of the group and neither resulted in important policy decisions.[29] The most fruitful source for a study of the committee's intentions are unsystematic and unfinished bodies of material, particularly the preliminary staff report of researchers at the Vienna Institute of Economic Research (WIW) and their informal notes.[30] The institute found time to submit only one finished report to the committee: it attempted to list the major problems that confronted the German planners in Southeastern Europe and suggested possible alternative solutions.[31]

It may seem surprising that a secondary agency such as the SOEG would attempt to draft a full-scale plan for Southeastern Europe despite the continued lack of Hitlerian directives. Actually, the entire field of planning in National Socialist Germany was less a forbidden area than it was a vacuum. Most Reich agencies were hesitant to proceed without Hitler's specific orders, but the SOEG had considerable experience in moving into areas of jurisdictional vacancy. The broad outlines of the Third Reich's New Order were clear enough; an ambitious

28. In August 1944, the committee was dissolved as unnecessary to the war effort. See Augenthaler to Schirach, 22 Aug. 1944, T-84, roll 196, frame 1562140. For a description of the short-term analyses, see below, pp. 156–58.

29. "Bericht über die erste Sitzung [des] Ausschusses für wirtschaftswissenschaftliche Planung," n.d., T-71, roll 14, frames 405696–98; "Geheimprotokoll über die zweite Sitzung des Zwölfer-Ausschusses über Fragen der Industrieplanung am 27. Juni 1942 . . . im Dienstzimmer des Herrn Vizepräsidenten der Südosteuropa-Gesellschaft, Gauwirtschaftsberater Rafelsberger," n.d., T-71, roll 49, frames 443706–24.

30. Some of these will be cited below. The most complete record of the institute discussions is Franz Nemschak, "Industrieplanung," April–Sept. 1942, T-71, roll 68, frames 568012–89.

31. WIW [Generalgutachten für die Arbeit des Wirtschaftswissenschaftlichen Planungsausschusses der Südosteuropa-Gesellschaft] (secret), n.d., T-71, roll 58, frames 556041–82. Not all of this extremely important document survived the war; this film contains only the greater part of it.

agency could rather easily utilize certain basic principles to propel itself into the forefront of Nazi planning agencies.

Certainly one of Hitler's more prominent *idées fixes* was his firm conviction that struggle is the natural form of relations between states or peoples and that only subordination of the weaker to the stronger assures a degree of relative stability.[32] Moreover, the sense of primacy of power permeated all actions of the National Socialist system. It is no exaggeration to say that all Nazi agencies agreed on the basic aim of the New Order: the attainment of the greatest possible degree of influence and power over the peoples and nations of Europe. To miss the power-centered aspects of all Third Reich plans is to miss the core of all New Order thinking in National Socialist Germany.[33] To be sure, there would be vigorous disagreements over methods and details, but if the SOEG kept the goal of German politico-military power at the center of its planning activities it would hardly be surprised by the nature of later decrees emanating from Hitler's headquarters.

If power represented the irreducible crystallization of the contents of the New Order, Nazi planners had next to turn to the further questions of "where" and "how much"—what were the geographic limits of the German sphere of control, and how directly should the Reich interfere in the affairs of the various subject peoples. There was a great deal of seeming confusion about the geographic area of the New Order among Hitler and the leaders of his party. The geographic extent of the German control was by no means self-evident. A prime consideration was the problem of the Axis. On the one hand, Hitler's own statements could be cited at the head of a list of Party protestations that the New Order would be a joint Italo-German creation;[34]

32. See, for example, Rauschning, *Gespräche*, p. 117; Hitler, *Secret Conversations*, entry 11 April 1942, p. 343; Bullock, *Hitler*, p. 313; Gruchmann, *Grossraumordnung*, pp. 74–75, 119.

33. In this connection, see Ribbentrop's extremely revealing remarks in Schmidt, "Aufzeichnung über die Unterredung zwischen dem RAM und dem italienischen Botschafter in Fuschl am 10. Juni 1943—Aufz. RAM 33/43g. Rs." (top secret), 11 June 1943, T-120, cont. 609, frames 0058, 0060–61.

34. This is true not only of his statements to satellite statesmen, but of Hitler's private conversations as well. See *Secret Conversations*, entry 13 May 1942, p. 388; Bormann, "Aktenvermerk—Besprechung des Führers mit Mussert—

at the same time, however, both he and other German leaders consistently tended to identify "Europe" with the "German sphere of Europe."[35]

The Italians did not have this problem. They envisioned not one Grossraum, but two closely allied, though separate, spheres; one headed by Rome, the other by Berlin. Each was to possess autarky, and have its own financial center and its own dominant currency. Geographically, the Italians included the Mediterranean, North Africa, and, less openly, Southeastern Europe within their own dominion.[36] The Germans regarded the Italian demands as excessive,[37] but they made no effort to arrive at a compromise between the two views. Instead, the German government simply avoided the issue by claiming that it could be resolved only through personal consultations between Hitler and Mussolini.[38]

NSB an 10.12.42" (secret), 14 Dec. 1942, T-120, cont. 2621, frame 381863; and Schmidt, "Aufzeichnung über die Unterredung zwischen dem Führer und dem Poglavnik in Anwesenheit des RAM im Führerhauptquartier am 23. September 1942—Aufz. Füh 36/42g. Rs" (top secret), T-120, cont. 607, frame 0226. This decision of Hitler received organizational realization in that other Nazi planning agencies (at least until September 1943) specifically excluded Italy and the Mediterranean from the geographic areas subject to German long-range planning. See Janke, "Vermerk . . . ," *IMT,* Doc. EC-121.

35. Hitler, *Secret Conversations,* entry 5 July 1942, p. 456; Ribbentrop, "Richtlinien für die Arbeit des Europa-Ausschusses—zu pers. gen. 324/44g," 5 April 1943, T-120, cont. 3155, frame E518689.

36. The best statement of Italian ambitions in the economic field is the memorandum of the Italian Minister for Trade and Foreign Exchange Regulations, Riccardi, "Der wirtschaftliche Wiederaufbau Europas" (ca. Oct. 1940), T-120, cont. 1095, frames 450134–37, 450148–49, 450155–56, 450159. For Italian ambitions and intrigues in Southeastern Europe, see Veesenmayer, "Gedächtnisschrift . . . vom 30. September 1942," National Archives Microscopy T-501 (hereafter cited as T-501), roll 265, frames 944/45. Among the published statements of Italian ideas on the New Order, see Italo Lunelli, *Pagina della nostra fede—Italia e Germania di fronte all'Europa* (Varese, 1942), especially pp. 241–53; Luigi Filippo de Magistris, "Noi e l'Africa," *Geopolitica,* IV (31 March 1942), 115–20; Giovanni Selvi, "Die Grundlagen der Neuen Ordnung," *Reich, Volksordnung, Lebensraum,* III (1942), 9–39.

37. RWM, Referat V Ld. 7, "Bemerkungen zur Aufzeichnung des Ministers Riccardi," 8 Oct. 1940, T-120, cont. 1095, frame 450132.

38. Schmidt, "Aufzeichnung über die Unterredung zwischen dem RAM und Staatssekretär Bastianini . . . am 9. April 1943 vormittags, RAM 20/43g. Rs." (top secret) 11 April 1942, T-120, cont. 609, frames 0051–50 [sic].

There can be little doubt that the Nazi leadership was unprepared to accept Italy's claim to equality in the shaping of the New Order, although the existence of an Italian subsphere within the German-dominated Europe was not incompatible with Hitler's basic visions on the structure of the New Europe. The New Order was in the first instance a system to secure permanent German power and control over the Continent. This meant that the heart of Europe, as well as all important politico-strategic areas, had to remain under Germany's permanent, direct control. These areas, the Reich, the annexed and acquired areas (including the northwest coast of France), the eastern territories, as well as selected other pieces of land such as the Iron Gate, the entire Danube, and the Kola Peninsula, would be under Germany's direct administration and would form a "first circle" of German power.[39] Between this iron core of the enlarged Reich and a type of new *Militärgrenze* guarding the approaches to the Grossraum lay the parts of Europe that could not escape German domination but would not feel the Reich's control as directly as the East or the protectorate. These states would be serflike (*hörig*) components of the New Europe.[40] In this same

39. Hitler, *Secret Conversations,* entries 13 Oct. 1941, 26 Feb. 1942, 13 May 1942, 29 June 1942, pp. 44, 275, 388, 438; Gruchmann, *Grossraumordnung,* p. 103. Hitler's ideas on the Danube had already received organizational realization as an intrasystem compromise. See Wehler, "Reichsfestung Belgrad," pp. 72–84. For the basic German policy directives on future aims in the East, see Wirtschaftsführungsstab Ost (OKW/Wi Amt Z 1/II Nr. 6250/42 geh.), *Richtlinien für die Führung der Wirtschaft in den neubesetzten Ostgebieten (Grüne Mappe),* Teil II (3rd ed; Berlin, 1942), pp. 16–17, 39. The best postwar treatment of this subject is in Alexander Dallin, *German Rule in Russia, 1941–45* (New York, 1957).

40. It is true that Hitler later in the war spoke of the need for abolishing the small states of Europe (*Goebbels' Diaries,* entry 8 May 1943, p. 357), but this statement belongs to the post-Stalingrad period during which Nazi demands increased in direct proportion to the decrease in the actual power of the Reich. The concept of the "power-ring" structure of the New Order was so prevalent among the various Nazi agencies that it can be categorized as an informal intrasystem compromise. See, for example, Hasselblatt, "Zusammenfassung der Denkschrift über die Tatbestände und Gefahren der völkerpolitischen Lage nach dem Sieg" (secret), ca. Nov. 1941, T-120, cont. 1536, frame D653087. (Hasselblatt's ideas were worked out in close collaboration with Undersecretary of State Luther.) Wiehl, "Aufzeichnung—betr.: handelspolitische Beziehungen der

vein yet a third gradation of German control within the interior of Europe consisted of Italy and her group of satellites. It is readily apparent that such an arrangement would not affect the Reich's position in its plenitude of ultimate power to control the affairs of the New Europe; the Italian sphere would exist only at the sufferance of the Reich.

Before the Italian armistice none of the major power segments in Nazi Germany questioned Italian control of such areas as Albania or Greece,[41] but Italian claim to other Balkan territories did not remain uncontested.[42] Hitler did reluctantly exclude Croatia from the German sphere,[43] but neither he nor other major government leaders seem to have contemplated yielding to the Italian demands for preponderance in other parts of the Balkans. The Führer's interest in Southeastern Europe was long standing[44] and persistent; his after-dinner conversations abound with references to Germany's past and future role in the Balkans. It was clear to the SOEG's planners that the question whether the Balkans would be part of the German Grossraum had already been answered. There remained only the determination of the degree of German control that should be exercised in the Balkans.

The SOEG's planners undoubtedly knew that Hitler tended to base such policy decisions on two basic considerations: the strategic-geographic location of the area and its political reliabil-

---

besetzten Gebiete mit dritten Ländern," 9 July 1940, T-120, cont. 1535, frame D652917. The SS recast the concept in the form of racial explanations, but it, too, kept the principle of differential treatment. See Heydrich, "Auszüge aus der Rede Heydrichs vor den Naziokkupanten," cols. 74–75.

41. After September 1943, even the Italian homeland was covetously eyed by Nazi Gauleiter. See Frederick W. Deakin, *The Brutal Friendship* (New York, 1962), pp. 614, 679; Gruchmann, *Grossraumordnung*, p. 111.

42. For a continuous and sharp criticism of Italian policies (and of the Foreign Ministry's appeasement of Italy), see the letters and reports of the German general in Croatia, Glaise-Horstenau, to the OKW, the Commanding General Southeast, *et al.*, T-501, roll 26, frames 1–401. The letters cover the period from 19 July 1941 to 13 Sept. 1942.

43. Hitler, *Secret Conversations*, entries 29 Oct. 1941, 12 May 1942, pp. 78, 384.

44. Rauschning, *Gespräche*, p. 118.

ity. A region that lay along the strategically significant approaches to the Continent or to the Reich was always marked
for direct German control, regardless of the political regime and
its attitude toward the Third Reich. In the Balkans such areas
included Bohemia-Moravia and the major part of the Danube
(along with Belgrade and hence Serbia).[45] Consequently, Slovakia, now surrounded almost entirely by inner-core territory,
could remain semiautonomous. As theoreticians and practi-
tioners of the leadership principle (*Führerprinzip*), Hitler and
his followers tended to gauge the political quality of a country
by the physical-racial appearance and pseudo or actual soldierly
bearing of its leaders.[46] In general, the leaders of the three remaining countries in Southeastern Europe, Admiral Horthy,
King Boris, and Marshall Antonescu, fared well under this sort
of scrutiny.[47] Thus, it is reasonable to postulate that Rumania
and Bulgaria would not be subject to direct German control.
The case of Hungary is less clear. Hitler grudgingly respected
the Magyars for their national fervor and ability to assimilate
even German ethnic groups within their borders,[48] but despite
this feeling (or perhaps because of it) the Führer was not unsympathetic toward an extension of the Reich's direct control into
all areas of the old Austro-Hungarian Empire.[49]

Politically, then, the New Order in Southeastern Europe
meant a division of the region into three areas of varying inten-

45. See Ziemke (the representative of the Foreign Ministry to the Reich
Protector in Prague), "Inhalt: Die Entscheidung des Führers—12.065/D Pol.2g
Rs." (top secret), 5 Oct. 1940, T-120, cont. 622, frame 032; and Friderici (liaison
officer of the German Armed Forces in Prague), "Betr.: Grundsätze der Politik
im Protektorat Nr. 22/40g Kdos.," 15 Oct. 1940, *IMT*, Doc. 862-PS; Hitler,
Secret Conversations, entry 29 June 1942, p. 438; Wehler, " 'Reichsfestung Belgrad,' " p. 81.

46. See, for example, "Ansprache des Führers vor den Oberbefehlshabern am
22. Aug. 1939," *DGFP*, D, VII, Doc. 192, p. 201.

47. See Hitler, *Secret Conversations*, entry 28 Aug. 1942, p. 542 (Horthy);
entries 2 and 4 April 1942, 16 Aug. 1942, pp. 315–16, 321, 512 (Boris); and
entries 27–28 and 9 Oct. 1941 [sic], 17 Oct. 1941, 11 Nov. 1941, 31 March 1942,
6 Sept. 1942, pp. 41, 56, 99, 314, 564 (Antonescu).

48. *Ibid.*, entry 26 Feb. 1942, pp. 274–75.

49. *Ibid.*, entry 9 Aug. 1942, p. 506; see also Gruchmann, *Grossraumordnung*,
p. 107.

sity of German control. From the central core of the Reich itself
a line of immediate German power would extend through the
protectorate, along the Danube, certainly including Serbia and
possibly encompassing Hungary as well, and finally flowing into
the eastern territory of direct German control in the Black Sea
and the Crimea.[50] Secure—or better, rendered harmless—behind
the initial power concentration would lie a group of pseudo-inde-
pendent, partially autonomous Grossraum members, Slovakia,
Rumania, Bulgaria, and perhaps Hungary, distinguishable from
the core areas by more mediate and indirect forms of German
control. Finally, the illusionary separate Italian Grossraum
would include Croatia, Greece, and Albania.

The basic purpose of the economic aspects of the New Order
was simple: the New Europe was to result in the "greatest possible increase in the German standard of living."[51] At a first glance,
such an aim seems not only a truism but also singularly uncon-
nected with the parallel political aims of the Third Reich. Surely
the Reich did not need to achieve a near monopoly of politico-
military power on the Continent to better the living conditions
of the German people. A program of economic development and
trade, mutually agreed upon by the various peoples of Europe,
could have accomplished the desired goal with more ease and
satisfaction. But merely to pose the question is to have missed
the primary raison d'être of all National Socialist activities—
an increase in power, control, influence. All else had to be secondary. The principle of the primacy of politics restricted the planning scope of economic projects, and structured planning efforts
to a considerable extent: the Reich economic planners knew that
the plans they might submit to the center—no matter how economically feasible—had little chance of adoption unless the economic measures proposed aided, or at least did not hinder, the

50. Hitler planned to Germanize the Crimea by resettling the Volksdeutsche
of Southern Tirol here. It is also significant in this connection that the Reich
Commissar for the Crimea, Alfred E. Frauenfeld, was an Austrian. See Hitler,
Secret Conversations, entry 2 July 1942, p. 445.

51. Göring to Funk, "Betr.: Kontinental- und Grossraumwirtschaft, V.P.
13873/5," 17 Aug. 1940, T-120, cont. 3665, frame E693069. See also Paul Einzig,
Hilter's"New Order" in Europe (London, 1941), p. 19.

attainment of the Reich's primary political goals. And once this realization permeated the thinking of the economic planning agencies, the broad outlines of the economic New Order in Europe, and particularly in the Balkans, became more concrete.

The Reich plans spoke of the need to interweave (*verflechten*) the economies of Europe. In itself, the principle, which implied a high degree of intra-European economic integration and consequently an international division of labor, was neither novel nor exploitative. As early as 1929, the French economist and technologist Francis Delaisi had developed a theory of two economically complimentary Europes, an industrial north and northwest, and an agricultural south and east.[52] Moreover, there is considerable evidence for believing that other countries of Europe, and again particularly the Balkan nations, were by no means unwilling to cooperate with the Reich in a long-range program of mutual economic development and trade.[53]

Neither Delaisi's plans nor the visions of the Reich's junior partners included what was for the Germans the major ingredient of all economic New Order planning, the element of control. Consequently, the economic integration of Europe envisioned by the Germans included several factors hardly vital from the point of view of increased economic efficiency or benefit. Thus, purely for control purposes the Germans planned a far-reaching infiltration of German "advisory" personnel into the professional and economic organizations of other European countries. Similarly, the Reich intended to force foreign businesses into German-dominated cartels.[54] The Germans endorsed in principle an increase of productivity in the New Europe, but, following the principles laid down in the Wohltat Pact, the increase in countries outside Germany should be undertaken by German development companies and should be restricted to products that

52. Francis Delaisi, *Les deux Europes* (Paris, 1929), pp. 10, 18, 28, and map, pp. 24–25.

53. Theo Suranyi-Unger, "Der Kampf um die Grossraumwirtschaft," *Zeitschrift für die gesamte Staatswissenschaft*, CI (1941), 417–47; Anton Reithinger, "Bei den Industrieausschussverhandlungen angeschnittene Wirtschaftsprobleme," 13 Jan. 1942, T-71, roll 14, frame 405593.

54. Funk to Göring, 6 Aug. 1940, *IMT*, Doc. PS-1093.

did not compete with established or planned German product lines.[55] International trade, too, was to increase, but the flow of products would travel along communication lines controlled by the Reich.[56]

Similarly, political considerations dominated the plans of the Third Reich's financial experts. In line with the Reich's political dominance, the New Europe would accept the reichsmark as a standard value, measure other currencies against it, and accept Berlin as the new financial center.[57] The dominating position of the reichsmark was an important part of the multipartite system of economic controls that would enable Germany to determine the entire price and wage structure as well as the standard of living in her sphere of control.[58] In the area of international finances, all Third Reich agencies also agreed that the Nazi Order needed a European-wide central clearing system.[59] Such an institution would provide the Germans with the complete knowledge of all foreign trade transactions in Europe and give them the means to manipulate the clearing accounts to their own advantage.

There was less general agreement on other aspects of the New Order's financial future. The geographic extent of the reichsmark currency area was not definite, and the institutional form and the functions of the central clearing system were quite contro-

55. "Richtlinien," enclosure in a letter of the Reich Ministry of Economics to the Reich Ministry of Justice, 23 Sept. 1940, *ibid.*

56. *Ibid.*

57. See the letter of an unidentified superior of Bergemann (an official of the RWM) to the latter, 2 July 1940, T-71, roll 59, frame 557493; Schultze-Schlutius (of the RWM, Dept V), "Vermerk," July 1940, *ibid.*, frame 557497. As early as July 1940, all German firms were advised that the Reichsmark had to form the basis of all future price arrangements with foreign business firms. See Schlotterer to Reichsstelle für Aussenhandel, "Betrifft: Faktuierung in Reichsmark," 16 July 1940, *ibid.*, frame 557515.

58. RWM, "Richtlinien," *IMT*, Doc. PS-1093.

59. Reichsbank, Volkswirtschaftliche Abteilung, "Der Zahlungsverkehr im europäischen Grosswirtschaftsraum" (conf. Reich matter), 20 July 1940, T-77, roll 679, frame 1886299; Schultze-Schlutius, "Ausbau des deutschen Clearingsystems zu einem europäischen Zentralclearing—V Ld (D) 2298/40g," 19 July 1940, T-77, roll 59, frames 557527–32; Neumann (of the Four Year Plan) to Reich Commissioner for the Netherlands et al., 24 July 1940, *ibid,* frame 557523.

versial. In general, the financial experts assumed that the war-occupied areas of Europe adjacent to the Reich (as well as Sweden and Switzerland)[60] would become domestic currency territory after the war, thus completing their political and economic integration into the Reich. Nations of the second circle, on the other hand, would keep their own currencies, pegged, to be sure, at a specific counter value to the reichsmark.[61] To handle the administration of the entire system the Ministry of Economics proposed the establishment of a new banking institution that would become "the supreme financial institution of the European Grossraum, the Bank of Europe." Its seat would be in Vienna.[62] The latter suggestion, embodying the ministry's familiar desire to decentralize the administrative structure of the New Order, understandably met with considerable opposition from the Reichsbank. In view of its own monopoly position, the German national bank opposed the establishment of any new central bank. Moreover, the Reichsbank regarded the choice of Vienna as the seat of the new bank as both absurd and incompatible with the prestige of the Greater German Reich.[63]

It is curious that while financial matters received quite detailed attention from Reich planning agencies, the social aspects of the New Order remained rather vague. Although the Grossraum propaganda ceaselessly extolled the New Order as the gate-

60. Gruchmann, *Grossraumordnung*, pp. 111–12.

61. Nazi economic circles were not agreed on whether the value relationship between the reichsmark and other European currencies was to be permanently set or periodically renegotiated. See the RWM memorandum, "Die Vereinfachung des Zahlungsverkehrs im mitteleuropäischen Raum," 9 July 1940, T-71, roll 59, frame 557502; Reichsbank, Volkswirtschaftliche Abteilung, "Währungsfragen im europäischen Wirtschaftsraum," 6 July 1940, T-77, roll 679, frame 1886332. The SOEG seemed to favor flexible exchange rates. See WIW, "Themenplan" [ca. Nov., 1942], 'Thema IX, 3,' T-71, roll 71, frame 571161.

62. Reichsbank, "Währungsfrage . . . ," *ibid.*, frame 1886332.

63. Despite its own concern for the prestige of the Reich and its opposition to the Bank of Europe (which may be categorized as an almost instinctive defense against encroachments of its own sphere of competence), the Reichsbank's other comments on the New Order merited far more attention than they received. The bank argued, for example, that the New Europe should be a "voluntary community of interest" not the result of force and coercion. *Ibid.*, frames 1886333, 1886336.

way to permanent economic prosperity for all of Europe, Third
Reich agencies made little effort to translate the undefined generalities into specific projects. Even internal discussions among
National Socialist agencies spoke of the social aspects of the
New Europe only in terms of their propaganda value.[64] The
reason for the strange silence is inherent in the primacy of political goals of the National Socialist New Order. There was no
need for detailed social welfare schemes in the foreseeable
future because improved social conditions of life for Germans,
not to mention other peoples, was a low priority concern of the
New Order. In the National Socialist reorganization of the Continent even the social welfare of the German people was of
secondary concern. Above all Germans would have the political
function of supplying the human material to enable the regime
to establish and maintain its systems of permanent power. In
turn, the other nationalities of Europe would supply the
economic means which would free the Germans for their political
roles.

The SOEG assigned itself the task of drafting specific economic plans for Southeastern Europe, plans which it expected
would be acceptable as regional details of the Reich's overall
New Order concept. As parts of a greater whole, the Society's
drafts were subject to certain evident tests of acceptability to
the center, and in this sense, the broader framework of German
plans limited the scope and variability of the SOEG's own project. But the basic outline was also a great aid to the Society,
because it provided a foundation and a structure for its regional
project. Thus, within the context of the power-rings concept,
the countries of Southeastern Europe, with the exception of the
Protectorate and Serbia, fell into the second and third categories.
Moreover, since the Reich had always emphasized its economic
interest in all of the Balkans, the categorization of the Balkan
countries could only mean that Germany would continue to
insist upon certain economic rights in the Italian sphere, while

64. See Mackensen to Foreign Ministry, "Nr. 1249 vom 16.4.," 16 April 1942,
T-120, cont. 1054, frames 421206–08.

the nations of the second ring would become, in terms of their economic future, tabulae rasae for the Reich planners—they were planning objects in the fullest sense of the term. The SOEG could begin its efforts by asking whether it was more practical from the German point of view to exploit or to develop the economies of Southeastern Europe.[65]

A decision was reached that it was more expedient to develop than to exploit, though the development had to proceed along lines that would assure that the "structure of Southeastern European industry and its further evolution would correspond permanently to the German interests."[66] And along with its final aim, the specific methodology of the economic New Order in the Balkans had been predetermined: Southeastern Europe had to find its place in the Reich-imposed international division of labor.[67] Moreover, since it was agreed that the primacy of politics prohibited a full-scale vertical economic diversification in the subject areas of Europe,[68] the Balkan countries were predestined to an economic future as agricultural or at best semi-industrial states.[69]

It must be emphasized that this basic, overall judgment on the economic New Order in the Balkans was not merely a paper theory; the plans had already reached the stage of preliminary execution. Nazi propaganda stressed that agriculturally oriented

65. The German words are quite literally *ausbeuten* and *entwickeln*. See *Generalgutachten*, p. IV, T-71, roll 58, frame 556044; Franz Nemschak (of the staff of the WIW), "Besprechung über das Thema: Industrialisierung des Südostens im Zusammenhang mit der Industrieplanung für den Wiener Freihafen (Dr. Kratz, Dr. Seifert, Dr. John)," 19 June 1942, T-71, roll 67, frames 566648–49.

66. *Generalgutachten*, T-71, roll 58, frame 556044.

67. [Rabitsch?] "Gedanken zum Generalgutachten," 8 May 1942, *ibid.*, frame 555919.

68. WIW, *Die voraussichtliche Entwicklung des Wiener Hafenumschlages* (for official use only) (Vienna, 1941), T-84 roll 202, frame 1568501. This study was technically not part of the industrial planning project, but it was written by the staff of the WIW, was undoubtedly compiled at the request of Rafelsberger in his capacity as *Gauwirtschaftsberater* of Vienna, and, as the title indicates, was to detail needed Viennese adaptations to the New Order; Berend and Ranki, "Expansion," p. 314.

69. "Europa—Aufbau ohne Schema—Ein Rumänien Interview Staatssekretär Landfrieds," *Berliner Börsenzeitung*, 5 April 1942.

economies were natural in Southeastern Europe, and German negotiators during the wartime bilateral industrial and trade negotiations made the message even more pointed.[70] Indeed, the Germans were so confident of their ability to impose such a division of labor on the Balkans that they had already prepared market analyses of Southeastern Europe to guide the expected influx of German manufactured goods into the Balkans after victory was achieved.[71]

While the industrial and the agricultural interests in Germany agreed that secondary manufacturing facilities should not be created in the Balkans, they tended to define the "natural" limits of economic diversification in Southeastern Europe rather differently. For the industrialists a "natural" industry was one that could be competitive (*lebensfähig*) in the new Grossraum.[72] This was understood to be any production facility that increased the volume of needed German imports, but did not materially reduce the flow of German exports.[73] And even these concessions would be bound by all of the political limitations on economic developments in the subject areas. In effect, this interpretation of the New Order left the Southeastern European nations with only two major directions in which they might develop their economic future: the mining and perhaps refining of their natural resources, particularly those metals and ores that Germany did not possess in abundance,[74] and the intensification and di-

70. Berend and Ranki, "Expansion," pp. 319–20, 339.

71. See Rolf Grünwald, *Südosteuropa als Absatzmarkt für Konsumfertigwaren—eine Strukturuntersuchung des Wiener Instituts für Verbrauchs- und Absatzforschung* (Vienna, 1944), 2 parts T-84, roll 79, frames 1367621–731, 1367732–52.

72. Heinrichsbauer, "Wiener Messe und Südostindustrialisierung," *Donauzeitung*, 20 Sept. 1941, p. 17 (p. 1 of the *Sonderbeilage* "Wiener Messe"); Breza, "Grenzen der Industrialisierung," n.d. [ca. Feb. 1942], T-71, roll 71, frames 571318–19.

73. [Kelter], "Die deutsch-ungarischen Wirtschaftsbeziehungen" (strictly confidential), ca. July 1944, T-71, roll 52, frame 447677; Hartmut Krohm, *Die Textilindustrie Südosteuropas* (Vienna, 1944), p. 38.

74. German economists foresaw a promising future for mining operations in Southeastern Europe. See Franz Nemschak, *Der türkische Bergbau und seine wirtschaftlichen Probleme* (Prague, 1944), pp. 19, 54; Kurt Wagner, *Grossraum-Technik* (Berlin, 1944), p. 130.

versification of their agriculture and agricultural processing industries.[75]

The agricultural interests enthusiastically supported the future of mining in Southeastern Europe, and they agreed that agricultural production had to be increased.[76] Most agricultural experts even supported agricultural diversification in Southeastern Europe, since the Balkan countries were climatically suited to grow the industrial and oleaginous plants that the Reich would need for its own consumption and production.[77] These concepts in planning for the postwar period did not inaugurate policy changes, since German support for postwar agricultural diversification in the Balkans would merely continue the direction of the Reich's prewar and wartime technical aid, monetary credits, and long-term contractual agreements.

The unanimity of the German agencies did not go beyond a universal agreement that the Balkan countries needed to develop their primary production facilities. The manufacturing interests were willing to permit the establishment of agricultural processing industries in Southeastern Europe,[78] but the agricultural interests foresaw only a narrow scope for such developments. The latter contended that the Southeast European states should be restricted to the manufacture of semifinished farm products; the Balkan countries should merely perform those op-

75. Berend and Ranki, "Expansion," p. 317. The authors cite (unfortunately without giving its origin) an official German memorandum found in the files of the Hungarian Foreign Ministry.

76. "Zusammenarbeit mit Deutschland—Gespräch mit dem bulgarischen Landwirtschaftsminister Bagrianov," *Südost-Echo,* 22 March 1940, p. 2.; "Argumente für eine rumänische Agrarreform," *ibid.* 31 Jan. 1941, p. 6; Albert Brummenbaum, "Die Intensivierung der europäischen Landwirtschaft als Gemeinschaftsaufgabe," *Deutsche Agrarpolitik,* I (April–May, 1943), 218–22.

77. See Christiansen, "Südosten," p. 519. This view was not universally accepted. As late as 1942, Acting Minister of Agriculture Backe wrote that Southeastern Europe should remain primarily a grain-producing area. See Herbert Backe, *Um die Nahrungsfreiheit Europas, Weltwirtschaft oder Grossraumwirtschaft* (Leipzig, 1942), pp. 225–26.

78. For example, the industrialists would have permitted local Balkan industries to process textile raw materials up to and including the weaving of the cloth. Only the manufacture of the cloth into clothing would be performed by Reich firms. See, Krohm, *Textilindustrie,* p. 14.

erations (for example drying and pulping) necessary to prevent spoilage of the products during their journey to the processing plants in the Reich. All additional preparations, as well as all secondary manufacturing steps had to be performed by firms located in Germany.[79] The New Order should tolerate agricultural processing industries in Southeastern Europe only if the particular industry manufactured solely for the domestic market of the Balkan country, and if in addition, the industry could manufacture its product entirely from raw materials available within the borders of the country. Hence, a canning industry in a country like Croatia, which produced no steel, was out of the question. However, since Croatia grew large quantities of low quality wines (while Germany did not), the Croatian facilities for the production of wine vinegar should be further developed. Industries that could not be fit into either of these categories presumably should be dismantled or pass directly into German hands as part of the New Order.[80]

The divergent plans of German industrial and agricultural interests had one factor in common: neither provided a meaningful solution to the Balkans' greatest economic problem, that of agrarian overpopulation. Between the two world wars, the existence of this problem had been the primary motivating factor for the passionate (and at times ill-considered) interest in rapid

79. Alex Walter, "Die nationalsozialistische Agrarpolitik und die Neuordnung Europas," *Deutsche Agrarpolitik* I (Jan. 1943), 124–25; Hanel's marginalia on Heinrichsbauer to Rischka, Ulmansky, Hausmann, and John, 17 May 1943, T-71, roll 75, frame 576444; Rischka, *Erster Jahresbericht*, pp. 33, 37; Schneider (head of the Industrial Committee of the *Gruppe Ernährung und Landwirtschaft*) to SOEG, 23 Sept. 1943, T-71, roll 56, frame 453013. The new boldness and ruthlessness that characterized the German plans after the fall of France is particularly well illustrated by the German attitude toward the development of agricultural processing industries in the Balkans. As part of the Wohltat Pact, Germany had specifically promised assistance in the development of the agricultural processing industry in Rumania. See Article I of the "Vertrag über die Förderung der wirtschaftlichen Beziehungen zwischen dem Deutschen Reich und dem Königreich Rumänien," *ADAP*, D, VI, Doc. 78, p. 76.

80. Ulmansky, "Betrifft: Plan für die Entwicklung einer kroatischen landwirtschaftlichen Industrie," 15 June 1943, T-71, roll 66, frames 565201–06. Ulmansky discusses only Croatia, but it seems reasonable to extend the basic principles to the remainder of Southeastern Europe. See also Rischka, *Jahresbericht*, p. 37.

industrialization schemes in Southeastern Europe.[81] To curtail or even reverse these moderate beginnings could only result in transforming a large part of Europe into a chronically depressed area. It is a particularly poignant commentary on the New Order that such a development was by no means unwelcome to the Third Reich economic planners. The Reich actually preferred to maintain a sizeable gap between the German and the Balkan standards of living. An oversupply of labor in the Balkans would result in depressed wage scales for Southeastern workers, keep the cost of Balkan exports to the Reich minimal, and hence benefit the German consumer.[82]

It might have been argued that the strict segregation of Grossraum members into primary and secondary industrial states would result in a labor shortage in the latter, so that the Reich would be forced to encourage Balkan laborers to travel to Germany and close the German labor gap. But that solution was equally unacceptable. Journeys into the Reich would make the differences in the standards of living of the German people and their own countrymen all too readily apparent to Balkan workers and hence bring with it the possibility of more dissatisfaction among the subject peoples.[83] Moreover, such arrangements were equally distasteful to the National Socialist *Volkstumspolitiker*—the dangers of blood mixtures and interracial marriages, to use the Nazi terminology, would be significantly increased.[84] A simpler solution was to pronounce the dogma that Balkan peoples were racially incapable of becoming skilled, industrial workers, a postulate that could then be supported by the best efforts of Nazi pseudoscience.

81. The Nazis were fully aware of this. One of the SOEG's research topics was entitled, "Die agrarische Übervölkerung als Haupttriebkraft der Industrialisierung im Südosten." WIW, "Arbeiten für die Industrieplanung" [ca. Feb. 1942], 'Thema II, 8,' p. 3, T-84, roll 196, frame 1561761.

82. WIW, *Voraussichtliche Entwicklung,* T-84, roll 202, frame, 1568502; Nemschak "Besprechung über das Thema . . . ," 19 June 1942, T-71, roll 67, frame 566649.

83. Seifert, "Wanderarbeiterproblem—Dispositionsvorschlag I," T-71, roll 58, frame 556102.

84. *Ibid.;* see also Walter Thoms, "Der betriebliche Arbeitseinsatz," in *Europäische Wirtschaftsgemeinschaft,* ed. Verein Berliner Kaufleute und Industrieller and Wirtschaftschochschule Berlin (Berlin, 1942), p. 74.

The SOEG's planning committee gave the task of dealing with the labor problem in a statistical study to Hans F. Zeck.[85] Zeck's analysis was ostensibly an empirical, on-the-spot examination of the habits and aptitudes of Balkan workers employed in the Viennese area on wartime assignments. He assumed that his sample, Vienna, would be sufficiently representative to make his conclusions valid not only for all Balkan nationals working in the Reich but also for the Balkan peoples as a whole.[86] To enable other Grossraum planners to compare the abilities of Balkan workers with those of other subject peoples,[87] Zeck refrained from devising his own grading system. Instead he adapted tables devised by the German Labor Front's (DAF) Institute on Labor Research (*Arbeitswissenschaftliches Institut*) that had been used for its investigations of workers from the occupied Russian and Polish territories.[88] The result was a system of grading the degree of difficulty of the work done by a majority of the workers in the sample (on a scale of 1–8) and of rating their individual ability for industrial work on a descriptive scale of 1–29.[89]

Zeck's empirical evidence supported—or, rather, was twisted to support—the standard theses of Third Reich racial science. Most of the Balkan laborers performed semiskilled work in categories 3 and 4. In general, they worked in groups led by a German foreman. In accordance with Nazi race-centered research methods, Zeck compared the skill of individual workers by comparing the average of one nationality with the average of another. The test results showed that Slovaks rated 2 and 4 on the 29-point scale, while Greeks at the other extreme, ranged

85. Hans F. Zeck, *Erfahrungen mit dem Einsatz südosteuropäischer Arbeiter unter besonderer Berücksichtigung der Verhältnisse im Landesarbeitsamtsbezirk Wien—Niederdonau* (strictly confidential) (Vienna, 1943), T-84, roll 86, frames 1375886–934. Zeck had previously written a popular study, *Die deutsche Wirtschaft und Südosteuropa* (Leipzig, 1939).

86. Zeck, *Erfahrungen*, T-84, roll 86, frame 1375889.

87. *Ibid.*, frame 1375896. Some of the limits of the study were clear even to Zeck. He admitted that many of his subjects for the study were not the most qualified workers the Balkan nations had available; the governments kept those at home. See *ibid.*, frame 1375902.

88. For a description of the various categories, see *ibid.*, Tables 6 and 9, frames 1375929, 1375933.

89. *Ibid.*, Tables 5 and 10, frames 1375929, 1375934.

from 14 to 19. The other nationalities spread between the two. No national group contained workers classifiable in category 1, that is, none were dependable (*zuverlässig*), as this category was described.[90]

Supported by his statistical "evidence," Zeck then wrote an analysis of the Balkan racial character. He felt his figures showed that the Balkan peoples were irresponsible, extremely naive, and capable of only primitive thought patterns. Consequently, a complete industrialization of the Balkans was out of the question; Balkan industrial workers, while generally suitable for a variety of semiskilled tasks, could not equal the quality of performance of Western European workers. On the other hand, a further development of agriculture in Southeastern Europe was fully justified, since Zeck found that Balkan agricultural workers were often superior to their German counterparts.[91]

With pseudoscientific proof in hand that the Balkan nations could not develop full-scale economies, the German planners need only to turn to the development of communication lines in the area. Since all factions of the German economic interests were, literally, attempting to get something out of and into Southeastern Europe, there existed unanimous agreement on the need for improved transportation and communication lines in and to the Balkans.[92] Within the borders of the Balkan countries

90. *Ibid.*, frames 1375904–05, 1375907.

91. *Ibid.*, frame 1375898. The conclusion agreed fully with the proposals advanced by the SOEG's agricultural affiliates. See Kurt von Rischka, "Die Beziehungen der deutschen Landwirtschaft zu der des Südostens," *Wiener Landwirtschaftliche Zeitung*, XCII (10 Jan. 1942), 8; Christiansen, "Südosten," p. 520. The SOEG's affiliate for agricultural research concentrated its work in such areas as the improved planting of soybeans and other oil producing plants, and animal husbandry. See Südost-Argrarinstitut, "Kurzer Tätigkeitsbericht, 1944," 8 Aug. 1944, T-84, roll 196, frames 1562457–59; Arbeitsgemeinschaft für Raumforschung (Wien) ed., *Wegweiser zu den in Wien vorhandenen Hilfsmitteln für die Raumforschung in den Gebieten der Ostmark, den Sudetenländern und im Südostraum: 1. Nachtrag (Ergänzungen und Berichtigugen, 1943)* (for official use only) (Vienna, 1943) T-71, roll 48, frame 567548.

92. It should be kept in mind that the economic reasons existed in addition, but not in opposition to the politico-strategic considerations that led to the general agreement (of Hitler as well as the major power segments) to retain permanent German control of the Danube. See Wehler, "'Reichsfestung Belgrad,'" p. 83.

improved road and rail service was necessary in order to expedite the sale of German industrial and manufactured products in both the urban and the rural areas of Southeastern Europe. At ˙the same time, the New Order necessitated the construction of rapid transportation trunklines between the Balkan countries and the Reich to facilitate the transportation of Balkan exports to the Reich.[93]

In theory, all types of transportation facilities were to be improved and expanded, but in practice the National Socialists focused most of their attention on the Danube River. It was to become the German-controlled (*deutschbestimmte*) main traffic artery connecting Germany and Southeastern Europe.[94] There were sound economic reasons for this emphasis. The National Socialists insisted on processing the raw or semifinished Balkan imports in the Reich. Hence, most of the shipments from the Southeast would consist of relatively bulky cargo. The most efficient and least expensive manner of shipping such relatively unperishable and nonfragile consignments was by sea or waterway.[95] Channeling much of the incoming traffic by way of the Danube would have the advantage of freeing the rail lines for handling perishable imports, and, above all, the less bulky manufactured goods that the Reich would send to Southeastern Europe. To enable the river to handle this vast expansion of traffic, the National Socialists had grandiose engineering plans for its improvement. The channel was to be deepened so that seagoing

93. Hassell ["Allgemeine Gesichtspunkte der SO-Verkehrsplanung"], 15 Jan. 1943, T-71, roll 71, frames 570864–66. In citing this study by Hassell, the author does not wish to imply that this prominent member of the German resistance either believed in or supported the Nazi Grossraum plans. However, the basic points of the Grossraum communication plans as they applied to the Balkans were summarized admirably in the document. In the SOEG's project, Hassel had the task of coordinating the research relating to transportation in the Balkans. See Hassell to Heinrichsbauer, 25 May 1943, *ibid.*, frame 570886.

94. Wehler, " 'Reichsfestung Belgrad,' " p. 83.

95. Brandl, *Vorschläge zum Ausbau der Donau als Grosschiffahrtsstrasse* (Vienna [1941]) p. 5; Brandl, "Beitrag zur Wasserwirtschaft an der mittleren und unteren Donau" (Spring, 1942), T-71, roll 69, frame 568572. This view of the Danube's role was common among Nazi writers. See Goetz Weissleder, *Donauraum und Rhein-Main-Donau-Kanal, eine verkehrspolitische, geschichtliche und geographische Studie* (Jena, 1944), p. 26.

ships from the Black Sea and the Mediterranean could sail as
far north as Vienna, thus bypassing Budapest as the major
port on the Upper Danube.[96] Indeed, if the plans for the Rhine-
Main-Danube canal[97] had come to fruition it would have been
possible for seagoing ships to sail from the North Sea to the
Black Sea without reloading their cargoes.[98]

The New Order was never reality, but it is possible to gain
at least a limited picture of what its reality would have meant
to the economies of Southeastern Europe. The Reich never
feared to treat the future as present, and the Vienna Institute
of Economic Research (WIW), in its study *Die voraussichtliche
Entwicklung des Wiener Hafenumschlages,* did its best to translate the generalities of future benefits into the less exhilarating,
but more meaningful language of statistical projections. According to the anticipating calculations of the institute, the tonnage
of goods to be unloaded in the port of Vienna was to increase
from 1.448 million tons (1938) to a postwar maximum of 7.8
million tons.[99] The study also reached the conclusion that both
the export of cheap mass goods from Germany and the import
of raw materials would decline, the former because Germany
would concentrate on high-value manufactured items, the latter
because Southeastern Europe was primarily to export semifinished products, not raw materials.[100] It was therefore clear that
most of the weight increase would result from Balkan exports
to Germany. The German shipments to Southeastern Europe
would yield a high capital value, but presumably be of relatively
low weight in terms of cost per unit. Actually, the tonnage
figures are not even of prima facie comparability, since, presum-

96. Brandl to Rafelsberger, 3 Nov. 1941, T-71, roll 69, frames 568727–29; Broschek (of the Port of Vienna Administration) to Rafelsberger, "Betrifft: Arbeits-
kreiss für Donaufragen, KZ-1903/42/Sev." (confidential), 17 April 1942, T-71
roll 52, frame 447455; Rafelsberger to Liebel, "Ihr Schreiben vom 28.11.42,—
Donau-Schiffahrt, Wirt 9384," 10 Dec. 1942, T-71, roll 64, frames 563015–17.
    97. On this project, see Weissleder, *Donauraum,* and the literature he cites.
    98. For the projected role of Vienna in the anticipated cross-Europe connec-
tions, see below, pp. 137–39.
    99. WIW, Voraussichtliche Entwicklung, T-84, roll 202, frames 1568492–93.
    100. *Ibid.,* frames 1568507–11.

ably, a far greater percentage of the Balkan exports to the Reich would reach Vienna as semiprocessed goods than before the war. The weight difference between a ton of dried fruit and a similar shipment of fresh fruit represents a very considerable increase in the harvest of the particular crop by the peasants of the Southeast. And these projected benefits were the result of a system labeled "development"; one can only wonder how "exploitation" would have differed.

The New Order was the intended exercise of permanent German hegemony in Europe. The system was a by-product of the success of German arms, its initial imposition upon the subject peoples would have been the result of force, and, the Nazis knew, it could have been maintained only by an elaborate system of perpetual controls.

As part of the second ring of German power Southeastern Europe was subject to indirect or limited German control. The terms were relative; they signified only that the Balkans were not destined to become a second *Generalgouvernement,* but it was also not intended that the Reich would permit the Southeast any meaningful degree of political or economic independence of action.[101] The distinctions did imply, however, that the exercise of German control would be more subtle than in the first power ring; specific channels of German influence would often be veiled rather than clearly visible, and when they were overt, the control factors would be cast in forms of pseudocontractual agreements between the Reich and the Balkan nations.

Whatever the specific fetters that would bind the nations of Europe, the foundation of the New Order would have been Germany's overwhelming military potential. As long as it loomed before the suppressed peoples, the New Order would be assured of success. No need would exist to demonstrate Germany's military might by actual occupation measures: the expectation that

---

101. For a discussion of the various degrees of autonomy (not sovereignty) permissable for the non-German countries in the New Order, see Werner Best, "Grundfragen einer deutschen Grossraumverwaltung," in *Festgabe für Heinrich Himmler* (Darmstadt, 1941), pp. 40, 42, 54–57.

an oppressor has the power to control the actions of the suppressed is in itself a significant control device in the hands of
those who possess the potential force.[102] It is unlikely that—aside
from some military bases, military instructors' cadres, and so
forth—the Balkans would have experienced any actual pro-
longed German military occupation in the New Order.

While the existence of the Reich's armed might would prevent
attempts at large-scale, government-backed rebellion in the
Southeast, the Germans could not be content with such purely
negative control if their detailed substantive plans were to bear
fruit. Among the positive control devices, the SS-sponsored
schemes to re-establish the old Austro-Hungarian *Militärgrenze,*
and the activities of the Volksdeutsche in the New Order would
have involved the most direct extension of German influence
into the political and economic life of the Balkan nations. The
former was an adaptation of Himmler's and Hitler's plans for the
East. A series of nationally and religiously homogenous villages,
peopled by SS-approved Balkan *Wehrbauern,* would have
guarded the approaches to the Reich in Bosnia and on the Dal-
matian coast. These areas would in effect have become German
colonial territory, inhabited by a Nazified population fiercely
loyal to the SS, Hitler, and the Reich.[103]

The place of the Balkan Volksdeutsche in the New Order was
not always clear. Hitler at one point considered resettling at
least some of the ethnic Germans in the interest of improving
relations between the Reich and the host countries,[104] but such
sentiments did not reach beyond the discussion stage. In the
course of the various resettlement actions, only 10 percent of

102. Herbert Simon, "Notes on the Observation and Measurement of Political
Power," *Journal of Politics,* XV (Nov. 1953), 511.

103. See "Richtlinien für die Sicherung des Landfriedens in Bosnien—13. SS-Di-
vision Ic 77/44g. Kdos." (top secret), 9 March 1944, T-120, cont. 2898, frames
458515–17.

104. See Schmidt, "Aufzeichnung über die Unterredung zwischen dem Führer
und Reichsverweser Horthy in Anwesenheit des RAM in Schloss Klessheim
am 17. April nachmittags—Aufz. Füh 26/43g. Rs." (top secret), 18 April 1943,
T-120, cont. 609, frames 120–21; Hitler, *Secret Conversations,* entry 26 Feb.
1942, p. 275.

the total population was ever taken out of Southeastern Europe (and these from peripheral areas), and no plans to resettle all or even a large part of the Volksdeutsche were ever drafted.[105] Instead, Hitler had decided by the spring of 1943 that the remainder of the ethnic groups should remain in their host countries.[106] The Balkan Volksdeutsche were to become the local and regional elite of the future, "an element of cohesion . . . and a necessity for the incorporation of the Southeast into the central European Grossraum."[107]

The decision did not come suddenly. The forced wartime treaties between the Reich and the Southeastern states had virtually transformed the ethnic groups from tolerated minorities into privileged inhabitants of states within states. The Volksdeutsche leaders, appointed and controlled by an SS-affiliate, the Liaison Office for Ethnic Germans, were arrogant men whose sense of loyalty was limited to the SS, Hitler, and the NSDAP. While the war was still raging, the ethnic Germans in Slovakia had established a German Labor Front unit,[108] and Andreas Schmidt, the leader of the Volksdeutsche in Rumania not only created NSDAP offices and formations but proudly noted that "my ethnic group has sworn loyalty to the Reich Leaders of the

105. Koehl, *RKFDV*, p. 53. Before the wholesale evacuation in 1944–45, the office of the RKFDV resettled 230,690 persons from the Balkan countries. The total number of ethnic Germans in the area was 2,250,000. See RKFDV, *Die Umsiedlung—Stand 1. Juli 1942*, Himmler Files, cont. 398, drawer 2, folder 35; Schechtmann, *European Population Transfers*, p. 29.

106. Büro RAM, "Vermerk g. Rs." (top secret), 9 March 1943, T-120, cont. 255, frame 184249.

107. Luther, "Vortragsnotiz, D VIII 515g" (secret), 5 Nov. 1942, T-120, cont. 3124, frame E505297.

108. Ribbentrop to Lorenz, 16 Nov. 1941, T-120, cont. 1536, frame D653142.

109. Andreas Schmidt, *Leistungs- und Lagebericht der Deutschen Volksgruppe in Rumänien vom 1. Juli 1942 bis 1. September 1944* ([Kronstadt], 1944), T-120, cont. 1003, frames 393140–44, 393158–59; Schmidt to Gottlob Berger (Chief of the SS-Main Office), 6 Dec. 1943, Himmler Files, cont. 391, drawer 1, folder 7. This sense of loyalty to the Party and the SS also increasingly lessened the authority of the Foreign Ministry, nominally the superior agency of the Vomi, in the field of ethnic German affairs. See Ribbentrop's bitter complaints on this score in Ribbentrop to Lorenz, 16 Nov. 1941, T-120, cont. 1536, frame D653141.

SS."[109] For the future, there remained only the transformation from autonomous organizations within states to dictatorial organisms over states. During the war the Balkan Volksdeutsche had merely removed their settlement areas from the de facto jurisdiction of the host countries; in the New Order they would not be content with this role. They would become guarantors of the docility of the Balkan governments. If the collaborator regimes proved obstinate, the Volksdeutsche leadership would assume direct control (or at least exercise direct influence) to assure continued domination of the Reich and its New Order in the area.[110] In the economic sphere, the Reich's pressure for the elimination of Jewish influence in the Balkans had already prepared the road for a new Volksdeutsche managerial class.[111]

Important as their role in the New Order was, the ethnic Germans were simply agents in the field, their actions and policies directed by Reich German officials. All German planners agreed that the New Order needed a new type of Grossraum administrator, a man who was an active Party member, who would act as representative of the Party, and who would have the "example of the Führer before him at all times."[112] As usual, disagreements arose over the jurisdictional aspects of the New Order administration; the Foreign Ministry, the Party, the economic interests all claimed legitimate control functions over the new bureaucracy. The Foreign Ministry endorsed a network of German advisors, disguised as attachés and subject to the direction and supervision of the German ministers in the Balkan nations.[113]

110. Vomi to Foreign Ministry, "Betr.: Lösungsvorschläge für Ungarn IX/11/III/19 Ra/Stf.," 21 March 1944, T-120, cont. 1003, frames 393221–31. The document refers to wartime problems, but it seems reasonable to project its conclusions to the postwar era.

111. See below, pp. 152–53.

112. See, for example, Werner Best, "Grundfragen einer deutschen Grossraum-Verwaltung," and Wilhelm Stuckart, "Die Neuordnung der Kontinente und die Zusammenarbeit auf dem Gebiete der Verwaltung," *Reich, Volksordnung, Lebensraum,* I (1941), 60 and 24 resp.

113. Some of these "advisors" had already informally taken up their duties during the war. See Rischka to Heinrichsbauer, 27 Feb. 1941, T-71, roll 131, frame 634975. After the war their tasks would have been formalized and the

The Economics Ministry continued to oppose rigid centralization and attempted to develop an institutional framework for its own subcapital concept.[114] The ministry would reserve all major policy decisions to its own Berlin headquarters, but with the establishment of the SOEG in February 1940 it was well on its way toward creating an important regional executive agency for the Southeast. Thereafter the system lacked only executive offices in the various Balkan countries. Funk was naturally enough unable and unwilling to use the diplomatic officials attached to the Foreign Ministry for this purpose, particularly since he felt he had another ready-made system of established organizations at his disposal—the various bilateral chambers of commerce. These organizations had originally been founded as private associations of German and foreign businessmen to promote business contacts and international trade, and were thus relics of a liberal era in an age of government-controlled economics by the time the war began. Since they had no organic functions in the Nazi system, they appeared more than ripe for a thorough Nazification at the hands of the Ministry of Economics.

Their transformation into Grossraum administrative units directed by the Economics Ministry began in the fall of 1940, when the ministry moved to divest them of what remained of their liberal, international character.[115] By October the chambers

---

scope of their functions expanded. Zeck, "Aktenvermerk—Betr.: Unterredung mit SS-Obersturmbannführer Smagon am 6.I. 1944," 7 Jan. 1944, T-71, roll 64, frame 564574.

114. The ministry was by no means alone in its dislike of the Foreign Ministry. It was well-nigh an axiom of all SS planning that the New Order could succeed only if the Foreign Ministry were eliminated as a serious factor of influence. See Berger to Himmler (secret), 2 Sept. 1944, Himmler Files, cont. 390, drawer 1, folder 6; Berger to Himmler, "Betr.: Reise nach Kroatien VS-Tgb. Nr. 725/43g. Kdos." (top secret), 13 July 1943, T-175, roll 119, frame 2645154. It is likely that, once the New Order was established, the Foreign Ministry would have been rapidly eclipsed by its rivals. Most of the wartime "advisors," while active within the framework of the embassies, were in fact SS and Party officials.

115. Rafelsberger, "Aktenvermerk- Betrifft: Südosteuropagesellschaft" (confidential), 4 Sept. 1940, T-71, roll 74, frame 575613; Dellbrügge (*Regierungspräsident* of Vienna) to Landfried, 26 Sept. 1940, T-71, roll 57, frame 453596.

of commerce in areas under direct Axis control had become unilaterally German affairs, with only German firms as members
and administrative offices staffed solely with German officials.[116]
Funk was unable to complete his task before formidable opposition made its appearance. The opposition of the Balkan governments could be ignored, but the matter took a more serious turn
when their voices were joined by those of the Foreign Ministry
(which saw the proposals as yet another attempted invasion of
its sphere of competency) and by some sectors of the German
private business community, which feared additional governmental supervision of business activities. Characteristically, Funk
retreated in the face of the opposition. Late in 1940, while still
advocating the transformation in principle, he declared that he
regarded its realization as impractical for the time being.[117]

Funk's withdrawal came during the period of massive setbacks
for the SOEG, and the Society, which had fully expected to
gain control of the organizations,[118] once more found itself left
to its own devices. (To be sure, for a time the characteristic tendency toward centralization in the Nazi system aided rather
than hindered the SOEG.) In the spring of 1941 the chambers
of commerce were further *gleichgeschaltet;* all (including the

116. This development was particularly encouraged by Schlotterer. See Heinrichsbauer to Rafelsberger ["Bericht über eine Berlin-Reise, 2.-4. Okt. 1940"],
5 Oct. 1940, T-71, roll 74, frames 575561–62; Heinrichsbauer to Bergemann, 12
Oct. 1940, T-71, roll 68, frame 567343; [Industrie- und Handelskammer Vienna],
"Deutsche Handelskammern und wirtschaftliche Vereinigungen im Ausland
(Nach dem Stand vom 1.X.1940)" n.d., T-71, roll 56, frame 453182. All-German
chambers of commerce had been established in France, the Netherlands, Den-
mark, and Poland.

117. Kratz to Dellbrügge, "Betr.: Südosteuropa-Gesellschaft—Auf Ihr Schreiben vom 30.10.1940, Nr. 137," 31 Oct. 1940, T-71, roll 72, frame 572177; Rafelsberger, "Aktenvermerk-Besprechung bei Herrn Staatssekretär Landfried," 12 Nov.
1940, T-71, roll 74, frame 575496; Rafelsberger, "Aktenvermerk uber die Besprech-
eung mit Reichswirtschaftsminster Funk in Berlin," 21 March 1942, T-71, roll 58,
frame 555751.

118. The SOEG had already begun negotiations with the Netherlands' Chamber
of Commerce in the hope of concluding an agreement whereby the former
recognized the SOEG as its agent for the entire Balkan area. See Heinrichsbauer
to Rafelsberger, 21 Nov. 1940, T-71, roll 74, frame 575483; Heinrichsbauer to
Rost van Tonnigen (president of the Netherlands Bank), 25 Sept. 1941, T-71,
roll 48, frame 442391.

international ones) adopted new, uniform constitutions.[119] Moreover, as the German armies occupied additional areas of Europe, unilateral chambers of commerce followed in their train. In some instances, as in Croatia, they were new establishments, in others transformations of previously bilateral organizations (for example, in Greece).[120]

The decisive factor in the SOEG's success, however, was its alliance with two powerful segments of the Nazi system not associated with the Economics Ministry: the Party *Auslandsorganisation* (AO) and the German Advertising Council (*Werberat der Deutschen Wirtschaft*). Throughout the war the AO pressed for more Party control over German economic and commercial activities in foreign countries, and consistently opposed soft conciliatory policies in the Balkans.[121] In the fall of 1940 the president of the council, Heinrich Hunke (who was also the Gau economic advisor for Berlin and who maintained close connections with the SS), joined the assault forces.[122]

Other circumstances favored the triumvirate. As international organs, the chambers of commerce were supervised by the Foreign Ministry, but as all-German agencies, supervision would fall to the AO. The Foreign Ministry attempted to preclude a further growth of the AO by subordinating some of the organization's activites to the direction of the ministry, but Ribbentrop suffered a severe defeat: in August 1941 his efforts were sharply reprimanded by Hitler.[123] Henceforth the anti-Ribbentrop forces could boast of an indirect Führer mandate. On

119. "Deutsch-Ungarische Handelskammern," *VWN* (Wochenbericht 19–26 May 1941), p. 3.

120. Reichsgruppe Industrie to Wirtschaftsgruppen, Industrieabteilungen der Wirtschaftskammern, Mitglieder des Südostausschusses, "Betr.: Deutsche Handelskammer in Griechenland, Athen, SO IV 4434/42," 25 Nov. 1942, T-71, roll 52, frame 452559; Reichsgruppe Industrie to above and in addition to Mitglieder des Länderausschusses Kroatien, "Betr.: Deutsche Handelskammer in Kroatien, Zagreb," 25 Nov. 1942, *ibid.*, frame 452557.

121. Misch to Heinrichsbauer, 26 Oct. 1941, T-84, roll 137, frame 1439915; Gerlach to Heinrichsbauer, 19 Aug. 1943, T-71, roll 62, frame 560487.

122. Heinrichsbauer to Rafelsberger, 5 Oct. 1940, T-71, roll 74, frame 575562. Hunke was also a member of the SOEG's presidium.

123. Bormann to Ribbentrop, 2 Aug. 1941, T-120, cont. 3288, frame E570420.

the other hand, relations between the AO, the Ministry of Economics, and the SOEG were excellent.[124] Funk had earned the AO's particular appreciation by his earlier directive assigning the supervision and selection of all future German business and commercial personnel outside the Reich to the AO.[125]

Together the AO and the SOEG, with Funk's benevolent but passive support, set out to infiltrate and undermine the uncooperative administrations of the existing chambers of commerce. Only then, would the "conquered" agency affiliate itself with the SOEG. Leading officials of the AO assumed important posts in the various chambers of commerce. Gerlach, the head of the Croatian AO unit, became president of the new chamber of commerce in Croatia. In Bucharest the AO's economic adviser was simultaneously first vice-president of the Rumanian-German chamber of commerce. When the AO was unable to establish a controlled chamber of commerce or infiltrate an established group, it founded its own group which then operated alongside the recognized organization. In Bulgaria, for example, the AO-sponsored Association of Reich German Businessmen in Sofia (*Arbeitsgemeinschaft reichsdeutscher Kaufleute in Sofia*) was to replace the Bulgarian-German chamber of commerce when the time was ripe.[126]

The SOEG had full confidence in the success of the AO's program of subversion. The Society consistently preferred closer liaisons with even the unreconstructed chambers of commerce to more dealings with the German commercial attachés in the

124. The SOEG and the AO maintained close and cordial relations throughout the war. See Heinrichsbauer to Rafelsberger, 20 Dec. 1940, T-71, roll 74, frames 575393–94; Gerlach to SOEG (Augenthaler), "Betr.: Zusammenarbeit AO–S.O.E.G. [sic]," 24 Feb. 1944, T-71, roll 62, frame 560483.

125. Gerlach to Heinrichsbauer, 3 April 1942, T-71, roll 62, frame 560517. The Foreign Ministry was proportionately displeased. See same to same, 19 Aug. 1943, *ibid.*, frame 560487.

126. Kutsche (of the AO) to Heinrichsbauer, 11 Nov. 1942, T-71, roll 68, frames 567135–36. At the same time the AO expanded its own administrative apparatus in the Balkans to impressive proportions. See, for example, Rudolf Empting, "Kroatien im Spiegelbild der Landesgruppe der Auslandsorganisation der NSDAP, Juni 1941–Juni 1942" (Zagreb, 1942), T-81, roll 136, frames 172982–173059.

Balkan countries.[127] As chambers of commerce came under the control of the AO, the SOEG entrusted its representation in the country entirely to them.[128] When, on the other hand, the older element was still in firm control of a chamber of commerce, as was the case in Bulgaria, the SOEG insisted that the official representing the SOEG should receive orders only from the SOEG and the Advertising Council, not from the chamber of commerce itself.[129]

It is clear that the future administrative control of German Balkan policies would have been carried out in a close partnership between the AO and the SOEG. The SOEG would exercise regional control from the New Order's Southeast capital and assure effective coordination of the main policies through the chambers of commerce, now affiliated with and subordinated to the Society. The AO, in turn, would control the cadre personnel. It would select administrative officials for duty in Southeastern Europe, assuring that they were politically reliable, active, fanatical Party members.[130]

Germany's impregnable politico-military power position left

127. See Heinrichsbauer to Kratz, "Betr.: Südost-Handelskammern," 9 Sept. 1942, T-84, roll 196, frame 1376535.
128. For example, in Croatia and in Rumania. At the time the SOEG concluded its agreement with the Rumanian group, the latter was still an international body, but the vice-president (who was also economic advisor of the AO) assured the SOEG that he had eroded the authority of the traditionalist officials. See SOEG and Deutsche Handelskammer in Kroatien, "Vereinbarung zwischen der Deutschen Handelskammer in Kroatien und der Südosteuropa-Gesellschaft e.V." (draft) [Jan., 1942], T-84, roll 87, frames 1377782–83; SOEG and Rumänisch-Deutsche Handelskammer, "Vereinbarung zwischen der Südosteuropa-Gesellschaft, Wien (SOEG) und der Rumänisch-Deutschen Handelskammer, Bukarest (Rude-Kammer)," 12 Feb. 1943, T-71, roll 49, frames 444291–92; Musmacher (vice-president of the chamber of commerce) to Heinrichsbauer, 12 Feb. 1943, *ibid.*, frame 445293. The executive secretary of the chamber of commerce, Paul Schön, was also a former official in the Foreign Commerce Department of the AO's Central Office.
129. Heinrichsbauer to Kratz, "Betr.: Errichtung einer Aussenstelle der Südosteuropa-Gesellschaft in Sofia," 14 Nov. 1942, T-84, roll 86, frame 1376670.
130. Stadler (of the SOEG's field office in Zagreb) to Heinrichsbauer, 13 March 1942, T-84, roll 87, frames 1377645–46; Rafelsberger, "Aktenvermerk über die Besprechung mit Reichswirtschaftsminister Funk in Berlin" (secret), 21 March 1942, T-71, roll 58, frame 555752.

her a limitless choice of economic controls to parallel her political and personnel fetters in the Balkans. The most basic and open form of economic control was the Reich's refusal to become a part of the international division of labor in the New Order.[131] This freedom would allow Germany to be independent of any economic developments in her satellite states, while the latter, with their perpetually incomplete vertical and horizontal economic systems, could not escape the economic influence of the Reich. But the National Socialists did not intend to limit their overt influence to noninvolvement in the international division of labor. The Germans' intention to dismantle all undesirable industrial facilities, their plan to establish prominent bastions of indirect and direct economic influence in the satellites,[132] and their anticipated control of the European currencies are equally obvious methods of economic control. As in the case of the political controls, most of the veiled forms of influence would have assumed the form of pseudocontractual or legal agreements. In the economic field the most far-reaching institutional innovation in the New Order would have been the creation of vast international vertical-horziontal cartels.[133] It is true that the creation of the new institutions would require a revolution in traditional legal economic thinking and its emphasis upon the nation as the logical economic unit, but National Socialist planners were more than willing to become legal pioneers.[134]

131. WIW, *Voraussichtliche Entwicklung*, p. 82, T-84, roll 202, frame 1568573.

132. For example, Rafelsberger proposed that all key economic positions (*Schlüsselstellungen*) that is, the Hungarian National Bank, the textile and cement industries, and the insurance business, should pass into direct German control, while the SS planned to acquire permanent ownership of the Manfred Weiss munitions works. See Rabitsch, "Industrieplanung (Besprechung zu Dr. Seiferts Besuch bei Rafelsberger 8.5. [1942])," n.d., T-71, roll 58, frame 555922; Rafelsberger to Veesenmeyer [sic] (secret), 23 March 1944, T-71, roll 58, frame 555794; [Veesenmayer] to RAM, "Nr. 213 vom 26.5.44" (top secret), 26 May 1944, T-120, cont. 2723, frame 422050.

133. The agricultural interests had no faith in the indirect control methods. See Heinrichsbauer to Rischka, 24 May 1943, T-71, roll 75, frame 576421; Hanel to Rischka, 26 May 1943, *ibid.*, frame 576417.

134. See Ernst Krieck, "Germanische Rechtsgesinnung," *Deutsches Recht*, X (10 Feb. 1940), 219; Hans-Helmut Dietze, "Deutschland—der Feind des Völkerrechts? Entwicklung und Widerlegung einer westeuropäischen Ideologie,"

Thus to some Third Reich jurists it was axiomatic that the New Order would mean the introduction of German law into all of Europe; and while less radical authors did not go this far, there was general consensus among National Socialist jurists that the Grossraum required a new system of international law, and that the new code must be based on the principles of the National Socialist Party law. As in the case of the new laws, the subject nations were spared the actual establishment of the cartel system, but the Nazis were well along in laying the theoretical ground work. The Economics Ministry had already authorized a new industrial organization, the Reich Association (*Reichs-vereinigung*); the SOEG and Vienna city authorities endeavored to correlate their economic plans with the expected operation of the cartels; and National Socialist economists were constructing theoretical models.

In 1941 Arno Sölter published a description and analysis of cartellization in the New Order under the title *Das Grossraum-kartell.*[135] Sölter postulated that the foundation of the economic reorganization of Europe was Germany's clearly acknowledged position as dominant power (*Führungsmacht*) on the Continent.[136] Political preponderance enabled the Reich to administer Europe along vertically organized lines without regard for political boundaries or sensitivities.[137] Sölter surmised that the various vertical components of each branch of industry would be united into a Europe-wide trust (*Grossraumkartell*), which

---

Deutsches Recht, X (9 and 16 Nov. 1940), 1911; Hans-Helmut Dietze, "Vom deutschen Verfassungsrecht zum europäischen Verfassungsrecht," *ibid.,* XI (12 and 19 April 1941), 804. For a description of the legal position of the NSDAP in the German state as well as the Nazi view of the German constitutional law under the Third Reich, see Gottfried Neesse, *Partei und Staat* (Hamburg, 1936); Gottfried Neesse, *Die Nationalsozialistische Deutsche Arbeiterpartei—Versuch einer Rechtsdeutung* (Stuttgart, 1935); Ernst Rudolf Huber, *Verfassungsrecht des Grossdeutschen Reiches* (Hamburg, 1939).

135. Arno Sölter, *Das Grossraumkartell—ein Instrument der industriellen Marktordnung im neuen Europa* (Dresden, 1941). This was one of a series of studies issued by Daitz' research institute.

136. *Ibid.,* pp. 33–35, 41, 42. Sölter did accord Italy a preferred position beside Germany.

137. *Ibid.,* pp. 83–84, 127.

would then regulate, in part as agent of the various governments (the cartel agreements would have the legal force of
international treaties), both the production and the marketing
of its entire product line.[138] Since the secondary manufacturing
operations and the major financial resources of any industrial
branch would almost certainly be in the hands of the Reich
interests, the new cartels would obviously in every case be
clearly dominated by German economic interests. Sölter did not
deny this. He also assumed that, in the future, German would
be the official language of all cartel agreements and the reichsmark the basis of all price arrangements.[139]

The Nazi regime had always preferred to channel much of
its actual control through organizations that were nominally associations of private interests, rather than destroy the old organizations and then establish revolutionary new ones. The Grossraumkartell, under the designation of Reich Association, was
an extension of this concept. The Reich Associations, the first
of which appeared in 1942, were deliberately structured to com-
bine aspects of economic self-government with functions of the
Ministry of Economics. The scope of their jurisdiction was vast:
they would have allocated raw materials among the cartel members, drawn up detailed production plans, marketed the products
in the Reich and abroad,[140] set prices, concluded price agreements,
and determined agreements with other cartels. Indeed, the Reich
Association was comparable in scope and function only to the
vast agricultural monopoly in Nazi Germany, the Reich Food
Estate.[141]

138. *Ibid.*, pp. 87–88, 93, 140.
139. *Ibid.*, pp. 151, 155–57. The latter provision had already become official
government policy for all international trade in German-dominated Europe.
See above, p. 113, n. 57.
140. The Reich never favored marketing organizations controlled and administered by the Balkan countries. See "Leistungsgrenzen der Handelsmonopole,"
Südost-Echo, 15 April 1941, pp. 1–2; [Wirtschaftsgruppe Gross-, Ein-, and Ausfuhrhandel to Economics Ministry], "Betr.: Aussenhandelsmonopole in
Kroatien" [ca. May, 1941], T-84, roll 87, frames, 1378340–41; Schubert, "Aktennotiz über eine Besprechung beim Auswärtigen Amt am 10.7.1941," 10 July
1941, *ibid.,* frames 1377293–94; Janovsky, "Bericht über die im RWM . . . ,"
T-71, roll 56, 555524.
141. "Reichsvereinigung und Grossraumkartell," *Chemische Industrie,* LXV
(12 June 1942), 233. *Grossraumkartelle* did not exist solely on paper. In 1942

Like the New Order itself, the future cartels would be huge entities; it could be argued that they, like the New Order, could be administered more effectively from a series of regional managerial offices in various cities than through an overly cumbersome central administration, geographically remote from the actual scenes of economic activity. The seat of all future cartels would no doubt be Berlin, but the organizations would need management centers between the raw material facilities in the Balkans and the central headquarters in Berlin. It was in this connection that Vienna envisioned a glorious economic future for itself, paralleling its rise to political prominence. It was to become the turntable of German-Balkan economic relations, or, as one non-Viennese author put it, the "Hamburg of the East."[142] While the city had no ambitions to become a center of heavy industry, it did want to be the most important port of transit to and from the European Southeast. Consequently, plans for the city's future development were closely correlated with the position assigned the Balkans in the New Order. Anticipating the vast increase in imports of raw and semiraw materials, Vienna hoped to effect large-scale improvements in its transportation and warehousing facilities. The harbor would be expanded and improved,[143] and in the hope of attracting not only terminal freight from the Balkans but also through-freight shipped from

---

the Slovakian cement industry, for example, associated itself (or was forced to take this step) with the German cartel—clearly a step toward the creation of an all-European cement cartel. See Mussap (the SOEG's representative in Bratislava), "Monatsbericht über die wirtschaftliche Lage in der Slowakei im April 1942," n.d., T-71, roll 70, frame 569793.

142. German publicists were generally agreed on Vienna's future economic importance as the major transportation hub (*Umschlagplatz*) between Germany and the Balkan states. See, for example, Walther Croll, *Wirtschaft im europäischen Raum* (Vienna, 1940), p. 110; Walter Schneefuss, *Donauräume und Donaureiche* (2nd ed., Vienna, 1944), pp. 26–27; Franz Egert, "Die Mittlerstelle der Ostmark in Güteraustausch und Verkehr des neuen Europas," *Weltwirtschaftliches Archiv*, LV (March, 1942), 272–73.

143. Rafelsberger, "Wirtschaftsplanung im Reichsgau Wien," *Deutsche Volkswirtschaft*, IX (21 April 1940), 377–78; see also [Heinrichsbauer?], "Bericht über eine Besprechung bei Beigeordneten Rafelsberger über ein Wirtschaftsprogramm für die Stadt Wien," 12 Oct. 1940, T-71, roll 74, frames 575543–44.

all parts of Europe to the Southeast, the city authorities planned to develop Vienna into an important rail center.[144]

The city was not content to dispatch the goods arriving from the Balkans; they would leave the city only after additional processing or manufacturing. Vienna needed to establish "every kind of processing industry (*jederlei Veredelungsindustrie*)."[145] In the New Order, Vienna would abound with industrial facilities that utilized the cheap Balkan products and turned them into German manufactured goods: mills, fruit and vegetable canneries, tobacco processing plants, slaughter houses and meat packing plants, facilities for the manufacture of vegetable oils, animal fodder industries, chemical plants, paper and textile manufacturing plants—all would have testified to Vienna's booming economic future in the New Order.[146]

A Europe ruled by a fanatical Nazi administrative corps, economic exploitation between states as a permanent feature of European life—the SOEG's plans for the New Order in the Balkans reveal a frightful glimpse of a relentless, methodical totalitarian future. The Nazis' New Europe would have institutional-

144. Rischka to Office of the Gauwirtschaftsberater in Vienna (Broschek), "Programm für die Besprechung mit den Vertretern des Reichsverkehrs Ministeriums, Agr/G/73 C 10/A Dr. R/5/43," 17 Feb. 1943, T-71, roll 75, frames 576581–82; [NSDAP, Gau Wien], Gauwirtschaftsberater, *Grundlagen zum Gauwirtschaftsplan von Wien—Teilausarbeitung I—Ausbau der Wiener Hafenanlagen* (secret) (Vienna, 1942), pp. 97–98, T-84, roll 202, frames 1568463–64; "[Tagesordung, Teilnehmerliste und Protokoll der] Besprechung von Verkehrsfragen im Reichsgau Wien am 2. u. 3. März 1943" (confidential), T-71, roll 58, frames 555680–81. Heinrichsbauer was untiring in stressing Vienna's future position in the transit trade on his various travels in northern and western Europe. See Heinrichsbauer, *Nordeuropa-Südosteuropa-Eindrücke von einer Skandinavienreise Ende Juli–Anfang August 1942* (confidential) (Vienna, 1942), pp. 8–9; "Der Südostauftrag Wiens, Gespräch des Reichsleiters Baldur von Schirach mit dem Hauptschriftsleiter der 'Donauzeitung' [Oberascher]," *Donauzeitung*, 9 Aug. 1942, p. 2.

145. Rafelsberger, "Wirtschaftsplanung," p. 378. Vienna was also suggested as the seat of tremendous (*gewaltige*) processing industries by economists outside Austria. See Walter Schmidt, "Die Verkehrsträger Grossdeutschlands vor neuen Aufgaben in der Europäischen Grossraumwirtschaft," in *Probleme des europäischen Grosswirtschaftsraumes,* ed. Bruno Kiesewetter (Berlin, 1942), pp. 115–16.

146. WIW, *Voraussichtliche Entwicklung*, T-84, roll 202, frame 1568529.

ized permanent categories of false heroes and real helots. Despite propagandistic claims to the contrary, the New Order was not planned as a system of cooperation but of subordination. In essence, the aim of the New Order was power; its content little more than the machinery necessary to attain and maintain the degree of influence that the Nazi central leadership desired in Europe.

For it was hunger for power that motivated all Nazi actions. To be sure, the German standard of living would have increased and the Viennese economy would have boomed, but these advantages were only means to an end: they strengthened the Reich's political stature in the postwar Europe. For the life of the non-German peoples of Europe, the New Order could hold out little promise but years of toil, subsistence standards of living, and political impotence for all but a minute number of pro-Nazi collaborators. The sole purpose of economic life in the satellites was to help provide the Reich with the material means to continue the oppression of the subject peoples.

Composed of a structured Reich with its ethnic German islands in Europe and deprived, dependent nations, the New Order gives the appearance of the most one-sided of exploitation systems. This is true, of course, though in a larger sense the Nazi New Europe would have been Sartrean hell: a system of political and economic oppression that chained alike arrogant masters and servile subjects, the one to perpetual vigilance lest the captives rebel, the other to hopeless existence as exploited peoples.

5 | The Premature Conquerors: The SOEG and Germany's Wartime Policies

THE spectacular (though Pyrrhic) German victories in 1940 and 1941 imparted a mixture of elation and fear to almost all of National Socialist officialdom. On the one hand, the unprecedented sweep of German arms seemed to open up virtually unlimited opportunities for agential expansion in the conquered areas of Europe. "Thinking big" acquired completely new meanings,[1] and the postwar future

---

1. In the summer of 1941, for example, Hitler noted that autarky should be thought of in Continental rather than national terms. See "Äusserung Hitlers zum Reichsminister Dr. Todt vom 20.6.1941," as quoted in Hans-Adolf Jacobsen, *Der Zweite Weltkrieg in Chronik und Dokumenten* (Darmstadt, 1959), p. 230; Henry Picker, *Hitlers Tischgespräche im Führerhauptquartier 1941–1942*, ed. Gerhard Ritter (Bonn, 1951), pp. 51–53, 102. In this connection it should be mentioned that the expected circulation of German books and articles throughout Europe was cited as one reason for the abrogation of the drive to force the adoption of the Gothic (*Fraktur*) print in German publications. See "Auch

appeared chronologically very near to the wartime present. At the same time, precisely because the final victory seemed so near, German agencies became fearful of being outmaneuvered by more future-oriented rival factions in the system, and virtually every segment of the National Socialist power structure lost interest in the problems of the immediate war effort.[2] Instead, they hastened to dispatch into the Reich's new and old satellites advance units of what they felt would soon be treaty-sanctioned groups of German controllers and advisors. From mid-1940 to the Battle of Stalingrad, the German-dominated areas of Europe became simultaneously laboratories for the practical application of the New Order plans and, since these plans were manifestations of the continuing rivalries among National Socialist agencies, battle grounds for the persisting intrasystem struggles.[3]

As an outpost of the economic power segment in the Third Reich, the SOEG speedily established its own field staff in the Balkan countries. In general, the SOEG selected its agents from the ranks of Germans who were already resident in Southeastern Europe as employees of another official or semiofficial Reich agency. The reason, it may be assumed, was both to save time and to avoid jurisdictional battles with other agencies over the release of disputed personnel. By the end of 1941 the Society maintained full-time agents in Zagreb and Bratislava, while

---

eine wichtige Rationalisierung," *Wirtschaftspolitische Parole,* VI (20 Oct. 1941), 635.

2. See, for example, Thomas (chief of the *Wehrwirtschaft- und Rüstungsamt*) to Speer, "Betr.: Rationalisierung in Verwaltung und Wirtschaft zum Zwecke der Freimachung von Kräften aller Art für die Kriegsführung. Antrag auf Erlass von Verordnungen für Verwaltung und Wirtschaft, Nr. 15753/42g" (secret), 10 March 1942, in National Archives Microscopy No. T-77 (cited hereafter as T-77), roll 571, frames 1749350–51.

3. The lack of concern with immediate war needs until Stalingrad was by no means confined to Balkan policies. See Burton H. Klein, *Germany's Economic Preparations for War* (Cambridge, Mass., 1959), pp. 202–03; Erich Schneider, "Grösse und Verfall der Wissenschaft im Zweiten Weltkrieg," and Hans Kehrl, "Kriegswirtschaft und Rüstungsindustrie," in Werner Picht et al., *Bilanz des Zweiten Weltkrieges* (Oldenburg, 1953), pp. 256–57, 276; Erich Welter, *Falsch und richtig planen* (Heidelberg, 1954), p. 11.

part-time representatives had taken up their duties in Bucharest, Budapest, Belgrade, and Sofia. The Society's full-time representatives were Peter Mussap (Bratislava) and Karl Schubert (Zagreb). Mussap had been deputy commercial attaché at the German embassy in Slovakia, and Schubert apparently came from the ranks of the Austrian NSDAP's economic administration.[4] Captain Heinz Buchas (Bucharest) was a member of the German Military Economic Mission to Rumania; Dr. Gerhard Misch (Budapest) was a correspondent of the *Eildienst,* the publication of the German Advertising Council, and also worked for the German-Hungarian Chamber of Commerce in Budapest; Anton Kreuzbauer (Belgrade) served as administrative advisor (*Kriegsverwaltungsrat*) on the staff of the German Plenipotentiary for the Economy in Serbia (*Bevollmächtigter für die Wirtschaft in Serbien*); while Dr. Franz Holzinger (Sofia) was associated with the German Academic Institute (*Deutsches Wissenschaftliches Institut*) in Sofia.[5]

Unlike other German agencies, the SOEG's wartime field officers had reportorial rather than executive functions: the representatives sent a steady stream of reports on current economic and political developments in their various countries to the Vienna central office.[6] Many of the reports were published in the SOEG's economic newssheet *Vertrauliche Wirtshaftsnachrichten* or they provided research data for the various theoretical analyses connected with the SOEG's long-range planning activities.[7] Others reached a variety of government and Party officials

4. See Mussap to Rischka and Heinrichsbauer, "Betr.: Besichtigungsfahrt der slow. Wirtschaftsdelegation," 12 Jan. 1944, T-71, roll 69, frame 569373. Schubert became *Gauwirtschaftsberater* of Vienna at the beginning of 1944.

5. Hanel to Hanslik (of the *Donauländische Raiffeisenverband*), 20 Nov. 1941, T-71, roll 65, frame 564187. In Turkey the SOEG was briefly represented by Anton Dechant (before he was ordered to the SS school at Bad Tölz), and its unimportant part-time agent in Greece was Lieutenant General (Ret.) Hervay, who also represented the Vienna Fair, Inc. (*Wiener Messe AG*), in Athens.

6. Heinrichsbauer to Hervay, 30 Dec. 1941, T-71, roll 66, frames 564662–63. The SOEG stressed the importance of objective reporting. See Max Stadler (Schubert's successor in Zagreb), "Bericht," 1 Nov. 1942, T-71, roll 51, frame 446388; Heinrichsbauer to Stadler, 18 Aug. 1942, *ibid.*, frame 446436.

7. See above, pp. 72–75, 103ff., for an analysis of the *VWN* and the SOEG's planning activities.

and thus became part of the overall flow of intelligence data available to the Nazi leadership.[8]

The statistical and descriptive material sent by the SOEG's Balkan agents served the German aims in Southeastern Europe in at least two ways. On the one hand German businessmen benefited from what was in essence often industrial or agricultural espionage. More significant, however, was its governmental usefulness. The reports constituted part of the background information that enabled German delegates at German-Balkan negotiations to counter effectively Balkan evasiveness and objections to increased German economic demands. The Germans in 1941 faced an unpleasant dilemma. The degree of control to which they aspired had grown in proportion to the number of military victories won by the Reich's armies, but the machinery for translating the goals into the reality of power had been inherited from the prewar era of ostensible mutual respect and cooperation. Moreover, since the center refused to permit drastic alterations in the German treatment of the nominally sovereign Balkan nations, the possibilities of altering the machinery remained rather circumscribed. The goals had become totalitarian, but the executory means remained liberal-democratic. It was frustrating.

The maze of bilateral committees inherited from the prewar era was indeed formidable. To begin with, there were the Governmental Committees (*Regierungsausschüsse*). Like most nations during the depression, the Balkan and German governments had instituted tight controls over the volume and conduct of foreign trade. The bilateral Governmental Committees had the task of supervising the execution of commercial treaties between the Reich and its Southeastern partners. They met at

8. A typical confidential report by Misch was sent to the following officials (described as the "small circle") : Dellbrügge (*Regierungspräsident* of Vienna), Rafelsberger, Gerlach (an official of the NSDAP's *Auslandsorganisation*), Chlan and Querner (both of the Viennese office of the SD), Ronneberger (the editor of the SOEG's *Vertrauliche Wirtschaftsnachrichten*), Kurt Knoll, Buzzi, and Kelter (of the *WIW*). See the marginalia in Misch to SOEG, 13 April 1944, T-71, roll 58, frame 555466. The report is on frames 55466–67.

periodic intervals to remove bottlenecks and negotiate differing interpretations of treaty terms. Since the war did not modify the governments' control of foreign trade, these agencies continued to function. Within the Reich governmental framework, they worked under the jurisdictional control of the Foreign Ministry.

The Wohltat Pact of March, 1939, by introducing joint industrial and agricultural development projects, ushered in a new phase in German-Balkan economic relations. In this context the need for new bilateral coordinating agencies was obvious, and in the spring of 1941 the Germans took steps to extend the basic concept of the Wohltat Pact to include the remainder of the independent Balkan nations. New institutions, called Industrial Committees (*Industrieausschüsse*), were established in Germany and the Balkan nations. The agencies were to conduct periodic bilateral discussions resulting, it was hoped, in the formulation of plans to integrate Southeastern Europe's existing and future industrial facilities into the New European Order. However, these committees, like the Governmental Committees, had outlived their usefulness before the members met across the negotiating table. The Governmental and Industrial Committees were suitable as organs of compromise and negotiation, but by 1941 the entire concept of mutual cooperation had become a meaningless propaganda term. Reich propagandists continued to celebrate all periodic bilateral sessions as steps on the road to a New Europe of mutual cooperation and interdependence,[9] but a careful study of their minutes (which Heinrichsbauer received regularly) reveals a considerably less harmonious picture. Southeastern industrialists and economic officials, understandably reluctant to become economic vassals of an increasingly arrogant Reich, showed no enthusiasm for the joint planning sessions. Time after time scheduled meetings were postponed and when German pressure finally forced the calling of

9. Ludwig Imhoff, "Europas neue Wirtschaftsordung im Entstehen," *Schulungsbrief*, IX (Folge 4/5/6, 1942), 26; "MWT in erfolgreicher Arbeit," *Südost-Echo*, 14 Nov. 1941, p. 2.

a session, there were further delays in putting decisions into effect.[10]

The Germans soon realized that the Industrial Committee negotiations yielded only disappointing results, and began to diagnose the factors that led to the failure. The verdict was neither astute nor accurate: German economic officials felt that the planning activities of the various German agencies needed to be better coordinated. As a cure, the Reich Industry Group in mid-1941 established yet more committees, so-called National Committees (*Länderausschüsse*), one for each of the Balkan countries with the exception of Albania and Turkey. These had the primary task of coordinating the drafting of the specific German proposals that would be put before the bilateral Industrial Committees, although it was also hoped that the committee members would pave the way for the eventual adoption of the German projects by cultivating the goodwill of individual Balkan businessmen. To prevent an excessive parochialization of planning activities in Germany, the Reich Group somewhat later added still another committee, the Southeast Committee (*Südostausschuss*), to coordinate the work of the national committees. It was headed by a I. G. Farben executive, Max Ilgner, and included Heinrichsbauer among its members.

Here, then, was the cumbersome German machinery established to lead the Reich on the path toward progressive German economic penetration of the Balkans. The Governmental Committees continued to negotiate trade agreements between Germany and Southeastern Europe; the National Committees worked on industrialization projects for the individual countries. These were then coordinated on an area-wide basis in the Southeast Committee,[11] before being finally presented to the international Industrial Committees. The SOEG played an important

10. Heinrichsbauer to Reinhardt (*Ministerialdirigent* in the Reich Ministry of Economics), 6 Dec. 1941, T-71, roll 14, frame 404825.

11. Reichsgruppe Industrie, "Entwurf einer Geschäftsordnung für den Südost-Ausschuss und die Länderausschüsse der Reichsgruppe Industrie," 2 Sept. 1941, T-71, roll 14, frames 404951–53; Ilgner to H. Lenze (of the Reich Industry Group) "[Vortrag in Wien]," 12 Dec. 1941, *ibid.*, frame 575731.

role in this complex process. Heinrichsbauer, Rafelsberger, and Rischka all served as German delegates for at least some of the Industrial Committees' negotiations and the SOEG's central office handled all technical arrangements for the meetings when they were held in Vienna.[12]

The Germans were wrong in their analysis of what ailed the lagging Industrial Committee sessions. The problem was not lack of coordination, but lack of cooperation. For the National Socialists the task ahead in the Balkans was one of control, subordination, permeation; for the Southeastern nations it quickly became a search for the best means of preventing precisely that end result. What might have become a genuine experiment in regional economic cooperation rapidly deteriorated into a contest between a militarily and politically superior exploiter and a number of wily victims.

That the relationship deteriorated to this level was a direct consequence of the National Socialists' power-oriented policy goals, and the necessity for all German agencies to accept these goals before they could hope to participate in the process of political interaction in the Third Reich. There was another way of dealing with the Balkans, and the Germans were fully aware of it. Throughout the war, German propaganda never tired of extolling the advantages of economic interdependence between the Balkans and the Reich. And there was a great deal of substantive merit in its protestations. The Balkans and Germany actually did have complementary economic structures. Germany needed Rumanian oil. Rumania could purchase German machine tools cheaper than she could manufacture them. There was no

12. Heinrichsbauer to Funk, 3 April 1941, T-71, roll 14, frame 404804; Heinrichsbauer to Schmidt (executive secretary of the Vienna Chamber of Industry and Commerce), 22 April 1941, T-71, roll 65, frame 564329; Heinrichsbauer to Foreign Ministry, 14 Oct. 1941, T-71, roll 48, frame 442977; Hanel to Rischka, "Betr.: Deutsch-Rumänische Industrieausschussberhandlungen vom 21. bis 24. Jänner 1942," 20 Jan. 1942, T-71, roll 131, frame 1634748; Zentralvereinigung der slowakischen Industrie, Deutschland-Ausschuss und Reichsgruppe Industrie, Slowakei-Ausschuss, "Protokoll über das Ergebnis der ersten gemeinsamen Tagung des deutschen und des slowakischen Industrieausschusses in Pressburg vom 4.–6. Februar 1942" (hereafter cited as "Slowakei, Industrie-Protokoll, 4.–6.2.1942"), T-84, roll 88, frame 1378183.

reason why Hungary should not buy steel products from Germany and export the products of her own expanding aluminum industry to the Reich. Moreover, the absence of internal tariffs and the introduction of a common currency throughout Central and Southeastern Europe could provide immense advantages to the entire area.

The concept of interdependence is irrevocably associated with the notion of partnership and mutual respect, but the Reich's aims and partnership were antithetical. The Germans in 1941 and 1942 came not as partners but as masters. Their aim was not to chart the outlines of a mutually advantageous economic future, but to draw the blueprint for a unilaterally beneficial German domination of the Balkans. The disillusionment began with small, but jarring discourtesies and callousnesses. Various German agencies allowed their officials to ship privately large amounts of food and other goods to Germany, without registering the shipments as Balkan exports.[13] The Germans manipulated price adjustments to reduce the benefits for the Southeastern nations.[14] The victor-and-master attitude became more glaringly apparent as the Germans moved to consideration of larger economic questions. The Reich's public interest in a tariff-free Continent was a propaganda sham: at one point the Foreign Ministry asked Breza, the SOEG's assistant executive secretary, to work out a standard model commercial treaty incorporating the concept, but the project was quietly dropped after only one discussion between Breza and an official of the ministry.[15] In-

13. Bergemann to Augenthaler (in the Reich Ministry of Economics), 11 April 1941, T-71, roll 68, frame 567299; Misch to Heinrichsbauer, 13 Feb. 1942, T-84, roll 137, frames 1439822–23.

14. See, for example, Janovsky (executive secretary of the Department of Export of the *Wirtschaftsgruppe Gross- Ein- und Ausfuhrhandel*), "Bericht über die in RWM stattgefundene Aussprache über die bulgarischen Verhandlungsergebnisse," n.d. [ca. Oct. 1941], T-71, roll 56, frame 555524.

15. Breza to Hudeczek (a *Geheimrat* in the Foreign Ministry), 1 Nov. 1941, T-71, roll 51, frames 447176–78. When Kratz returned to the subject in July 1942, a *Ministerialrat* in the Economics Ministry explained that "it was true that a European customs union had been frequently mentioned in . . . Funk's speeches, but for the time being there was no possibility of serious negotiations on the subject." See Kratz to Heinrichsbauer, "Betr.: Europäische Zollunion," 13 July 1942, T-84, roll 86, frame 1376659.

stead, the Reich's representatives pressed ever more vigorously for a reduction of Balkan tariffs to permit an increase in German exports to Southeastern Europe.[16] As if to confirm their lack of interest in meaningful economic cooperation, the National Socialists also refused to export significant quantities of raw materials to the Balkans, pressing instead for larger shipments of unfinished products to Germany.[17]

From 1941 to the end of 1942 the Germans and the Balkan nations engaged in hidden, but nevertheless bitter warfare. The countries of Southeastern Europe had no great difficulty in determining their intended role in the New Order. As politically and nationalistically conscious people, they resented the planned barriers to the free development of their national economic institutions and opposed the German attempts to control their economic future. However, their political and military impotence made open defiance a foolish gesture. Instead, they had to restrict their opposition to more subtle means. The Germans possessed the politico-military power to subdue the Balkan resis-

16. Reichsgruppe Industrie to Wirtschaftsgruppen et al., "Betr.: Neue Vereinbarungen mit Kroatien, SO IV/12360/41," 11 Dec. 1941, T-71, roll 75, frames 575736–40; Reichsgruppe Industrie, "Bericht über das Ergebnis der fünften gemeinsamen Tagung des deutschen und bulgarischen Regierungsausschusses in der Zeit vom 11. April bis 11. Mai 1942 in Sophia," 13 June 1942, T-84, roll 88, frames 1378422–23.

17. See, for example [Reichswirtschaftskammer, Arbeitsgemeinschaft der Industrie- und Handelskammern], "Bericht über das Ergebnis der gemeinsamen Tagung des deutschen und des ungarischen Regierungsausschusses in Budapest vom. 4–16. Januar 1940," n.d., T-84, roll 136, frames 1438393–94, and Enclosure I to this report, "Zusatzkontingente für die deutsche Ausfuhr nach Ungarn," *ibid.*, frames 1438395–99; Bulgarischer und Deutscher Industrieausschuss, "Protokoll über die erste Tagung der deutsch-bulgarischen Industrieausschüsse," 14 May 1941, T-84, roll 88, frames 1378474–80; Reichsgruppe Industrie, "Übersicht über die bisher erfolgte Auswertung des Protokolls der 2. gemeinsamen Tagung des deutsch-rumänischen Industrieausschusses in Wien vom 21. bis 24. Januar 1942," 6 Nov. 1942, *ibid.*, frame 1378525. These conclusions are also supported by two excellent postwar analyses: Eliza Campus, "Die hitler-faschistische Infiltration Rumäniens 1939–1940," *Zeitschrift für Geschichtswissenschaft*, V (No. 2, 1957), 223; and Berend and Ranki, pp. 314, 317–18, 319. The attempt of all three authors to brand the pre-1945 Hungarian and Rumanian governments as willing Third Reich collaborators must be largely discounted as a consequence of post-1945 political pressure.

tance, but for internal political reasons they were unable to employ their full potential. Consequently, they too fought with a restricted arsenal. The refusal of the center to permit the naked use of power forced German agencies to stay within the established bilateral institutions in their attempt to subdue the Balkan countries and enlarge German agential fiefs in the New Europe. The duellists therefore had to develop a wide variety of subtle thrusts and parries to fight their often grotesque battles.

The obvious first step toward German control of the existing industrial facilities in Southeastern Europe was the transfer of Balkan industrial stocks to German ownership. Consequently, the German delegates to the Industrial Committee sessions consistently sought to open opportunities for German investment and to prevent the passage of laws prejudicial to foreign (that is, German) investments in the Balkan countries.[18]

The Balkan nations countered by encouraging state capitalistic and monopolistic enterprises, and by exploiting the economic rivalry of the two Axis partners.[19] When the Southeastern countries were reluctant to permit German *Beteiligungen* (literally participations; the word conveyed the concept of purchasing stock in Balkan enterprises by German companies or banks with the object of controlling a sizeable minority and, if possible, a majority of the voting stock in the firm),[20] on a normal com-

18. Kratz to Heinrichsbauer, "Betr.: Südostausschuss der Reichsgruppe Industrie–Sitzung am 11. Nov. 1942," 13 Nov. 1942, T-71, roll 14, frames 405123–24; Reichsgruppe Industrie, "Bericht über das Ergebnis der 7. gemeinsamen Tagung des deutschen und des bulgarischen Regierungsausschusses in Berlin in der Zeit vom 10.4. bis 24.5.1943," 15 June 1943, T-84, roll 88, frames 1378416–18.

19. Lajos Jocsik, *German Economic Influences in the Danube Valley* (Budapest, 1946); Otfried Ulshöfer, *Einflussnahme auf Wirtschaftsunternehmen in den besetzten nord- west- und südosteuropäischen Ländern während des 2. Weltkrieges, insbesondere der Erwerb von Beteiligungen (Verflechtung)* Tübingen, 1958), pp. 43–44, 54; Schubert, "Aktennotiz über eine Besprechung beim Auswärtigen Amt am 10.7.1941," 10 July 1941, T-84, roll 87, frames 1377293–94; Lemr, "Aktenvermerk über eine Besprechung mit dem Direktor der Aussenhandelsstelle [in Croatia] Dr. Kalas," 13 Dec. 1941, *ibid.*, frames 1377831–32.

20. As was true of all aspects of German Balkan activity, intrasystem control of such transactions was divided among a number of agencies. The

mercial basis, the Germans exploited the economic and political vulnerability of the Southeast. The Balkan nations needed outside capital if they hoped to institute any large-scale industrialization projects. The Reich was the only major available credit source and in providing investment funds, the Germans took great care to channel them into fields of "natural expansion."[21]

The German economic drive in the Balkans also took full advantage of the Reich's political superiority in the area. By no means all *Beteiligungen* reflected new German investment in the Balkans. Many stock transferrals were gained by the more or less forced liquidation of French and Belgian investments in the Balkans.[22] The German business community also greedily fell heir to the benefits that resulted from the Reich's political pressure for the elimination of Jewish influence from all phases of public life in the satellite countries. Aryanization was the propagandistic euphemism for overall programs of forcible expropriation of Jewish property and the removal of Jewish influence from economic and professional life in the Balkan countries. It was one of the early steps in a process that led to the physical extermination of the Jews,[23] though the SOEG and German busi-

---

Foreign Organization (AO) of the NSDAP had to approve the sending of all German business officials to the Balkans, the Foreign Ministry examined the possible repercussions on German foreign policy of participation, the SS had a voice in all transfers involving the expropriation of Jewish property, the corporative organizations selected the actual participating German firms, and the Reich Ministry of Economics conducted the transfers. See Reichswirtschaftsminister, "Allgemeiner Erlass Nr. 108/41 D.St/R.St Betr.: V3; Auslandsgründungen und Erwerb von Auslandsbeteiligungen: im Anschluss an RE 9/38 D.St/Ue.St," 24 Dec. 1941, T-71, roll 62, frame 560518; Ulshöfer, p. 92.

21. Hinterschweiger (head of the Austrian field office of the *Reichsgruppe Industrie*), "Bericht über das Ergebnis der Reise nach Bukarest," 25 July 1941, T-71, roll 66, frame 564676; Misch to Heinrichsbauer, 31 Oct. [1941], T-84, roll 137, frames 1439900–03. In 1941, 46.33%, and in 1942, 30.00% of the stock in companies newly established in Croatia during the two years was owned by Germans. See *Italienischer Einfluss*, p. 33.

22. This aspect of the German economic drive is covered in detail in Ulshöfer, and in Yves Bouthillier, *Le Drame de Vichy* (Paris, 1951), II, 122ff.

23. Raul Hilberg, *The Destruction of the European Jews* (Chicago, 1961), pp. 435–36, 455, 461–65, 476–82, 488ff.

nessmen restricted their concern to its economic aspects.[24] Actually, the term *aryanization* does not quite express the German aims. The Germans designated the first step in the process of expropriating Jewish business properties de-Judization (*Entjudung*). This meant simply the elimination of Jewish ownership, and laws to this effect were passed by the Balkan governments without undue pressure from the Reich. However, initially such laws provided merely for the transfer of the property to a national of the country, but the Germans were interested in Germanization (*Germanisierung*) of the property, that is, its transfer to German ownership. The Germans showed relatively little interest in removing the Jews from the economic life in the Balkans if they could not be replaced by German influence. Despite German zeal in acquiring Jewish businesses, the Balkan countries countered this threat as effectively as the demand for stock transfers by utilizing state capitalistic devices. For example even in Slovakia, the politically least independent of the Balkan dependencies, of 9,987 Jewish enterprises expropriated by March 1941, only 1,910 had been aryanized (here meaning redisposed to Slovaks or Germans); the remaining 80 per cent were still under the trusteeship of the Slovak government.[25]

German plans for participation in Balkan economic life did not end with attempts to acquire Balkan investment portfolios. Perhaps even more significant were the recurring demands for close production and even personnel integration between the Balkan and German economies. The German negotiators tried to associate Balkan industrial facilities with German-dominated cartels[26] and were eager to help the Balkan nations model the

24. For a revealing glimpse of a prominent businessman's attitude on aryanization, see Stöger (of the *Reichsgruppe Handel*), "Zusammenfassender Bericht über die Ergebnisse meiner Beobachtungen in Bezug auf den Handel [in Rumänien] während der Zeit vom 22.1. bis 22.2. 1941," 24 Feb. 1941, T-71, roll 66, frames 565076–77.

25. See Mussap, "Die Lösung der Judenfrage in der Slovakei/Dr. Vosek/[sic]," 10 March 1943, T-71, roll 70, frame 569599.

26. "Protokoll der deutsch-ungarischen Industriebesprechungen, Budapest vom 16.–19. September 1941," n.d., T-84, roll 88, frame 1378376; Mussap, "Monatsbericht über die wirtschaftliche Lage in der Slowakei im April 1942," n.d., T-71,

structure of their economic associations on that of the Reich Industry Group.[27] The Balkan negotiators could hardly miss the clear German expectations to dominate the Balkan economic associations and thus possess one more lever of control over the economic policies of the Balkan governments.[28]

All of these more or less commercial methods to extend Germany's influence in the Balkans yielded disappointing results. The economic interests could have resorted to massive terror and expropriation measures easily enough, but that would have required authorization from the central leadership, and as noted before, it refused to clarify its position. Instead, the economic interests harnessed the two Trojan horses that could be used very effectively to permeate Balkan economic life and undermine its independence: the ethnic Germans and ostensibly private, semiofficial organizations such as the SOEG. The Balkan Volksdeutsche played an important and not very laudable role in the German economic expansion into Southeastern Europe. It is true that prior to the extension of the war to the Balkans the various ethnic groups (with the exception of Yugoslavia) had not become active agents of National Socialism,[29] but by the spring of 1941 the Volksdeutsche had succumbed to the spell of the New Order. A new spirit of power and status conscious-

roll 70, frame 569793; Mussap, "Betr.: Deutsch-Slowakische Regierungsausschuss-verhandlungen," 24 May 1943 (strictly confidential, not for publication), *ibid.*, frame 569509.

27. "Protokoll über die erste gemeinsame Tagung des Deutschen und des Rumänischen Industrieausschusses in Bukaret [7–23 July 1941]," 23 July 1941, T-84, roll 88, frames 1378611–25; Breza, "Deutsch-bulgarische Industrieausschüsse . . . ," *ibid.*, frames 1378231ff.; "Slowakei-Industrie Protokoll—4.–6.2.42," ibid., frame 1378168; Reichsgruppe Industrie, "3. Tagung der deutsch-rumänischen Industrieausschussverhandlungen in Bukarest vom 8. bis 12. Februar 1942—Deutsche Verhandlungswünsche," 29 Jan. 1943, T-71, roll 56, frame 452539; Heinrichsbauer to Rafelsberger "[Reisebericht Ungarn, Bulgarien, Thrazien]," 19 May 1941, T-71, roll 53, frames 449065–68.

28. Buchas, "Ordnung der inneren Wirtschaft Rumäniens als Voraussetzung für die Einbeziehung Rumäniens in die Südosteuropa-Wirtschaftsplanung," 27 July 1942, T-71, roll 55, frames 451430–33. See also above, pp. 129–33.

29. Louis de Jong, *Die Deutsche fünfte Kolonne im Zweiten Weltkrieg,* tr. Helmut Lindemann (Stuttgart, 1959), p. 230.

ness permeated the ethnic German community; leaders of the various German national groups and their superiors in the Liaison Office for Ethnic Germans[30] took a second look at their very far-reaching plans for the complete political and economic autonomy of the ethnic Germans in Southeastern Europe. The Rumanian Volksdeutsche, for example, were reported to have realized that the German victory in the West gave them an opportunity "finally to rise to a sort of master class (*Herrenschicht*)."[31]

While most, though not all,[32] of the political plans were shelved until the end of the war, the ethnic Germans performed a number of very useful services in the economic field during the war itself. As citizens, and in some cases as governmental officials, of a Balkan country they were often in a position to supply the Germans with statistical material that Reich Germans as foreigners could not obtain.[33] More odious still was their role in the aryanization process. As noted before, the Balkan countries attempted to prevent excessive German inroads into their economic lives by restricting the transfer of expropriated Jewish businesses to Reich Germans. Several nations passed laws prohibiting foreigners from owning more than 50 per cent of the stock of companies operating within their boundaries. The Reich deliberately used the Volksdeutsche to circumvent these restrictions. When Reich Germans subscribed to 50 per cent of the shares of a "de-Judacized" company, ethnic Germans to 10 per cent and Balkan nationals to the remaining 40 per cent, the letter of the law was kept, but the intent was clearly vio-

30. On the development of the Vomi as a control agency for the German minorities, see MacAlister Brown, "The Third Reich's Mobilization on the German Fifth Column in Eastern Europe," *Journal of Central European Affairs,* XIX (July 1959), 131–35, 148.

31. Stöger, "Zweiter Rumänienbericht über die Zeit vom 1. bis 31. März 1941," n.d., T-71, roll 66, frame 565003.

32. In Transnistria (the Rumanian-occupied part of the Soviet Union between the Bug and the Dnestr), for instance, the Volksdeutsche were governed directly by the Vomi. See Kratz to Mayerzedt, "Betr.: Transnistrien—Sitzung bei der Volksdeutschen Mittelstelle am 17.9.1942," 23 Sept. 1942, T-84, roll 86, frame 1376456.

33. Heinrichsbauer to Misch, 23 Oct. 1943, T-84, roll 137, frame 1439397.

lated.[34] In effect, the ethnic Germans had put their loyalty to
the Reich before their obligations as citizens of the Balkan nations, and the company was not merely aryanized but
Germanized.[35]

As an ostensibly private organization, the SOEG became another of the Reich's Trojan horses, and the Society's contribution
to the German economic drive was significant. The SOEG's
agents found that Southeastern government officials were considerably more willing to talk to them than to official German
agents, and the SOEG became an important source of confidential data for various important Reich offices.[36] The SOEG's role
in the aryanization process was to function as an unofficial detec-
tive agency. Always remaining fully aware that its own influence
and importance was directly dependent upon the economic prosperity and political importance of its home base, Vienna, the
Society was extremely active in helping Viennese and Austrian
businessmen locate and purchase suitable Balkan properties. Indeed, one of the major functions of the SOEG's field offices was
to conduct constant searches for available properties and to act
as the Society's on-the-spot representatives in the purchase
negotiations.[37]

The German machinations could hardly increase the Reich's
popularity in Southeastern Europe, but nations need not be pop-

34. "Intensivierung der Züchtung von Soja und anderen Ölpflanzen," *Gospo-
dorstvo* (3 March 1942), T-84, roll 87, frame 1377655. The article was translated
and sent to the SOEG by its Zagreb field office.

35. The Balkan nations were not unaware of the doubtful loyalty of the
ethnic Germans, and their governments attempted to limit their influence in
the aryanization process. See Vomi to Deutsche Volksgruppe in Kroatien,
"Betrifft: Beteiligung der Deutschen Volksgruppe in Kroatien an der Arisierung
Az 8864-A/Hg," 19 Sept. 1941, T-77, roll 548, frame 1724188; Vomi to
Reichsführer-SS, "Betrifft: Beteiligung . . . Az 8864-787/41-H/Hg," 20 Sept.
1941, *ibid.*, frame 1724187.

36. Jung (Misch's assistant) to Heinrichsbauer, 25 March and 31 July 1942,
T-71, roll 63, frames 561547-48, 561542; Misch to Augenthaler, 19 May 1944,
T-71, roll 56, frames 452172-73.

37. Heinrichsbauer to Misch, 19 and 25 Sept. and 28 Oct. 1941, T-84, roll
137 frames 1439438-39, 1439927, 1439904; Stadler, "Die Aufgaben der Abteilung
Südosteuropa-Gesellschaft e.V. in der Deutschen Handelskammer in Kroatien,"
28 July 1942, T-71, roll 51, frame 446449.

ular in order to achieve their aims.[38] During the postwar Stalin era the Russians exploited Southeastern Europe with methods not unlike those of the National Socialists.[39] However, if a nation adopts a policy of unilateral exploitation, it must be in uncontested control of the area to be exploited. In 1945 the Allies had achieved victory, and the Russians were unchallenged masters of Southeastern Europe. In 1941 and 1942 the Germans had only the illusion of victory. It was not a very firm foundation for a policy of unconcern, arrogance, and consistent neglect of the Balkans' needs and interests.

Although both the weight of indirect evidence[40] and the pleas of some unheeded voices[41] should have been sufficient to pierce the veil of illusion, for most German agencies, including the central leadership, the brittleness of the New Order was not apparent until the Battle of Stalingrad. The disaster on the Volga, however, brought the Reich leadership face to face with the necessity of fighting a long and bitter war. This required

38. The Germans were by no means unaware that their aims were extremely unpopular in Southeastern Europe. However, it was widely felt that the inevitable victory of German arms made popularity or even cooperation unnecessary. See, for example, Buchas to Heinrichsbauer, 4 Oct. 1942, T-71, roll 55, frame 451182.

39. Erich Klinkmüller and Maria E. Ruban, *Die wirtschaftliche Zusammenarbeit der Ostblockstaaten* (Berlin, 1960), pp. 125, 128, 238–39, 256–57; Fritz Schenck, *Magie der Planwirtschaft* (Cologne, 1960), pp. 84, 97, 104–05.

40. During the latter part of 1941 and throughout 1942, it became clear that the Germans were increasingly unwilling (or unable) to supply the industrial needs of the Balkan countries. German promises of deliveries came to be stated in extremely vague terms and, even then, fewer goods arrived than had been promised. See Reichsgruppe Industrie, "Bericht über das Ergebnis der 4. gemeinsamen Tagung des deutschen und des bulgarischen Regierungsausschusses in der Zeit vom 22.9. bis 15.10.1941 in Sophia," 8 Nov. 1941, T-84, roll 88, frames 1378461–62; Kratz to Heinrichsbauer, "Betr.: Südostausschuss der Reichsgruppe Industrie—Sitzung am 11. Nov. 1942," 13 Nov. 1942, T-71, roll 14, frame 405134. However, the propaganda illusion of German capabilities was maintained; the decreased deliveries do not seem to have been reflected in German statistics—including confidential figures.

41. See, for example, Thomas (head of the *Wehrwirtschafts- und Rüstungsamt* to Speer, "Betr.: Rationalisierung in Verwaltung und Wirtschaft zum Zwecke der Freimachung von Kräften aller Art für die Kriegsführung. Antrag auf Erlass von Verordnungen für Verwaltung and Wirtschaft, Nr. 15753/42g" (secret), 10 March 1942, T-77, roll 571, frames 1749350–51.

not only a thorough mental reorientation for the leaders and the German people, but also a reversal of the policies that regarded the immediate needs of the war effort as matters of secondary importance.[42]

After January 1943 the overconfident master had to become the calculating supplicant. The relationship between the Reich and the Southeast was reversed—but not quite. While the Reich's sphere of control was shrinking daily, its military control of the Southeastern region remained undisputed until almost the very end of the conflict. Moreover, the erstwhile master had a very pronounced tendency to regard his ill fortunes on the battlefronts as temporary setbacks whose importance should not be overemphasized. The staffs necessarily put aside the long-range plans on which they had been working, but the practical tasks of securing immediate aid for the National Socialists' military survival never really aroused their sustained interest.[43]

Nevertheless, the Germans reluctantly turned their attention to the more immediate work of integrating the productive capabilities of the Balkan nations into the overall strategic needs of the Reich. The nations of Southeastern Europe now became important not only as suppliers of oil and troops for the Eastern front, but also as locations for important industrial facilities, and, above all, as exporters of grain and foodstuffs.[44] The Reich

42. On this development and the difficulty of persuading even the highest German echelons to look realistically at Germany's critical situation after Stalingrad, see Günter Moltmann, "Goebbels' Rede zum Totalen Krieg am 18. Februar 1943," *Vierteljahrschefte für Zeitgeschichte,* XII (Jan. 1964), 13–43.

43. In May 1943, the Reich Ministry of Agriculture reminded the SOEG that, whatever the needs of the moment, it remained a fundamental goal of German policy to prevent the development of an agricultural processing industry in Southeastern Europe. Even later that year at least some of the SOEG's time and energy was spent in investigating the long-range economic implication of the intra-Axis rivalry in the Balkans. See Walter (*Ministerialdirektor* in the Reich Ministry of Agriculture) to Heinrichsbauer, 13 May 1943, T-71, roll 61, frame 559755; *Italienischer Einfluss,* pp. 25, 27, 45.

44. Before 1943 the Reich's leadership, while considering the possibility of utilizing the industrial capacity of the Southeast to supplement the Reich's output of munitions and armaments, immediately dismissed the idea as not worth serious discussion. See Führer und Oberster Befehlshaber der Wehrmacht, "Vereinfachung und Leistungssteigerung unserer Rüstungsproduktion, WiRü

had imported large quantities of Balkan grain before the war, but after June 1941 the potential Ukrainian riches blinded the Nazis, and their interest in the Balkans shifted to the long-range development of oleaginous plant cultures. Even the 1942 harvest excited little more than routine interest in Berlin; the Armed Forces High Command (OKW) was primarily concerned with the problem of securing the Ukrainian grain.[45] Here again, only the battle of Stalingrad brought about a new interest in short-term exploitation of Balkan agricultural assets. Suddenly, military experts began to suggest that the Balkan countries might contribute more to the war effort by keeping their peasants in the fields than by sending them as ill-equipped troops to the Eastern front.[46] The Reich also showed a new interest in all aspects of the manufacturing potential of the Balkan countries; the capacities for agricultural processing,[47] and the production facilities for finished products received close scrutiny —and not merely to discover the most efficient method of dismantling them.

The SOEG quickly joined the new search for the short-term exploitation of the Balkans. In the spring of 1943 the Society issued the first of its Industry in the Southeast (*Industrie im Südosten*) reports. These were dry, objective compendia of economic assets—raw materials and manufacturing or refining facilities—in the Balkan countries. The first study analyzed the bauxite and aluminum industry; it was quickly followed by a

---

Amt/Rü (IIa) Nr. 3750/41g. Kdos." (top secret), 3 Dec. 1941, T-77, roll 511, frame 1680933.

45. OKW, WiRü Stab Ia, "Auszugweise Abschrift aus Br. B. Nr. 109/42gK." (top secret), 1 June 1942, T-77, roll 667, frame 1870465.

46. OKW, WiRü Amt, W Stab Ia, "Notiz für W/Ausl." (secret, urgent), 25 March 1943, T-77, roll 511, frame 1680668. The suggestion was ascribed to Warlimont.

47. Straubinger to Heinrichsbauer, "Betrifft: Südosteuropa-Gesellschaft— Untersuchung der Wirtschaft des Südosteuropäischen Raumes," 12 July 1943, T-71, roll 70, frame 570387; Kelter (of the WIW), "Vermerk," 29 Nov. 1943, T-71, roll 66, frames 565461–62. A study in the SOEG's *Industrie* series was devoted to the sugar industry in Hungary. Wiener Institut für Wirtschaftsforschung, ed., *Die Zuckerindustrie in Ungarn, Stand April 1944* (confidential) (Vienna, 1944.)

more ambitious analysis of chrome, manganese, lead, zinc, iron, and copper findings.[48]

Studies and learned staff memoranda could perhaps provide an accurate picture of what the Balkans had to offer, but they could hardly have a meaningful impact on the war effort until statistical bauxite ore had been converted into aluminum and manufactured into airplanes, or the products of a cement plant in Rumania had become part of a military fortification in the East. The Germans could determine potential on their own, but to bridge the gap between paper capacity and productive reality they needed to meet two other prerequisites: the Balkan nations had to cooperate and the Reich agencies had to curtail their murderous infighting.

After the turn of the tide, the National Socialists found themselves in the position of the sorcerer's apprentice. Before 1943 the Germans had shown no concern for the wishes and interests of the Southeastern nations; after Stalingrad, the Balkans refused to make the Reich's cause their own.[49] This is not to say that Southeastern Europe openly rebelled. As long as the Reich's forces had the strength to subject the Balkans to military occupation, the countries saw no alternative to fulfilling at least some of the Reich's import demands. But as the Reich became economically more vulnerable, the Southeastern nations became more uncooperative.

Resistance to German demands could take a variety of

48. WIW, ed., *Die Bauxit- und Aluminiumwirtschaft der südosteuropäischen Länder* (secret) (Vienna, 1943), T-84, roll 79, frames 1367327–452. Later in the year, after the Italian armistice, the SOEG issued a similar analysis of the aluminum resources of Italy and the former Italian areas in the Balkans. See WIW, ed., *Die Bauxit- und Aluminiumwirtschaft in Italien* (Vienna, 1943), T-84, roll 222, frames 1592658–92; Forschungsstelle für den Südosten, *Die Bodenschätze der südosteuropäischen Länder* (strictly confidential) (Vienna, 1943–44), 2 vols.

49. Even the Rumanian ambassador in Berlin, Jon Gheorghe, by no means unsympathetic, was reported to have commented in October 1943, "it is important the we have a good harvest, it is not important that we sell it [to the Reich]." See the enclosure, "Betrifft: Einstellung von königl. Rumänischen Gesandten Exc. Gheorghe, II a/1024/43g," in Backe to Himmler (secret), 27 Oct. 1943, Himmler Files, Cont. 390, drawer 1, folder 7.

forms—agricultural products, for example, were statistically hidden. Since the size of the harvest determined the amounts shipped to Germany (the Germans theoretically received any surplus left after the needs of the Southeastern nations had been met) the falsification and nonpublication of agricultural statistics became an effective method of resisting the Germans. The nations of the area passed laws and decrees specifically formulated to keep statistical information a closely guarded secret, and agricultural statistics became a prized commodity in the Balkans.[50] Passive resistance was effective only in the "independent" countries of Southeastern Europe; nations such as Yugoslavia, which were under actual military occupation, had to turn to more active means. In Croatia and Serbia, partisan activities tied down large numbers of German troops and through attacks on the transport system, particularly in 1943 and 1944, constituted a serious obstacle to German efforts to ship exports to the Reich.

The increasing Balkan disengagement from the German war effort might have been averted or at least mitigated if the 1943 shift of German aims had been accompanied by equally radical changes in mental attitude and thoroughgoing efforts to increase administrative coordination among German agencies.[51] The latter change never came. A number of factors were responsible. German propaganda, including intra-adminsitrative information, still consistently underestimated the gravity of the Reich's posi-

50. Misch to Heinrichsbauer, 1 April 1943, T-84, roll 136, frame 1439578, and the enclosure to this letter, *ibid.*, frames 1439579–82; Heinrichsbauer to Straubinger, 23 Oct., 1943, T-71, roll 52, frames 448348–49. In this connection the Germans made excellent use of the SOEG's reportorial facilities. The Society's agent in Hungary estimated the Hungarian wheat and rye crop of 1943 at 34.2 and 8.2 million quintals respectively. Postwar authorities give it as 35.7 and 8.3 million quintals. See Misch, "Die Aussichten der ungarischen Ernte 1943 . . . ," 11 June 1943, T-71, roll 61, frames 559866–67; Slavcho D. Zagoroff, Jenö Vegh, and Alexander B. Bilimovich, *The Agricultural Economy of the Danubian Countries 1933–45* (Stanford, Cal., 1955), p. 223.

51. There were some important officials, particularly among the military, who did see the need for an end to the proliferation of policies and the execution of policies. See, for example, Glaise-Horstenau (The German commanding general in Croatia) to Warlimont, 15 Feb. 1943, T-501, roll 264, frame 560.

tion. Stalingrad was a major but not a decisive defeat; after
all, had not Göring called it a Thermopylae on the path to total
victory?[52] In the victory-centered atmosphere it was obviously
difficult to persuade German agencies to concentrate all their
efforts on immediate war aims, despite the mounting indications
that reforms were long overdue.[53] By the beginning of 1943 the
trade relations of the Reich and the Balkan nations were becoming daily less symbiotic and more one-sided. The Germans' inability to maintain their level of exports, together with the
mounting inflation in the Balkan countries, had resulted in very
considerable clearing balances in favor of the Southeastern countries.[54] The Germans showed no great concern over the Reich's
monetary debts, but the Balkan countries demanded a reduction
of the clearing deficits.[55] The Germans first attempted to reduce

52. See the excerpt from Göring's speech of 30 Jan. 1943, in O. W. Vacano
et al., eds., *Sparta der Lebenskampf einer nordischen Herrenschicht* (2nd ed.,
Bücherei der Adolf-Hitler Schulen, 194[3]), p. 120.

53. The specific effects of this continuing schizophrenia were often grotesque.
For example, at least some of the SOEG's officials did not regard the July
1943 Allied bombings of Hamburg as a total calamity: the situation might
be used to get some of the Hamburg agricultural processing plants permanently
located in Vienna. See Hecke (of the *Gruppe Ernährung und Landwirtschaft*)
to Rafelsberger, "Betrifft: Verlegung von Lagerei- und Produkten-Verarbeitungs-
betrieben von Hamburg nach Wien," 24 Aug. 1943, T-71, roll 75, frames
576299-300.

54. Between 1940 and 1942, Germany's total clearing debts to all countries
with whom she maintained trade relations increased 6 or 7 billion reichsmark.
See Klein, *Germany's*, p. 93. In large measure this was a result of the inflation of
Balkan prices. Rumanian wholesale prices, for instance, increased from an index
figure of 100 (August 31, 1939) to 712.1 at the end of 1942 and 1085.3 at the end
of 1943. However, the rate of exchange for the lei and the reichsmark increased
only by one-third—from 1 RM to 40 lei in August 1939 to 1:60 in June
of 1944. See Jörss (an official of the *Werberat der Deutschen Wirtschaft* in
Rumania), to Werberat der Deutschen Wirtschaft, Abteilung Ausland, 16 June
1944, T-71, roll 53, frame 449171. The price indexes were confidential figures
estimated by FINCOM, a Rumanian financial institute.

55. See "Niederschrift über die am 26. und 27. Mai 1943 in Budapest stattgefundene Zwischenbesprechung der Präsidenten und Geschäftsführer der Delega-
tionen für die deutsch-ungarischen Industriebesprechungen," 27 May 1943, T-84,
roll 88, frame 1378203; "Bericht über das Ergebnis der in der Zeit vom 22.
Februar bis 15. März 1943 in Budapest stattgefundenen 24. gemeinsamen Tagung

the debt without sacrificing their newly acquired economic entrenchment in Southeastern Europe. They suggested, for example, that the cost of Balkan orders placed with German plants be deducted from the German debt immediately, although the orders themselves could not be filled until after the war.[56] The Balkan countries were not enthusiastic; they demanded more concrete sacrifices. They recognized that the Reich could not supply current production goods, but they pointed to the measures the Reich could take immediately: relinquishing her stock holdings in the Balkans and relocating major industrial facilites there.

The Southeastern demands might have been met successfully either by rapid German concessions or by coordinated refusals of all German agencies. Instead, they became the occasion for yet another round of bitter infighting among the German Balkan offices. Only the objects of disagreement changed: after 1943 the agencies simply fought over the best means of persuading the Balkans to aid the Reich's war effort. While some offices advocated pleading with the Balkan governments to be more cooperative, others saw military occupation as a far more effective guarantee of German success.[57] And, paradoxical though it was, the more desperate the German position in the war became, the less influential were the voices of moderation in the National Socialist hierarchy.

---

des Deutschen und des Ungarischen Regierungsausschusses" (confidential), 22 April 1943, *ibid.*, frame 1378201; Jon Gheorghe, *Rumäniens Weg zum Satellitenstaat* (Heidelberg, 1952), p. 284.

56. Reichsgruppe Industrie, "Anlage zum Rundschreiben vom 11. Januar 1943–SO IV/110/43," 9 Jan. 1943, T-71, roll 56, frames 452545–46; Reichsgruppe Industrie, "Bericht über das Ergebnis der in der Zeit vom 22. Februar bis 15. März [1943] stattgefundenen 24. gemeinsamen Tagung des Deutschen und des Ungarischen Regierungsausschusses," n.d., T-84, roll 88, frame 1378201.

57. After the Germans occupied Hungary in March 1944, one of the officials affiliated with the SOEG reported ecstatically that "compensations, clearing agreements, payment modalities, etc. are no longer important. Hungary now works and delivers as if she were a German federal state [*Bundesstaat*]. Moreover, all important posts are filled by German officials, so that all has to run as we wish." See Reuss (correspondent of the SOEG's *Vertrauliche Wirtschaftsnachrichten* in Budapest) to Oberascher, 20 June 1944, T-71, roll 63, frame 562415.

The collapse of Fascist Italy represented a particularly significant milestone in the history of the power relationships among the various German agencies concerned with Balkan policy. The Foreign Ministry had been the leading spokesman for a German policy that would take Italian and Balkan sensibilities into account; after September 1943, "tougher" organizations (such as the NSDAP's *Auslandsorganisation* and the SS) and "tougher" men moved to the foreground. The new State Secretary of the Economics Ministry, Franz Hayler, his deputy, Otto Ohlendorf, and the recently appointed Reich Commissioner for Price Control (*Reichskommissar für die Preisbildung*), Hans Fischböck, all advocated more rigorous treatment of the Balkan satellites.[58] For the new men, the ultimate answer to all of the Reich's problems in Southeastern Europe was force and terror.

The long policy debates suceeded only in disengaging the Balkan nations even more from the Reich's war effort. In addition, force itself, in view of the German setbacks in the USSR and Sicily, was clearly becoming counterproductive by the end of 1943. Unless the Southeastern countries contributed meaningfully to the German war needs, it would be doubtful if the center could spare the forces necessary to put the area under military occupation. The needs of the moment therefore forced the Germans to be accommodating. They agreed to relinquish some of their recently acquired Balkan stocks, but, in a curious reversal of roles, it was now the Germans' turn to delay the execution

58. Hayler was head of the *Reichsgruppe Handel* when he replaced State Secretary Landfried in November 1943. Ohlendorf came to the Economics Ministry from the SS, although he was also executive secretary of the *Reichsgruppe Handel* under Hayler. He had been head of *Amt* III of the *Reichssicherheitshauptamt*, headed one of the Einstzgruppen, and had administered SS-controlled business ventures in the concentration camps. Like his chief, he retained his other posts when he became an official in the Economics Ministry. See *Who's Who in Germany*, II, 116; "Hayler und Ohlendorf," *Donauzeitung*, 21 Nov. 1943, p. 5; Hilberg, *Destruction*, p. 187. Rittershausen (head of the Finance Institute at the University of Breslau and one of the members of the SOEG's Price Committee) to Heinrichsbauer, 10 Dec. 1943, T-71, roll 62, frame 561242; Gerlach (President of the German Chamber of Commerce in Croatia and head of the Croatia Group of the NSDAP-AO) to Heinrichsbauer, 11 Jan. 1944, T-71, roll 52, frame 447550; see also, "Devisenkurse in der Preispolitik," *Donauzeitung*, 7 Nov. 1943, p. 5.

of bilateral agreements. Substantial stock sales were made only in Hungary, and as late as October 1943, sales in Slovakia involved only stock owned by residents of the Protectorate, not by Reich Germans.[59] Relocations were also seriously hampered by the persistence of the old German attitude. As part of the relocation plans, the SOEG sometime in 1943 did issue what was obviously intended as the first in a series of studies of the energy and power resources in the Balkans (indispensable prerequisite knowledge for relocations) but aside from airplane production, no substantial relocations were made in 1943.

The motives were clearly political. The Germans did not become very enthusiastic about relocations in Hungary until the summer of 1944—after they had militarily occupied the country.[60] The Germans were equally reluctant to reverse their earlier decision to limit secondary industrial development in the Balkans to a minimum. They did acquiesce in the construction of new plants, but again only as a last and temporary expedient. An analysis of the cement industry in the Balkans, published by the SOEG in 1944, relied heavily on data supplied by the German cement industry; it concluded that an expansion of cement production facilities in the Balkans was not important.[61]

These appeasement measures were overlong in coming and obviously distasteful to the Germans. They could not become the foundation of a new German-Balkan spirit of partnership

59. "Ungarn, Regierungsausschuss, 22.2–15.3.1943," T-84, roll 88, frame 1378201; Mussap to Heinrichsbauer, 30 Oct. 1943, T-71, roll 70, frame 569419.

60. On relocations, see Reichsministerium Speer, Abt. Techn. Planung Ost, "Fragebogen zur Industrieverlagerung nach der Slowakei," 13 July 1943, *ibid.*, frame 569452; WIW ed., *Stand und Möglichkeiten der Energieversorgung der Slowakei* (secret) (Vienna, 1943), T-84, roll 131, frames 1432975–1433025; [Reich Ministry of Economics], Referat II Ld II 4 to Reichswirtschaftsministerium, Referat II, Gr. 1, "Betr.: Ungarn: Bericht des Planungsamtes zur deutschen Wirtschaftslage 1943/44, III Ld. II 4/4396g Rs" (top secret), 19 July 1944, T-84, roll 136, frame 1438713.

61. Buchas to Augenthaler, 22 Feb. 1944, T-71, roll 55, frame 450891; Münchner Institut für Wirtschafts- und Konjunkturforschung and Deutsches Institut für Wirtschaftsforschung, eds., *Die Zementindustrie im Südosten* (secret) (Vienna, 1944), T-84, roll 79, frames 1367491–620. See also Janovsky, "Bericht über die wirtschaftlichen Verhältnisse in Ungarn und Rumänien im Jahre 1943" [ca. March, 1943], T-84, roll 88, frame 1378698.

since they were counterbalanced by other German policies that clearly demonstrated the National Socialists' disinterest in the long-term economic future of Southeastern Europe.

The "price negotiations" of 1943 are an example of such a negative German policy. The German concessions did succeed in temporarily reducing the Reich's clearing debts,[62] but the Germans made no effort to institute policies that would deal effectively with the two factors that would inevitably send the debt soaring again, the continuing inflation in Southeastern Europe and the discrepancy between German imports and Balkan exports. Unchecked, the two factors brought about steadily rising prices on Balkan exports—and hence a steadily mounting German paper debt. In the spring of 1943, the Germans took another look at the international price problem. As usual the campaign began with appeals to Axis solidarity: such minor problems as price discrepancies must not disturb the free flow of goods between the anti-Bolshevik partners.[63] Actually, even the Nazis were not naive enough to believe that such propaganda would convince the Balkan nations at this late date, and they coupled the ideological preface with some more practical and revealing proposals. They wanted a bilateral price freeze on goods involved in international trade, a suggestion that, at least on the surface, merited some serious discussion. Actually, it was something less than altruistic. While such agreements might maintain stable prices for goods shipped to and from the Reich, they could do little to curtail the galloping inflation of domestic prices (in large part the result of excessive Balkan credits to Germany) that plagued all of Southeastern Europe. In effect, the Germans asked for a system of dual prices in the Balkan countries, a domestic price and an export price. The Reich was not unaware that the latter would soon be appreciably lower

62. Hungary, for example, had an active balance of 149 million pengö in her trade with Germany during 1942; by the end of 1944 this had been reduced to 60 million pengö. See Berend and Ranki, "Expansion," p. 338.

63. Hans Fischböck, "Binnenländische und zwischenstaatliche Preispolitik," 28 May 1943, T-71, roll 53, frame 448631. This was a lecture delivered under the auspices of the SOEG to an audience that included the Balkan consuls stationed in Vienna.

than the former, but they proposed to get around this problem by suggesting that the Balkan exporter receive a governmental subsidy from his home government to compensate him for the price difference—hence giving the Reich additional, if indirect, credits.[64]

The Balkan nations did not find it difficult to discover the true import of the proposals and the Reich-sponsored official bilateral negotiations produced only the usual pattern of delays and evasions by the Balkan negotiators.[65] Confronted with barred official doors, the Reich attempted to introduce the SOEG as an inconspicuous, "private"[66] negotiating partner. In May 1943, Fischböck (a former vice-President of the SOEG), suggested that overtures by the Society take the place of formal government-level contacts. Under the auspices of the purportedly private SOEG, a small group of ostensibly equally private experts, Heinrichsbauer, Rafelsberger, an economics professor at the University of Breslau, and an official of Fischböck's office constituted themselves as the Price Committee (*Preisausschuss*). In this organizational form they began negotiations with a similar Hungarian group headed by the well-known Hungarian economist, Professor Suranyi-Unger. The proposals of the Price Committee differed little from the earlier official drafts, nor were they intended to. They had Fischböck's approval; indeed, a clause incorporating a mutual guarantee of export quotas was added at his personal suggestion.[67] The Hungarians, of

64. Fischböck, "Binnenländische . . . Preispolitik," *ibid., frame* 448628.

65. Hanel, "Aktenvermerk—Besprechung über den Preisausschuss der SOEG am 28. Mai 1943 im Wiener Rennverein," 1 June 1943, T-84, roll 136, frame 1439256.

66. The Balkan countries did not always see through this ruse; even then many Southeastern officials apparently accepted the SOEG as a genuinely private group. See Jung (Misch's assistant) to Heinrichsbauer, 25 March and 31 July 1942, T-71, roll 63, frames 561547-48, 561542; Misch to Augenthaler, 19 May 1944, T-71, roll 56, frames 452172-73; Geffers (Holzinger's successor in Bulgaria) to Heinrichsbauer, 6 Jan. 1944, T-71, roll 70, frame 569896; Misch to SOEG, 8 March 1944, T-71, roll 56, frames 452201-02.

67. "Entwurf 2—Richtlinien für die Preisgestaltung im handelspolitischen Warenverkehr (Auf Grund der Besprechung beim Reichskommissar für die Preisbildung in Berlin, am 2.6.1943)," n.d., T-84, roll 136, frame 1439261; "Vermerk zu Richtlinien für die . . . ," n.d., *ibid.,* frame 1439266.

course, could detect little difference and agreed only to an evasive and meaningless joint statement with the SOEG.[68]

Was all this, ultimately, an elaborate comedy of errors? Or were the Germans so naive as to think that unacceptable official proposals were somehow transformed into acceptable terms when offered by a private organization? Funk, for one, was naive. He had expected a miraculous transformation of the Balkan attitude. The minister was genuinely saddened by the rejection of the SOEG's draft proposals, and now saw no other solution to the problem except to raise German export prices, which would have meant a Hungarian counterincrease and the beginning of a new spiral.[69] Fischböck's use of the SOEG, however, was a more subtle maneuver than Funk had grasped. If they limited their scope to governmental-level actions, the National Socialists had essentially two paths open: they could either tolerate the Balkan rejection of their proposals and allow the price scissors to open still wider, or they could use (or threaten to use) force to obtain compliance with their wishes. The former decision involved an economic liability since the Balkans would become even more uncooperative, the latter a political commitment that might have equally adverse effects. The SOEG's action removed the Reich from the horns of the dilemma. The elaborate subterfuge underscored the Germans' serious concern about the price problem and reiterated their disadvantageous proposals—but it did not require additional official involvement or commitment. Moreover, the message seems to have been understood. In September 1943, the Hungarians agreed to both a mutual price freeze and a delivery guarantee for the most important products traded between Germany and Hungary.[70]

68. "Schlussprotokoll der Besprechungen zwischen dem Ungarischen Auschuss . . . und der Südosteuropa-Gesellschaft," 29 June 1943, T-71, roll 14, frames 404844–45.

69. Funk to Auswärtges Amt, "Betr.: Erhöhung der Preise und Löhne in Ungarn. Auf das Schreiben vom 5. Juli 1943-Pol IV a 3475-43-," 27 July 1943, T-71, roll 62, frames 561259–60; Funk to Fischböck, 27 July 1943, *ibid.*, frames 561257–58.

70. Clodius to Auswärtiges Amt, "Ha Pol IV a 4122," 31 July 1943, *ibid.*, frames 561262–64; Rittershausen to Hanel, 12 Sept. 1943, *ibid.*, frame 561273. The Bulgarian decision in June 1943 to agree to a price freeze may also have

German insincerity and heavy-handedness could produce equally insincere agreement to aid the German effort, but without a genuine spirit of cooperation, there remained a large administrative gap between Balkan paper agreements to ship surplus grain to the Reich and the arrival of a loaded box car at the German border.[71] Part of the difficulty was, of course, the passive and open resistance of the Balkan countries. The Germans compounded this overall policy difficulty by their continuing failure to coordinate their field efforts. In order to operate successfully in this twilight area of Southeastern official agreement and unofficial sabotage of the same agreement, the German's needed of flexible, decentralized, well-coordinated system of purchasing agencies. The machinery in use until 1943 was hardly the answer. Before the spring of 1943, only the centrally controlled *Reichsstellen* were authorized to purchase Balkan supplies and to supervise their shipment to the Reich. This system was not only administratively cumbersome, but discouraged initiative on the part of individual importers and made it impossible to utilize whatever private business ties existed between German and Balkan agricultural enterprises. In the spring of 1943—not least due to the SOEG's efforts—individual importers were permitted to purchase directly in the Balkans and ship to the Reich.[72] Similarly, some regional coordination programs were organized. The SOEG's Nutrition and Agriculture Group, for example, early in the year invited Viennese importers to a series of monthly discussions with the

---

been indirectly influenced by the SOEG's negotiations. See "Preisstop im Handel mit Bulgarien," *Donauzeitung,* 10 June 1943, p. 5.

71. The primary contributions to the war effort that the Reich expected from Southeastern Europe after 1943 were agricultural products. Even before 1939 some 70% of the Reich's imports from the Balkans consisted of raw or processed agricultural goods, and as late as 1943, 69% of the Hungarian exports to Germany fell into the category of agricultural products. It should be kept in mind that Hungary was the most industrialized of the Southeastern nations. See Berend and Ranki, "Expansion," p. 338.

72. Görnandt (of the *Gruppe Ernährung und Landwirtschaft*) to Rischka, "Betr.: Reichsstelle für Milcherzeugnisse, Oele und Fette," 25 Feb. 1943, T-71, roll 66, frames 564717–18; Rischka to Kratz, "Betrifft: FS 8407 vom 9. April 1943," 10 April 1943, T-71, roll 75, frames 576498–99.

Group's staff officials. The sessions were devoted to exchanging views on such pressing matters as transport problems, the rationalization of import procedures, negotiations with the *Reichsstellen,* and cooperation with ethnic German economic experts in the Balkans.[73]

This last matter became a particular concern of the SOEG during 1943. The SOEG's establishment of the Cooperative Institute (*Genossenschaftsinstitut*) was a futile but original effort to cut through a major Gordian knot of Nazi red tape. While the peasants and governments in the Southeastern countries practiced effective passive resistance, the German minorities continued—after their attitude in 1941 and 1942 they hardly had a choice—to cast their lot with the Reich. They were quite willing to export their agricultural products to Germany but they encountered a number of difficulties since their products often fell under the same export restrictions as those of their Balkan neighbors.[74] German governmental moves were of no great avail, and the SOEG again put on its "private" mask. The Cooperative Institute was rather hastily established in the spring of 1943, and, while the agency enveloped itself with the usual statement of long-range goals,[75] its actual purpose was to create rapidly an independent organization that could bypass official govern-

73. SOEG, Gruppe Ernährung und Landwirtschaft, "Betr.: Monatliche Dienstbesprechung der Geschäftsgruppe Ernährung und Landwirtschaft der Südosteuropa-Gesellschaft," 5 Jan. 1943, T-71, roll 76, frame 577688; "Betrifft: Dienstbesprechung der Gruppe 'Ernährung und Landwirtschaft' der Südosteuropa-Gesellschaft, 2/F/Dr. R./St," 9 March 1943, *ibid.,* frame 577664; Gruppe Ernährung und Landwirtschaft to Hausmann, "Betr.: Dienstbesprechung der Gruppe Ernährung und Landwirtschaft," 4 April and 5 and 29 June 1944, *ibid.,* frames 577661, 577656, 577660. Unfortunately, the solutions suggested and discussed within the course of these talks cannot be ascertained. The SOEG's files contain only the agendas for the meetings, not the minutes.

74. Volksdeutsche Mittelstelle, Amt X, Führung der volksdeutschen Wirtschaft (Heller) to SOEG, "Betrifft: Nicht-Verwertung Landwirtschaftlicher Erzeugnisse im Banat bei Rumänien, X/2/43," 16 Aug. 1944, T-71 roll 66, frame 565379; Volksdeutsche Mittelstelle to Augenthaler, "Betrifft: Arbeitsbesprechung Wien über Auftragsverlagerung in den deutschen Volksgruppen, X/8/71," 3 Aug. 1944, *ibid.,* frames 565380-85.

75. Südostgenossenschaftsinstitut, "Informationsschrift über das Südost-Genossenschaftsintitut der Südosteuropa-Gesellschaft" [May, 1943], *ibid.,* frames 564988-90.

mental agencies and establish direct contact with the Balkan and particularly the Volksdeutsche cooperative movement.[76] This, combined with the newly decentralized German purchasing system and a fuller utilization of the SOEG-sponsored import syndicates, was to provide an invisible breach in the Balkan governmental defences and through it drain Balkan exports into the Reich from behind the walls of Southeastern governmental prohibitions. That, at any rate, was the theory.

All such efforts were clearly exceptions. Far more usual was continuing administrative chaos and interagency rivalries. At the beginning of 1944, for example, the Hungarians permitted shipment of a sizeable quantity of grain to the Reich.[77] The Germans, of course, had to arrange for its transportation to Germany. Even this was not an easy task. The German-Hungarian negotiations were concluded on September 1; not until September 8 did the Ministry of Agriculture issue an order coordinating the work of its various transportation subdivisions, and even then coordination seems to have been limited to Berlin. A subsequent frantic telegram from a German field representative could point to no accomplishments, but listed only unsolved problems; there was no cooperation among the various German agencies in the field, preliminary planning was notable for its absence, and, no doubt as a result, there were no available boxcars. That was two weeks after the original negotiations had been concluded.

Before Stalingrad, Reich agencies sought to lay the basis for permanent German control of the Southeast of Europe. By and large they failed. After the defeat on the Volga, the Germans

76. *Ibid.,* frame 564989; Südostgenossenschaftsinstitut to Heinrichsbauer, 19 Oct. 1943, *ibid.,* frame 564961.

77. The story of this particular instance of German intrasystem bungling is contained in: Reichsministerium für Ernährung und Landwirtschaft, "Aufzeichnung über die Besprechung vom 25. August bis 1. September 1944 im kgl. ung. Ackerbau und im kgl. ung. Versorgungsministerium, zu V A 4–3995/44," 5 Sept. 1944, T-77, roll 593, frames 1774746–47; Reichsministerium für Ernährung und Landwirtschaft, "Anordnung I/2–99344 [sic]," 8 Sept. 1944, T-77, roll 591, frame 1774808; and "Fernspruch von Landesrat Wippern vom Stab, MVAchef Dr. Ackermann an MVOR Dr. Bath . . . vom 15.9.1944 5.20 Uhr," 15 Sept. 1944, T-77, roll 593, frame 1774790.

changed their goals and to some extent their tactics. They failed once again. There is considerable evidence that the actual German imports after 1942 fell far short of both the Reich's expectations and the Southeast's ability to deliver. Balkan passive and active resistance was an unqualified success. According to secret German figures, imports from the Balkans to Germany attained the following amounts and monetary values during the war years:[78]

Year	Volume (in 1000 T.) (includes foodstuffs, raw materials, finished and semifinished products)	Value (in Mills. RM)
1940	72,816	1,388
1941	74,246	1,378
1942	68,586	1,959
1943 (Jan.–June)	32,584	1,201

Thus, while the monetary value of the imports climbed steadily as the result of the inflation rampant in all of Southeastern Europe, the tonnage of goods reaching Germany actually decreased after the German drive for more imports began in 1943. If the second half of 1943 was comparable to the first six months of that year (and there is no indication that it was not) about 65,584,000 tons crossed the Balkan borders into the Reich—an amount well below the figures for 1942 and substantially below those of 1940 and 1941.

An examination of the most important category of Balkan exports to the Reich, agricultural products, substantiates these conclusions. The combined harvest of grain crops in the three most important Balkan producers (Bulgaria, Hungary, and Rumania) in the years 1941–43 showed the following figures:[79]

78. "Der Aussenhandel Deutschlands mit den südosteuropäischen Ländern" [ca. mid-1943] (secret), T-71, roll 14, frame 404906. This conclusion is made even more poignant if one takes into consideration that the German figures are likely to have been inflated in order to impress the center.

79. The International Institute of Agriculture (Bureau of the FAO in Rome), *International Yearbook of Agricultural Statistics 1941–42 to 1945–46* (Rome, 1946), I, 4, 10, 28.

Crop production
(in Mill. Quintals)	1941	1942	1943
Wheat	51.0	33.3	60.9
Rye	7.6	6.2	8.9
Corn	60.7	41.3	46.5

During the same years the total exports of these crops from the three countries, which, since virtually all exports went to Germany, was almost identical with the amount shipped to the Reich, showed the following amounts:[80]

Crop
(in Mill. Quintals)	1941	1942	1943
Wheat	2.2	0.3	1.9
Rye	0.1	0.08	0.05
Corn	2.5	1.3	0.86

Again the figures speak for themselves. Despite significantly better harvests in the Balkan area, the region's exports either decreased (rye and corn) from 1942 to 1943, or, as in the case of wheat, the 1943 exports were proportionately lower than the increase in the harvest of that crop for the year 1943.

The specific amounts the Balkan countries kept from the Germans can only be estimated, but the following example may indicate their magnitude. The SOEG's representative in Hungary estimated the Hungarian wheat and rye crop of 1943 at 34.2 and 8.2 million quintals, respectively, and he assumed the Hungarians' own combined needs of wheat and rye to be 31.5 million quintals.[81] This would leave an exportable surplus of 10.7 million quintals of wheat and rye available to Germany. However, the Hungarians only exported 1.5 million quintals of

80. *Ibid.*, II, 4–5, 36–37, 60–61.
81. Misch, "Die Aussicht der ungarischen Ernte 1943 . . . ," 11 June 1943, T-71, roll 61, frames 559866–67. These figures seem to be correct. Postwar sources give the harvest as 35.7 and 8.3 million quintals, respectively. See Zagoroff et al., *Agricultural Economy*, p. 223.

wheat and rye to the Reich.[82] Even assuming that some of the
remainder went to other Axis and neutral countries, it is clear
that about 70 percent of the surplus was hoarded by the Hungarian farmers or governmental agencies, a revealing statistic
on the German failure to get the Balkan countries to increase
their contribution to the German war effort.[83]

In occupied nations such as Yugoslavia actual German military presence prevented large-scale official hoarding, but partisan
attacks had equally serious effects. For example, according to confidential German reports, partisan actions rendered various parts
of the important railroad trunkline from Zagreb to Semlin completely unusable for a total of 3,179 hours during the months
September to December 1943.[84] Translated into proportions, this
meant that for more than a quarter of the time goods could
not be shipped to Germany over some part of the line.

Partisan activities also had an important indirect effect on
the German war effort in Southeastern Europe. During the latter
stages of the war, the ethnic Germans became the only completely loyal population group in the Balkans, and the Germans
increasingly drafted their male members into the Armed-SS
(*Waffen-SS*) and Army (*Wehrmacht*) units guarding German
installations in the Balkan countries against partisan attacks.
These actions in turn meant a continuous drain on the agricultural labor force of the Volksdeutsche, and hence a steadily diminishing productivity level for this important element of support for the Reich's policies.[85]

82. *Ibid.*, p. 228.

83. See also, Nicholas Kallay, *Hungarian Premier* (New York, 1954), pp. 301–02
for figures on the quantities the Hungarians kept from the Reich authorities.

84. Gerlach, "Wirtschaftslage in Kroatien, Ende Dezember 1943" (strictly confidential), 1 Jan. 1944, T-71, roll 52, frame 447576. Despite its appearance, the
figure is not a miscalculation. The report divided the distance into five parts
and treated each subdivision as a separate entity. For a description of the
transport situation in Serbia, see Gruppe Ernährung und Landwirtschaft, Wein-
ausschuss, "Protokoll über die am Dienstag den 20. Juni 1944 um 16.30 . . . stattgefundene Sitzung des Weinausschusses der Gruppe Ernährung und Landwirtschaft der Südosteuropa-Gesellschaft," n.d., T-71, roll 75, frame 575930.

85. Kasche (the German Minister in Croatia) to Auswärtiges Amt, "Betr.:
Sonderkontingent für Landmaschinen für die Deutsche Volksgruppe, WL 1
3817/42," 5 Oct. 1942, T-71, roll 61, frames 560044–48.

In large part the German failures in Southeastern Europe both before and after 1943 were the result of administrative inefficiency and shortsightedness. At the same time the National Socialist behavior factor must not be ignored. The permeation of all German actions with the policies and the spirit of National Socialism played a major role in alienating the Southeastern countries both before as well as after Stalingrad. There is no doubt that as a political and racial Weltanschauung, National Socalism was totally unsuited to be the ideological base of a politically united Europe. However, political differences do not necessarily prevent mutually advantageous economic relations. The Reich and Southeastern Europe represented economically complimentary regions, and the regimes in control of the Balkan nations before and during World War II were quite prepared to become Germany's economic partners.[86] It was only the Third Reich's inability to divorce its economic policies from National Socialist political goals that shattered the illusion of economic symbiosis. When it became apparent that the New Order meant an economic reorganization of Europe for the exclusive benefit of the Reich, the Balkan countries ceased to identify the "struggle against Bolshevism" as their own, and sought to disengage themselves from the German grip by all possible means.[87]

To some extent, the association of economic policy and political mentality was no doubt the result of the NSDAP's control of the German businessmen in the Balkans. Since the Party's foreign organization had to approve all business appointments outside the Reich, it is obvious that generally only reliable National Socialists were sent. But this is not the whole story. In a desire for profits, expansion, and power, they all too frequently ignored considerations of common business ethics. Their belief that German power would triumph in Europe was the basis for some extremely questionable business transactions. By their actions if not their words, they often agreed with the center's basic political decision that German might was indeed Euro-

86. Gheorghe, *Rumäniens Weg,* pp. 284ff.
87. *Ibid.,* pp. 284–89; Alexander Cretzianu, "The Rumanian Armistice Negotiations: Cairo, 1944," *Journal of Central European Affairs,* XI (Oct. 1951), 243–58.

pean right. The SOEG cooperated wholeheartedly in the German economic drive, and while its administrators cannot be accused of specific crimes, the Society's activities do illustrate the extent to which even lesser German agencies such as the SOEG devoted their energies to furthering the aims of National Socialism. Not only did the Society assist the central Reich agencies, its attempt to have Vienna get a "fair" share of the Balkan spoils led it to participate enthusiastically in the expropriation measures the Germans initiated in the Balkans. Unethical practices were countenanced or encouraged in Berlin, and they became magnified as German regional or special interest groups attempted to outbid and outmaneuver each other.

The result was the complete failure of the German economic policies in the Balkans. The various stocks purchased, the elaborate controls bought and acquired by the Germans in the period 1940–42, were either sold or lost their practical value after 1942. In the meantime, however, the German methods had led to such intense opposition to the Reich and its aims, that when Germany needed the Balkans' aid after Stalingrad, the Southeastern countries granted their assistance only grudgingly and, in terms of their overall ability, sparingly.

6 | Conclusion

In the panoramic sweep of recorded history, the twelve-year rule of the National Socialist regime occupies an insignificant chronological span. And yet this brief reign of terror left in its wake a heritage of immense proportions: the deliberate death of millions, the most disastrous war in history, the political division of Europe, the final eclipse of European world leadership—these were the fruits of the Third Reich. The legacy is staggering and totally negative. For this reason it was perhaps inevitable (and certainly necessary if the study of history is to have a curative value) that early postwar scholarly analyses of the National Socialist era emphasized the immediate and physical horrors that resulted from Adolf Hitler's brief reign. Moreover, in attempting to explain the seemingly unspeakable atrocities, these early accounts enveloped the Nazi regime and its leaders with an aura of unique and diabolical

175

greatness. To be sure, the greatness was that of unfathomable evil, but it had greatness and magnitude nevertheless.

Despite its apparent logic in the presence of the concentration camp horrors, this explanation of the "whys" of the National Socialist totalitarian system was both intellectually and politically distorted. On the one hand, it pictured the leaders of the Third Reich as almost Weberian ideal types representing pure evil in human form. In a sense they became superhuman figures, whose deeds were somehow outside the realm of normal human behavior. This also meant that the evil types who had guided Germany for twelve bloody years merely superimposed their rule on the German body social, so that it would be relatively simple to lift off, as it were, the layer of evil surrounding German society.

Time, the failure of the denazification campaign, and the Cold War revised and almost reversed the earlier picture of National Socialist totalitarianism. From a greater chronological distance the leaders of the Third Reich shrank to human proportions. While the denazification program was all but forgotten, scholarly analyses emphasized the humanity (not humaneness) of the regime's leaders. The Görings, the Goebbels, even Hitler himself were not great men; indeed, they were "insignificant characters." And the system, too, possessed "no greatness."[1] Not even the greatness of typological purity. As researchers uncovered more and more of the documents left by the National Socialist regime, the facade of monolithic evil intent crumbled to reveal what appeared to be the "real" National Socialist system: a bewildering array of petty feuds, political opportunism, and personalized rivalries among the various agencies. All this was indeed characteristic of the regime, but it is also a distortion to picture the National Socialists as all too human and the period as simply another twelve years of history, more disastrous perhaps, but not essentially different from other eras characterized primarily by war and bloodshed. The uniqueness of National Socialism in practice was not perhaps the quantitative degree of its vio-

1. The citations are from Joachim C. Fest, *Das Gesicht des Dritten Reiches* (Munich, 1963), p. 391.

lence but rather its ability to permeate German social life with its political and societal norms. During the Third Reich virtually all political (public) figures in Germany carried out the regime's immoral directives, even though (as numerous defense affidavits showed in the postwar trials) those same individuals often had little personal sympathy with the policy aims involved. Few of the executors of National Socialist policies were deliberately and personally evil; far more were normal men whose work resulted in institutionalized evil and immorality.[2] It is relatively easy to analyze and even to exorcise the former, and most of the Rudolf Höss's have paid their debt to humanity with their lives or long years in prison. Yet the political reformer should not and the historian cannot stop here, for the essence of totalitarianism lies not in a Rudolf Höss, but in the vast army of "normal" officials—even non-Party members[3]—who permitted their own nazification, or to put it another way, allowed the regime to make use of their talents and services. It is not difficult to demonstrate the emotional, the personal, the ideological difference between the administrator who had internalized and emotionally accepted the National Socialist myths and the official at the next desk who merely translated the perverse ideas into administrative reality while remaining inwardly unaffected. Such a demonstration is also, however, meaningless because it misses the wider historical significance of modern mass totalitarianism. It is the tragedy of totalitarianism that while the engaged and the disengaged official might be personally very dissimilar, the difference in the political effects of their actions is negligible. Indeed, it might well be argued that the ravings of a Streicher had fewer disastrous results than did the actions of the manufacturer who supplied Zyklon B to Auschwitz. The National Socialist regime was not a superstructure momentarily imposed upon an otherwise unaffected body social, but a

2. One of the major merits of Rolf Hochhuth's recent play *Der Stellvertreter* (Hamburg, 1963), is to have drawn this clear distinction in his characterizations of National Socialist types.

3. It might be noted here again that Funk did not become a Party member until 1930; and, according to Hanel, Heinrichsbauer never formally joined. Hanel Interview.

politico-ethical venom that permeated and saturated German society with norms of political behavior that were the deliberate negation of those prevailing in a *Rechtsstaat*. The norms were invented by the center, but the invention had practical effects only as the German officials and public figures accepted them as the basis of their current activities and postwar plans. The Weimar Rechtsstaat became a totalitarian organism when virtually all German officials agreed to pursue goals within the exclusively power-oriented behavior framework imposed by the center, rather than attempt to uphold the Rechtsstaat norms against the new standards.[4]

This politico-ethical permeation of an entire society was inaugurated by decrees from the center, but the enforcement and impact of those directives depended far less upon the actions of Hitler or Goebbels than upon the day-to-day activities of a district party leader, a grumbling civil servant, and the executive secretaries of such organizations as the SOEG. It is this level that converted Hitler's and Himmler's personal, willed, evil intentions into "normal," institutionalized Reich policies. The significance of these secondary agencies and officials must not, however, be overemphasized. Although they often had considerable decision-making power in enforcing and even determining the scope of actual directives, the center at all times set the policy goals and above all determined the norms of political behavior for the entire system.

The SOEG provides an excellent subject for an in-depth case study of the process whereby "normal" nontotalitarian German officials accepted the National Socialist political norms and thus simultaneously furthered their own political careers and the center's self-determined policy goals. The Society's organizational life was wholly contained within the National Socialist era; the SOEG did not exist before the Nazis came to power, and it ceased its activities only shortly before the Third Reich itself

4. The objection that terror and propagandistic devices made the rejection of the totalitarian norms practically impossible is not pertinent here: to say that there was no other choice does not deny that the basis of institutionalized totalitarianism was acceptance (for whatever reason) of the National Socialist norms by administrative officials and public figures throughout German society.

fell. Moreover, it was clearly a second-echelon organization; it did not initiate the behavioral norms, it received them, converted them into political activity, and spread them within its circle of political interaction.

From its establishment to its collapse, the SOEG was largely an autonomous organizational unit striving for political power—that is, engaged in politics—within the overall totalitarian system. Its behind-the-scenes exploitation of the neofeudal norms and its carefully staged public image functions alike were steppingstones to a position of intrasystem political power. Perhaps the most striking aspect of the SOEG's organizational development within the National Socialist system was its very ability to move, its relative freedom of action, vis-à-vis both its own superior agency and other Reich-level agencies. Although the central agency to which the SOEG was subordinated, the Reich Ministry of Economics, declined in power and prestige throughout the war, this had no appreciable effect on the SOEG, whose own position was becoming increasingly stronger during the same time span. It is indicative of the complexity of political infighting among agencies in the Third Reich that the same agency could rebuke the Ministry of Economics and yet add to the public image luster of its nominal subordinate. The Reich Ministry of Agriculture, for instance, which vigorously opposed the Economics Ministry's plans for the economic development of the Balkans, nevertheless cooperated fully with the SOEG, and high-ranking officials of the Ministry of Agriculture appeared as prominent speakers at several of the SOEG's functions. The Foreign Ministry refused to permit the SOEG's cultural ventures in 1940, but three years later it urged the SOEG to enter the field of German cultural propaganda in the Balkans. And the SS, equally concerned with weakening the power of the Economics Ministry, nevertheless graced the SOEG's Prague congress with the presence of Reinhard Heydrich, one of its most prominent officials. Clearly, the SOEG's public image was becoming brighter at the same time that the Ministry of Economics was losing its power, and, more significant still, the SOEG's stature grew in large part through the implicit support of precisely those agencies that were simultaneously undermining the authority of Funk's ministry.

The history of the SOEG is thus a case study of the process of politics under the National Socialist totalitarian regime. For all its outward appearance the regime was not, even during the war years, a monolithic, centrally directed dictatorship in which minute details of local and regional administration were directed from the central offices in Berlin. It is true that Berlin founded the SOEG, but it is equally apparent that the Society was left very much to its own devices once it had been established. Heinrichsbauer, not Funk, established the SOEG as a political success by coupling the umbrella form of organization (*Dachgesellschaft*) with his shrewd but tactful manner of adapting his dealings with other agencies to the neofeudal norms approved by the center. From a study of the SOEG it may be concluded that the operation of local and regional agencies in the Third Reich was by no means subject to detailed supervision and instruction from the Berlin central agencies; rather, once an agency had been given a general authorization to begin its operations, the organization then might well carry out its mission without further interference from Berlin, unless—and apparently only unless—the agency needed further and more specific authorization in its drive for expansion, or if it interfered with the interests of another organization and the latter agency in turn alerted its Berlin superiors. All of this is not meant to suggest that the center exercised no control over the activities of the system's components. There was indeed a form of control, but it was behavioristic rather than structural. Such forms of influence were less evident, but far more subtle and no less effective than structural straitjackets. The center maintained a position of unchallenged normative authority. The center decreed the basic goals of German policy and the center set the ethical norms of behavior for all components of the system.

At its most essential and yet most effective level, the control by the center consisted simply in the acceptance by all agencies in the Third Reich of the inviolability of its goals and norms of behavior. These conditions constituted an iron-clad framework within which all institutional development, struggle, and experimentation had to take place. No agency in the Third Reich ever seriously contemplated challenging the authority of the center. Consequently, intrasystem freedom of action, far from diminishing the authority of the center, increased its control and enhanced its image by casting it in the role of perpetual umpire, a role that also guaranteed the finality of its organizational authority. Institutional success in the system depended primarily on an implicit acknowledgment that the only criteria of political success was the accumulation and exercise of direct power. Within the European community, power could be used to subjugate the other peoples to the rule of National Socialism; within the system it could eliminate personal and institutional rivals. Through the acceptance of these conditions for organizational success within the system, the Heinrichsbauers— personally decent, humane, cultured middle-class Germans— in turn became to a greater or lesser degree institutionalized Höss's. They were not personally immoral, they merely institutionalized immorality as the price of political success in the system. And in doing so they advanced the center's overall policy goals as effectively as if they had personally subscribed to the ideas which Hitler set forth in *Mein Kampf* or Himmler put into his memoranda and speeches.

Acceptance of the center's goals was in effect universal among officials that staffed organizationally ambitious institutions in all parts of Greater Germany. The SOEG and its affiliates were staffed with both German and Austrian officials,[5] but there is no evidence whatever to suggest that the Austrian officials in the Society attempted to defy or oppose the German staff members. Indeed, Rafelsberger and Rischka, who were Austrians, urged the use of far more ruthless means to further National Socialist control of the Balkans than did the Society's German executive secretary; and such men as the top officials of the Vienna Institute for Economic Research (WIW) participated fully and even enthusiastically in the industrial planning project. Moreover, Viennese firms were as eager as those of the Reich

5. See below, Appendix.

to cooperate with the SOEG in obtaining their share of the Balkan spoils. There is no document in the SOEG's files that suggests a Viennese business enterprise ever refused to accept control of illegally obtained Balkan property; there are, however, several requests from prospective buyers for the SOEG's aid in locating suitable "aryanized" and expropriated properties in Southeastern Europe.

Substantively, the self-imposed behavioristic and hence political straitjacket of agencies under the National Socialist regime expressed itself most completely in the process of drawing up and executing the plans for the New Order. Consequently the work of the SOEG's Industrial Planning Committee is undoubtedly one of the most revealing windows into the operations of totalitarian politics. The SOEG's efforts show a great deal not only about National Socialist plans for the Balkans, but also about the use of the process of planning for political purposes in the National Socialist system. The output of plans of the Committee on Economic Planning could only be a concretization and specification of the center's overall goals. Similarly, the suggested methods of carrying out the center's policies are representative of National Socialist behavioral norms. In the most general sense, the essence of the New Order was an application of the center's a priori-determined goals dominated by race and power. Europe was to be organized in the German image and administered either directly or indirectly by National Socialist officials; in the New Europe the interests of the non-German peoples would have been incidental to the primary goal of assuring greater power and economic prosperity for the self-proclaimed *Herrenvolk.*

The Economic Planning Committee's difficulties in drawing up suitable plans illustrate the effectiveness (and shortsightedness) of the center's political control. The SOEG originally set out merely to draft economic goals and suggestions for putting these goals into effect in Southeastern Europe. This in itself was not an overly difficult task. The overall economic goal of the New Order was to increase the prosperity of the Reich. As the basic means of accomplishing this, the Germans intended to establish an international division of labor between the Reich and the Balkans. In general such an arrangement would have restricted the Southeastern European nations to the manufacture of agricultural and semi-finished industrial materials, which would then be exported to the Reich at low cost. At the same time Germany would sell her exports to the Balkans at high prices. Within the Balkan area Germany would be dealing within a seller's market, since the Southeastern European nations would not be permitted to manufacture products that Germany intended to sell to them. From the Balkan point of view there is, of course, nothing equitable or fair about this scheme, but from the German point of view it can be argued that buying cheaply, selling dearly, and eliminating competition was sound economic doctrine. These forms of economic imperialism might be economically and even politically feasible, but the SOEG's planners soon discovered that quite often the formulation of a desirable economic policy was irreconcilable with the center's basic political goals and behavioral norms. Thus, the SOEG's officials knew that their refusal to allow a complete manufacturing process to be performed in any one Balkan country was economically unwise, but, since the center feared the growth of industry in the Balkans might impede its absolute political control of the area, the prohibitions became part of the German plans. Similarly, maintaining the Balkan countries as sovereign nations was economically preferable; it was rejected as a long-range solution because it would have allowed some freedom of action for the Reich's subject peoples. In the last analysis, an organization like the SOEG that hoped to please the center had to incorporate in its planning contingencies for the possibility that at any time the Reich would forego economic advantages in order to achieve what was always the primary National Socialist aim—the attainment of naked power. Planning, like every other political activity in the Third Reich, was not a free search for pragmatic solutions to real problems but a means of applying answers that had been predetermined by the center's norms.

Acceptance of the totalitarian political norms was the prerequisite for intrasystem success, but the widespread acceptance

by all levels, agencies, and officials in the Third Reich in turn
was a major factor in the system's overall failure to achieve
its goals in dealing with extrasystem factors. In both the planning of policies and their execution the various German officials
took into account solely the intrasystem impact of the extrasystem variables with which they had to deal. The SOEG's plans
for the future of the Balkans provided no real alternative to
the Reich's complete political and economic domination in the
area. Knowledge of these intentions in turn understandably gen-
erated Balkan animosity to the German plans and thus helped
to defeat the overall German goals. Similarly, the swarms of
German Balkan agents who formed a vanguard (and later a
rear guard) for the New Order, created far more opposition to
the National Socialist plans and goals than any Allied propaganda could have done. Yet, in a sense, the agents—like the planners—had no choice. In order to be successful within the National
Socialist system they needed to behave institutionally in line
with the center's totalitarian norms. Whatever private doubts
a German official might have had about the wisdom of German
policies in 1940, 1942, or even 1944, his immediate political future depended upon his acceptance of the center's announcement
that the war had been won and that the New Order would
follow.

The inevitable result of the German Balkan policies and plans
was their utter failure. From 1940 to 1942 the Balkan states'
lack of cooperation could be, and generally was, ignored by
the Germans; the statement by the SOEG's representative in
Rumania that after the war Germany could dictate to the Balkans anyway,[6] was symptomatic of the National Socialists' mental attitude toward their role in Southeastern Europe before
the fortunes of war turned. After 1942 the Germans could not
remain oblivious to Balkan sentiments. The Reich's primary
interest in increased Balkan contributions to the immediate war
effort made the cooperation of the Balkan governments and peoples obligatory. However, the earlier attitude was not easily forgotten. The post-1942 drive for larger volumes of imports from

6. Buchas to Heinrichsbauer, 4 Oct. 1942, T-71, roll 55, frame 451182.

the Balkans was extremely unproductive; the earlier German policies had so disillusioned the Balkan nations that they were now completely unwilling to identify the Reich's cause and struggle as their own. And, in a sense, the Reich agencies too could not change their attitude. As long as Balkan activities and Balkan policies—be they long or short term—had an intrasystem political use, those agencies engaged in politics had to accept the center's definition of reality; a definition that never included an actual admission that the fortunes of war had turned against the Reich.

The history of the SOEG's organizational and institutional success thus reveals that the National Socialist totalitarian system of politics consisted not of two but of three layers of "reality." Behind an outwardly monolithic facade of glittering uniforms and pseudomilitary discipline lay organizational chaos and neofeudal jousts for power. But this second layer was also only part of the entire picture. Beyond was the subtle underlying unity of the system. What gave substance to the entire entity was not the outward propaganda image but the unity of shared goals and interests. The conflicts among the agencies were never over the basic issue of whether the National Socialist goals were morally right and should be carried out. The German and Austrian officials who had never had occasion to confer with Hitler could be entrusted with far-reaching authority in the knowledge that they would exercise it as the center intended them to. While the internal apparatus of the Third Reich presents a picture of organizational anarchy, the policy impetus is clear and monolithic. The new barbarian invaders of Europe might have feuded over their relative position behind the leader, but they all willingly rushed forward on the same path.

▲▲   Appendix

IT was suggested as part of the conclusion to this study that the analysis of the SOEG's history showed there was no appreciable difference in the degree to which Austrian and German officials were willing to carry out the Nazi aims and policies. In order to bring into sharper focus the image of the SOEG as a bi-national organization in which both German and Austrian officials cooperated wholeheartedly to further the Nazi aims, the following tabulation gives the nationality of the SOEG's leading officials. In this tabulation the term *German* designates officials who assumed positions in Austria after the Anschluss in March 1938, while the term *Austrian* refers to those who lived and worked in Austria prior to 1938.

A. National officers and the staff of the central office

NAME	POSITION	NATIONALITY
Walther Funk	Protector	German
Joseph Bürckel	President	German
Baldur von Schirach	President	German
Walter Rafelsberger	Vice-President	Austrian
Hanns Blaschke	Vice-President	Austrian
Hans Fischböck	Vice-President	Austrian
Günter Kaufmann	Vice-President	German
Richard Buzzi	Treasurer	Austrian
August Heinrichsbauer	Executive Secretary	German
Hans Augenthaler	Executive Secretary	Austrian
Robert Breza	Deputy Executive Secretary	Austrian
Leonhard Oberascher	Associate Executive Secretary	Austrian
Erika Hanel	Personal Secretary of the Executive Secretaries	Austrian

Totals Group A Austrian: 8
German: 5

B. Leading officials of the SOEG's affiliates

NAME	POSITION	NATIONALITY
Ernst Bierbrauer	head of the Forschungsstelle für den Südosten a. d. Montanistischen Hochschule, Leoben	Austrian
Hanns Blaschke	head of the Kulturpolitischer Arbeitskreis	Austrian
Ludwig Brandl	head of the Arbeitskreis für Donaufragen	Austrian
Rolf Grünwald	head of the Wiener Institut für Verbrauchs- und Absatzforschung	German [?]
Gertraud Hagmüller	administrative secretary of the Südostgemeinschaft Wiener Hochschulen	German
Erwin Hanslik	administrative secretary of the Südostgenossenschaftsinstitut	Austrian
Oskar Hausmann	administrative secretary of the Südostagrarinstitut	Austrian
Felix Kraus	administrative secretary of the Kulturpolitischer Arbeitskreis and the Gesellschaft der Freunde der Deutschen Akademie in Wien	German

NAME	POSITION	NATIONALITY
Karl Mayerzedt	head of the Gruppe Ernährung und Landwirtschaft	Austrian
Franz Nemschak	member of the staff of the Wiener Institut für Wirtschaftsforschung (WIW)	Austrian
Franz Neumaier	administrative secretary of the Photogrammetrisches Institut	Austrian
——Rabitsch	member of the staff of the WIW	Austrian
Kurt von Rischka	administrative secretary of the Gruppe Ernährung und Landwirtschaft	Austrian
Franz Ronneberger	editor of the *VWN*	German
——Schimitschek	head of the Südost-Institut für Wald- und Holzforschung	Austrian
Baldur von Schirach	president of the Gesellschaft der Freunde der Deutschen Akademie in Wien	German
Arnold Seifert	director of the WIW	German [?]
Adolf Staffe	head of the Südostagrarinstitut	Austrian
Sawa Ulmansky	administrative secretary of the Maisausschuss	German
——Ungerer	executive secretary of the Verein zur Wahrung der Main- und Donauschiffahrtsinteressen	German
Hans Würdinger	head of the Institut für Südostrecht	German

	Totals Group B	Austrian: 12
		German: 9[?]

C. Representatives of the SOEG in Berlin and in the Balkan Countries

NAME	CITY	NATIONALITY
Heinz Buchas	Bucharest	German
——Geffers	Sofia	German
——von Hervay	Athens	Austrian
——Kratz	Berlin	German
Anton Kreuzbauer	Belgrade	Austrian [?]
Gerhard Misch	Budapest	German
Peter Mussap	Bratislava	German [?]
Paul Schön	Bucharest	German
Karl Schubart	Zagreb	Austrian
Max Stadler	Zagreb	Austrian

Totals Group C   Austrian: 4[?]
German: 6[?]

Totals for the SOEG as a Whole   Austrian: 24
German: 20

▲▲ | # Bibliography

THE basic sources for this study of the *Südosteuropa-Gesellschaft* and National Socialist Balkan policies are captured and microfilmed German World War II records, particularly the SOEG's own files, and the Foreign Ministry materials. Almost all of the SOEG's correspondence, memoranda, and minutes of meetings survived the war, and were subsequently microfilmed by Allied authorities. The films are available from the National Archives in Washington, D.C. In most cases, the items in the films are the copies of documents retained by the SOEG's central office. The material, grouped by originating offices, is arranged in a series of folders. Within each folder the arrangement is chronological. In addition, the central office maintained some general alphabetical files and a file of confidential papers, arranged both alphabetically and chronologically. In general, the papers in the various folders are in good order; the material of the *Ausschuss für wirtschaftswissenschaftliche Planung* is, however, badly disorganized and scattered in several folders.

190

The list of unpublished protocols, reports, constitutions, and other materials given below is incomplete, but an effort has been made (1) to include some of the materials that are basic for the study of the SOEG itself, and (2) to list those materials which, whether originating with the SOEG or another agency, are of paramount importance for the study of National Socialist plans and policies in the Balkans during and after World War II.

Primary Sources
Unpublished Memoranda and Studies

Breza, Robert. "Der Arbeitsbereich des Ausschusses für wirtschaftswissenschaftliche Planung," Jan. 1942. T-84, roll 198, frames 1564676–721 (mimeographed).

———— [?] "Wirtschaftswissenschaftlicher Planungsauschuss der Südosteuropa-Gesellschaft—Zusammenfassende Darstellung der Vorarbeiten," Sept. 1942. T-71, roll 71, frames 570985–90.

Fischböck, Hans. "Binnenländische und zwischenstaatliche Preispolitik," 28 May 1943. T-71, roll 53, frames 448597–632.

Funk, Walther. "Vermerk über das Ergebnis meines Besuches in Bukarest und Budapest" [ca. Sept., 1942]. T-84, roll 6, frames 5642–44.

Germany, Reichsgruppe Industrie. "Bericht über das Ergebnis der fünften gemeinsamen Tagung des deutschen und bulgarischen Regierungsausschusses in der Zeit vom 11. April bis 11. Mai 1942 in Sophia [sic]," 13 June 1942. T-84, roll 88, frames 1378421–23.

————, ————. "Bericht über das Ergebnis der in der Zeit vom 8. 5.-12. 6. 1942 in Bukarest stattgefundenen 12. gemeinsamen Tagung des Deutsch-Rumänischen Industrieauschusses," 3 July 1942. T-84, roll 88, frames 1378536–42.

————, ————. "Bericht über das Ergebnis der in der Zeit vom 22. Februar bis 15. März in Budapest stattgefundenen 24. gemeinsamen Tagung des Deutschen und des Ungarischen Regierungsausschusses," April 1942. T-84, roll 88, frames 1378200–01.

————, ————. "Bericht über das Ergebnis der 7. gemeinsamen Tagung des deutschen und des bulgarischen Regierungsausschusses in Berlin in der Zeit vom 10. 4. bis 24. 5. 1943," 15 June 1943. T-84, roll 88, frames 1378416–18.

————, ————. "Bericht über das Ergebnis der 4. gemeinsamen Tagung des deutschen und des bulgarischen Regierungsausschusses in der

Zeit vom 22. 9.-15. 10. 1941 in Sofia," 8 Nov. 1941. T-84, roll 88, frames 1378461–64.

————, ————. "3. Tagung der deutsch-rumänischen Industrieausschussverhandlungen in Bukarest vom 8. bis 12. Februar 1943," 29 Jan. 1943. T-71, roll 56, frames 452535–41.

————, ————. "Entwurf einer Geschäftsordnung für den Südostausschuss und die Länderausschüsse der Reichsgruppe Industrie," 2 Sept. 1941. T-71, roll 14, frames 404951–54.

————, ————. "Protokoll über die erste gemeinsame Tagung des Deutschen und des Rumänischen Industrieausschusses in Bukarest (zu V Ld 12/37853/41)," 23 July 1941. T-84, roll 88, frames 1378611–25.

————, ————. Deutscher Industrieausschuss and Bulgaria, Bulgarischer Industrieausschuss. "Protokoll über die erste Tagung der deutsch-bulgarischen Industrieausschüsse," 14 May 1941. T-84, roll 88, frames 1378474–80.

[Germany, Reichsgruppe Industrie and Hungary, Bund der ungarischen Fabrik-Industriellen (GYOSZ)]. "Protokoll der deutschungarischen Industriebesprechungen, Budapest, vom 16.–19. September 1941," n.d. T-84, roll 88, frames 1378373–83.

[————] (Max Ilgner), and [————] (Tibor von Kallay). "Protokoll über die deutsch-ungarischen Industriebesprechungen in Wien vom 27. April bis 1. Mai 1942," 1 May 1942. T-84, roll 88, frames 1378348–72.

————, ———— and ————. "Protokoll über die 3. deutschungarischen Industriebesprechungen in Budapest vom 14. bis 18. September 1942," 18 Sept. 1942. T-71, roll 61, frames 559670–92.

————, ———— and Mitteleuropäischer Wirtschaftstag. "Vorschlag der Reichsgruppe Industrie und des Mitteleuropäischen Wirtschaftstages für die Wirtschaftsplanungen im südosteuropäischen Raum," 14 July 1941. T-71, roll 75, frames 575813–17.

————, ————, Slowakei-Ausschuss and Slovakia, Zentralvereinigung der slowakischen Industrie, Deutschland-Ausschuss. "Protokoll über das Ergebnis der ersten gemeinsamen Tagung des deutschen und des slowakischen Industrieausschusses in Pressburg vom 4.-6. Februar 1942," n.d. T-84, roll 88, frames 1378167-85.

———— [Reichswirtschaftskammer, Arbeitsgemeinschaft der Industrie- und Handelskammern?]. "Bericht über das Ergebnis der gemeinsamen Tagung des Deutschen und des Ungarischen Regierungsausschusses in Budapest vom 4.-16. Jan. 1940," n.d., T-84, roll 136, frames 1438393-99.

Janovsky, Karl. "Bericht über die im RWM stattgefundene Aussprache über die bulgarischen Verhandlungsergebnisse" [ca. Oct., 1941]. T-84, roll 88, frames 1378465–71.

———. "Bericht über die wirtschaftlichen Verhältnisse in Ungarn, Bulgarien und Rumänien im Jahre 1943" [ca. March, 1943]. T-84, roll 88, frames 1378694–711.

Kraus, Felix. "Aktvermerk—Betrifft: Gesellschaft der Freunde der Deutschen Akademie in Wien," 10 Nov. 1942. T-71, roll 60, frames 558397–426.

———. "Entwurf—Abkommen zwischen: Stadt Wien, Deutscher Akademie und Südosteuropa-Gesellschaft," 23 Oct. 1943. T-71, roll 60, frames 558487–89.

———. "Entwurf—Kulturpolitischer Arbeitskreis der SOEG," 4 Nov. 1941. T-71, roll 55, frames 451488–90.

———. "Südosteuropa-Gesellschaft und volksdeutsche Arbeit," 14 April 1941. T-71, roll 56, frames 452133–35.

Misch, Gerhard. "Auszug aus dem Protokoll über die in der Zeit vom 14.-19. IX. 1941 in Budapest abgehaltenen Industriebesprechungen," n.d. T-71, roll 74, frames 574633–36.

———. "Lage und Aussichten der ungarischen Schwerindustrie," 12 Sept. 1941. T-84, roll 137, frames 1440081–93.

———. "Nachkriegspläne der ungarischen Industrie," 1 Nov. 1943. T-84, roll 136, frames 1439371-85.

Mussap, Peter. "Betr.: Deutsch-Slowakische Regierungsausschussverhandlungen," 24 May 1943. T-71, roll 70, frames 569509–10.

———. "Die Lösung der Judenfrage in der Slowakei /Dr. Vosek/ [sic]," 10 March 1943. T-71, roll 70, frames 569596–600.

Nemschak, Franz. "Industrieplanung," April–Sept. 1942. T-71, roll 68, frames 568012–89.

Oberascher, Leonhard. "Aktenvermerk—Anregungen des Herrn Dr. Böhm zur Gesamtarbeit der SOEG," 3 Aug. 1944. T-71, roll 51, frames 446911–13.

Rabitsch. "Besprechung über die Industrieplanung im Südosten am 11.5. 1942, Dr. Seifert, Dr. John, Dr. Nemschak, Dr. Rabitsch," n.d. T-71, roll 58, frames 555913–14.

———. "Industrieplantung— Besprechung zu Dr. Seiferts Besuch bei Rafelsberger 8.5. [1942]," n.d. T-71, roll 58, frames 555920–22.

Rafelsberger, Walter. "Aktenvermerk—Besprechung bei Herrn Staatssekretär Landfried," 12 Nov. 1940. T-71, roll 74, frames 575496–97.

———. "Aktenvermerk über die Besprechung beim Reichsleiter am 18. Juni 1941," n.d. T-71, roll 74, frames 575173–77.

————. "Aktenvermerk über die Besprechung mit Reichswirtschafts-minister Funk in Berlin," 21 March 1942. T-71, roll 58 frames 555749-53.

Rischka, Kurt von to Straubinger. "Betrifft: Geplante Ressortbesprechung in Berlin," 24 April 1942. T-71, roll 131, frames 634639-52.

————. "Die mögliche Bedeutung der Südosteuropa-Gesellschaft als Organ der neuen europäischen Wirtschaftsgemeinschaft" [25 May 1943]. T-71, roll 14, frames 404846-57.

Schwarz-Meer Handels- und Industriegesellschaft m.b.H. "Satzungen der Schwarz-Meer Handels- und Industriegesellschaft," n.d. T-71, roll 131, frames 634572-73.

Seifert, Arnold. "Entwürfe Dr. Seifert—Industrieplanung, Souveränitätsfrage," n.d. T-71, roll 47, frames 441916-442101.

————. "Erläuterungen zum I. Organisationsplan," n.d. T-71, roll 47, frames 441989-97.

————. "Industrieplanung—Besprechung am 30.6.1942 im Amtszimmer des Herrn Staatskommissar Rafelsberger . . . ," n.d. T-71, roll 14, frames 405664-65.

———— [?]. "Die industriewirtschaftlichen Folgen des Rückganges (und Zuwachses) des deustchen politischen Einflusses auf Südosteuropa seit 1938" [18 June 1942]. T-71, roll 58, frames 556095-99.

Stadler, Max. "Die Aufgaben der Abteilungen Südosteuropa-Gesellschaft e.V. in der Deutschen Handelskammer in Kroatien," 28 July 1942. T-71, roll 51, frames 446449-50.

————. "Wien als Südosthandelsplatz—eine Standortanalyse," 1940. T-84, roll 87, frames 1377997-1378010.

Südosteuropa-Gesellschaft. "Aktion Gen. v. Unruh—Meldung Soeg [sic], 25.5.1943" [25 May 1943]. T-71, roll 65 frames 563753-916.

————. "Arbeitsplan der Südosteuropa-Gesellschaft," 1940. T-84, roll 196, frames 1562262-63.

————. "Geschäftsordnung der Südosteuropa-Gesellschaft" [ca. Oct., 1942]. T-84, roll 196, frames 1452264-76.

————. "Gliederung der Südosteuropa-Gesellschaft" [1943]. T-84, roll 196, frames 1562045-55.

————. (Hanel): "Im Rahmen der Südosteuropa-Gesellschaft in Arbeit befindliche Untersuchungen, Stand 15. Juni 1943" [June, 1943]. T-71, roll 14, frames 405496-512.

————. "Niederschrift über die am 8. Feber 1940 in Wien 62, Strasse der Julikämpfer 19, abgehaltene konstituierende Versammlung des Vereins 'Südosteuropa-Gesellschaft' mit dem Sitze in Wien 110, Hockegasse 73/75," n.d. T-71, roll 78, frames 579700–04.

————. "Satzung der 'Südosteuropa-Gesellschaft' " [ca. April 1941]. T-71, roll 78, frames 579667–71.

————, Ausschuss für wirtschaftswissenschaftliche Planung. "Bericht über die erste Sitzung [des] Ausschusses für wirtschaftswissenschaftliche Planung," n.d. T-71, roll 14, frames 405696–98.

————, ————. "Ergebnis der Besprechung über den Arbeitsplan des Wirtschaftswissenschaftlichen Planungsausschusses der Südosteuropa-Gesellschaft bei Min. Rat Reinhardt am 24.1. 1942," n.d. T-71, roll 14, frames 405699–701.

————, ————. "Geheimprotokoll über die Zweite Sitzung des Zwölfer-Ausschusses über Fragen der Industrieplanung am 27. Juni 1942 . . . im Dienstzimmer des Herrn Vizepräsidenten der Südosteuropa-Gesellschaft Gauwirtschaftsberater Rafelsberger," n.d. T-71, roll 49, frames 443706–27.

————, Gesellschaft der Freunde der Deutschen Akademie in Wien. "Satzung" [ca. Nov., 1942]. T-71, roll 60, frames 558407–08.

————, Gruppe Ernährung und Landwirtschaft. "Aktvermerk-Betrifft: Besprechung über die Gründung einer Schwarz-Meer Handels- und Industriegesellschaft," n.d. T-71, roll 131, frame 634581.

————, Hauptgeschäftführer (Heinrichsbauer). "Der Aufbau der Südosteuropa-Gesellschaft," Dec., 1942. T-84, roll 196, frames 1562056–58.

————, ———— (Heinrichsbauer). "Ergänzung zu dem Bericht: Tätigkeit und Aufbau der Südosteuropa-Gesellschaft" [Feb., 1941]. T-84, roll 196, frames 1562235–36.

————, ———— (Heinrichsbauer). "Tätigkeit und Aufbau der Südosteuropa-Gesellschaft," 10 June 1941. T-84, roll 196, frames 1562253–61.

————, ———— (Heinrichsbauer). "Tätigkeit und Aufbau der Südosteuropa-Gesellschaft" [Dec., 1941]. T-84, roll 196, frames 1562237–52.

————, ———— (Heinrichsbauer). "Tätigkeitsbericht der Südosteuropa-Gesellschaft" [ca. May, 1942]. T-84, roll 196, frames 1562156–73.

————, Südost-Genossenschaftsinstitut. "Bericht über die Tätigkeit des Südostgenossenschaftsinstitutes im Jahre 1943," n.d. T-71, roll 76, frames 577565–69.

————, ————. "Geschäftsordnung des Südost-Genossenschaftsinstitutes der Südosteuropa-Gesellschaft," n.d. T-84, roll 196, frames 1562559–70.

————, ————. "Informationsschrift über das Südost-Genossenschaftsinstitut der Südosteuropa-Gesellschaft" [ca. May, 1943]. T-71, roll 76, frames 577209–13.

————, ————. "Protokoll über den Ablauf der ersten Präsidialsitzung des Südostgenossenschaftsinstitutes der Südosteuropa-Gesellschaft vom 14. April 1943," 14 April 1943. T-71, roll 66, frames 564981–87.

————, ————. "Satzungen des Südostgenossenschaftsinstitutes der Südosteuropa-Gesellschaft" [ca. March, 1943]. T-71, roll 76, frames 577204–08.

————, Wiener Institut für Wirtschaftsforschung. ["Generalgutachten für die Arbeit des Wirtschaftswissenschaftlichen Planungsausschusses der Südosteuropa-Gesellschaft"] [ca. June, 1942]. T-71, roll 58, frames 556041–82.

————, ————. "Satzung des Wiener Institutes für Wirtschaftsforschung e.V., 27 Aug. 1940. T-71, roll 54, frames 450144–46.

———— and Deutsche Gesellschaft der Wirtschaft in Böhmen und Mähren. "Abkommen," 24 Nov. 1942. T-71, roll 57, frames 453888.

———— and Deutsche Handelskammer in Kroatien. "Vereinbarung zwischen der Deutschen Handelskammer in Kroatien und der Südosteuropa-Gesellschaft e.V." [June, 1942]. T-84, roll 87, frames 1377782–83.

———— and Rumänisch-Deutsche Handelskammer. "Vereinbarung zwischen der Südosteuropa-Gesellschaft, Wien (SOEG) und der Rumänisch-Deutschen Handelskammer, Bukarest (Rudekammer)," 12 Feb. 1943. T-71, roll 49, frames 444291–92.

———— and Ungarischer Ausschuss für Wirtschaftsorientierung. "Schlussprotokoll der Besprechungen zwischen dem Ungarischen Ausschuss für Wirtschaftsorientierung und der Südosteuropa-Gesellschaft über die Richtlinien für die Preisgestaltung im ungarisch-deutschen Warenverkehr," 29 June 1943. T-71, roll 14, frames 404844–45.

["Tagesordnung, Teilnehmerliste und Protokoll der] Besprechung von Verkehrsfragen im Reichsgau Wien am 2. u. 3. März 1943," n.d. T-71, roll 58, frames 555665–731.

Ulmansky, Sawa. "Betrifft: Plan für die Entwicklung einer kroatischen landwirtschaftlichen Industrie," 15 June 1943. T-71, roll 66, frames 565201–08.

———. "Protokoll—1) über die Besprechungen mit den Herren vom ungarischen Ausschuss für Wirtschaftsorientierung in der SOEG am. 20. Juli 1943—2) über die Besprechungen in der Landesbauernschaft Niederdonau am. 26. Juli 1943," 10 Sept. 1943. T-71, roll 66, frames 565159–61.

———. "Vorschlag betreffend Vereinheitlichung der Führung einer Aktion zur Maisnutzung in den Südoststaaten," 2 Dec. 1942. T-71, roll 64, frames 562770–71.

Primary Sources
Publications of the SOEG and Its Affiliates

Brandl. Ludwig. *Fahrwasserverhältnisse und Transportleistungen auf der Schiffahrtsstrasse der Donau.* Vienna: SOEG [?], 1943, Confidential.

———. *Grundsäzliches über die Schiffahrtsstrasse der Drau.* Vienna: SOEG [?], 1943.

———. *Vorschläge zum Ausbau der Donau als Grosschiffahrtsstrasse.* Vienna: SOEG, 1941.

Brandl, Ludwig. *Wasserstrassenverbindungen von der Donau zum Mittelmeer.* Vienna: SOEG, 1941.

Breza, Robert. *Währung und Wirtschaft Rumäniens von 1930 bis 1940.* Vienna: SOEG [?], 1941.

Chlebarov, Georgi S. *Die Tierzucht Bulgariens.* Prague: Volk und Reich, 1944.

Deutsches Institut für Wirtschaftsforschung. *Der italienische Einfluss auf die Industriewirtschaft in Südosteuropa seit Kriegsbeginn.* Vienna: SOEG, 1943. Secret.

Funk, Walther. *Die Länder des Südostens und die europäische Wirtschaftsgemeinschaft.* Vienna: Südost-Echo, 1944.

———. *Wirtschaftsordnung im Neuen Europa.* Vienna: Südost-Echo, 1941.

Grünwald, Rolf. *Südosteuropa als Absatzmarkt für Konsumfertigwaren. Eine Strukturanalyse des Wiener Instituts für Verbrauchs- und Absatzforschung.* 2 parts. Vienna: SOEG, 1944. T-84, roll 79, frames 1367621–731 and 1367732–52. [Part 2 is incomplete on the film; a complete copy of the study is available in the Nationalbibliothek in Vienna.]

Heinrichsbauer, August. *Eindrücke von einer Balkanreise im April/ Mai 1940.* Vienna: SOEG, 1940. Confidential.

————. *Nordeuropa-Südosteuropa—Eindrücke von einer Skandinavienreise Ende Juli-Anfang August 1942.* Vienna: SOEG, 1942. Confidential.

Kriege, Käte. *Schrifttumsnachweis über die serbische Forstwirtschaft und deren Grundlagen.* Prague: Volk und Reich, 1944.

Krohm, Hartmut. *Die Textilindustrie Südosteuropas.* Vienna: Volk und Reich, 1944.

Münchner Institut für Wirtschafts- und Konjunkturforschung and Deutsches Institut für Wirtschaftsforschung. *Die Zementindustrie im Südosten.* Vienna: SOEG, 1944. Secret.

Nemschak, Franz. *Der türkische Bergbau und seine wirtschaftlichen Probleme.* Prague: Volk und Reich, 1944.

Rischka, Kurt von. *Erster Jahresbericht über die Tätigkeit der Gruppe "Ernährung und Landwirtschaft" der Südosteuropa-Gesellschaft gemäss Paragraph 5 der Geschäftsordnung.* Vienna: SOEG, 1942. Confidential.

————. *Geschäftsbericht der Gruppe "Ernährung und Landwirtschaft" der Südosteuropa-Gesellschaft. Wein 1. December 1942.* Vienna: SOEG, 1942.

Stadler, Max. *Die Preisentwicklung in Kroatien seit 1941 und ihre Bestimmungsgründe.* [Vienna: SOEG], 1943. T-84, roll 105, frames 1399918–1400038.

Stradal, Hermann. *Betrachtungen über die voraussichtliche Entwicklung der Mineralölwirtschaft im Gau Wien.* Vienna: [SOEG], 1942. T-84, roll 202, frames 1568599–645.

Südosteuropa-Gesellschaft. *Agrarpolitische Vorträge der Südosteuropa-Gesellschaft.* Vienna: SOEG, 1940.

————, *Die Bodenschätze der südosteuropäischen Länder.* 2 vols. Vienna: [SOEG], 1943. Strictly confidential.

————. *Stand und Möglichkeiten der Ernergieversorgung des südosteuropäischen Raumes.* Vienna: [SOEG], 1941.

————. *Standorte der landwirtschaftlichen Erzeugung in der Türkei.* Vienna: SOEG, 1942. [A copy of this study is available in the library of the *Institut für Weltwirtschaft* in Kiel].

————. *Südosteuropa-Probleme.* Vienna: SOEG, 1940. [A copy of this brochure is available in the library of the *Institut für Weltwirtschaft* in Kiel].

————. *Verkehrspolitische Vorträge der Südosteuropa-Gesellschaft.* Vienna: SOEG, 1940. [A copy of this publication is available in the library of the *Institut für Weltwirtschaft* in Kiel].

————, Photogrammetrisches Institut. *Ubersichtskarten der über-schwemmten Landflächen im Gebiet der mittleren und unteren Donau im Jahre 1942.* [Vienna: SOEG, 1943]. In T-84, roll 86, frames 1375991–99.

————, Südostgemeinschaft Wiener Hochschulen. *Arbeitsbericht der Südostgemeinschaft der Wiener Hochschulen. Breslau* [?]: Schlesischer R. N. Druck R. Nischkowsky [1941]. A copy of this publication is available in the Nationalbibliothek in Vienna].

————, Wiener Institut für Wirtschaftsforschung. *Die Bauxit- und Aluminiumwirtschaft in Italien.* Vienna: SOEG, 1943.

————, ————. *Die Bauxit- und Aluminiumwirtschaft der südosteuropäischen Länder.* Vienna: [SOEG], 1943.

————, Wiener Institut für Wirstchaftsforschung. *Stand und Möglichkeiten der Energieversorgung der Slowakei.* Vienna: SOEG, 1943.

————, ————. *Die voraussichtliche Entwicklung des Wiener Hafenumschlages.* Vienna: SOEG, 1941. T-84, roll 202, frames 1568477–598.

————, ————. *Die voraussichtliche Entwicklung des Wiener Hafenumschlages II, Erdwiderung auf die Stellungnahme der Reichsstelle für Raumforschung.* Vienna: SOEG [?], 1941.

————, ————. *Die Zuckerindustrie in Ungarn. Stand April 1944.* Vienna: SOEG [?], 1944.

Wesemann, Hans Otto. *Das Verkehrswesen Südosteuropas.* Vienna: Südost-Echo, 1940.

Zeck, Hans F. *Erfahrungen mit dem Einsatz südosteuropäischer Arbeiter unter besonderer Berücksichtigung der Verhältnisse im Landesarbeitsamtsbezirk Wien-Niederdonau.* Vienna: SOEG, 1943. T-84, roll 86, frames 1375886–934.

Primary Sources
Diaries, Memoirs, and Letters

Anfuso, Filippo. *Die beiden Gefreiten—Ihr Spiel um Deutschland und Italien.* Translated by Egon Heymann. Munich: Pohl, 1952.

Ciano, Galeazzo. *The Ciano Diaries, 1939–1943.* Edited by Hugh Gibson. Garden City, New York: Doubleday, 1946.

————. *Ciano's Diplomatic Papers.* Edited by Malcolm Muggeridge and translated by Stuart Hood. London: Odhams Press, 1948.

————. *Ciano's Hidden Diary, 1937–1938.* Translated and edited by Andreas Mayer. New York: Dutton, 1953.

Fotitch, Constantin. *The War We Lost.* New York: Viking, 1948.

Frank, Hans. *Im Angesicht des Galgens.* 2nd edition. Neuhaus b. Schliersee: Eigenverlag Brigitte Frank, 1955.

Gafencu, Grigore. *Prelude to the Russian Campaign.* Translated by E. Fletcher-Allen. London: Muller, 1945.

Gheorghe, Jon. *Rumäniens Weg zum Satellitenstaat.* Heidelberg: Vowinckel, 1952.

Gilbert, Gustave M. *Nuremberg Diary.* New York: Farrar and Strauss, 1944.

Goebbels, Joseph. *The Goebbels Diaries, 1942–1943.* Edited and translated by Louis P. Lochner. New York: Doubleday, 1948.

Hassell, Ulrich von. *Vom andern Deutschland.* 3rd edition. Zurich: Atlantis, 1947.

Hitler, Adolf. *Hitler's Secret Conversations, 1941–1944.* Edited by Hugh R. Trevor-Roper. New York: Farrar, Strauss, and Young, 1953.

———. *Hitlers Tischgespräche im Führerhauptquartier 1941–1942.* Prepared by Henry Picker and edited by Gerhard Ritter. Bonn: Athenäum, 1951.

———, and Mussolini, Benito. *Les Lettres secrètes echangées par Hitler et Mussolini.* Introduction by André François-Poncet. Paris: Editions du Paris, 1946.

Hodza, Milan. *Federations in Central Europe.* London: Jarrolds, 1942.

Hoettl, Wilhelm. *The Secret Front.* Translated by R. H. Stevens. London: Weidenfelt and Nicolson, 1953.

Horthy, Nicholas. *Ein Leben für Ungarn.* Bonn: Athenäum, 1953.

Kallay, Nicholas. *Hungarian Premier.* New York: Columbia, 1954.

Knatchbull-Hugessen, Hughe. *Diplomat in War and Peace.* London: Murray, 1949.

Maček, Vladko. *In the Struggle for Freedom.* Translated by Elizabeth and Stjepan Gazi. New York: Speller, 1957.

Neubacher, Hermann. *Sonderauftrag Südost.* 2nd edition. Göttingen: Musterschmidt, 1957.

Papagos, Alexander. *The Battle of Greece, 1940–1941.* Translated by Pat. Eliascos. Athens: J. M. Scaziskis "Alpha" Editions, 1949.

Papen, Franz von. *Der Wahrheit eine Gasse.* Munich: List, 1952.

Rahn, Rudolf. *Ruheloses Leben.* Düsseldorf: Diederichs, 1949.

Rauschning, Hermann. *Gespräche mit Hitler.* New York: Europa, 1940.

Rosenberg, Alfred. *Das politische Tagebuch Alfred Rosenbergs aus den Jahren 1934/35 und 1939/40.* Edited by Hans-Günther Seraphim. Göttingen: Musterschmidt, 1956.

Rintelen, Enno von. *Mussolini als Bundesgenosse.* Tübingen: Leins, 1951.

Schacht, Hjalmar. *76 Jahre meines Lebens.* Bad Wörishofen: Kindler and Schiermeyer, 1953.

Schenk, Fritz. *Magie der Planwirtschaft.* Cologne: Kiepenheuer and Witsch, 1960.

Schirach, Henriette von. *The Price of Glory.* Translated and adapted by Willi Frischauer. London: Muller, 1960.

Schmidt, Paul. *Statist auf diplomatischer Bühne.* Bonn: Athenäum, 1949.

Ullmann, Hermann. *Pioniere Europas. Die volksdeutsche Bewegung und ihre Lehren.* Munich: Arbeitsstelle für Heimatvertriebene/ Süd, 1956.

Waldeck, Rosie G. *Athene Palace.* New York: McBride, 1942.

Primary Sources
Document Collections, Official Directories,
Trial Transcripts and Statistical Yearbooks

Austria, Wiener Volksgericht. *Der Hochverratsprozess gegen Dr. Guido Schmidt vor dem Wiener Volksgericht.* Vienna: Österreichische Staatsdruckerei, 1947.

Eristov, Madeleine and Michel, translators. *Documents Secrèts du Ministère des Affaires étrangères d'Allemagne. Vol. II. Hongrie (1937–1943).* Paris: Dupont, 1946.

Germany, Kommandierender General und Befehlshaber in Serbien, Generalbevollmächtigter für die Wirtschaft in Serbien. *Die Wirtschaftslage im Bereich des Kommandierenden Generals und Befehlshabers in Serbien—Dritter Gesamtbericht.* [Belgrade: Gebevoll. f.d.Wi. in S.,?], 1944.

————, OKW, Wirtschaftsführungsstab Ost. *Richtlinien für die Führung der Wirtschaft in den neubesetzten Ostgebieten (Grüne Mappe)* Berlin: OKW, June 1941. T-77, roll 5, frames 717851–878.

————, ————, ————. *Richtlinien für die Führung der Wirtschaft in den neubesetzten Ostgebieten (Grüne Mappe) Teil II.* Third ed.; Berlin: Zander, 1942. T-580, roll 477, folder no. 200.

————, Reichsgau Wien, Statistisches Amt. *Statistische Übersichten für den Reichsgau Wien.* Vienna: Ueberreuther, 1943 and 1944. Secret.

————, Reichsgruppe Industrie, Geschäftsführung. *Gliederung der Reichsgruppe Industrie.* 3rd edition. Berlin: Lühe, 1941.

————, Reichskommissar für die Festigung des deutschen Volkstums. *Die Umsiedlung—Stand 1. Juli 1942.* Manuscript Division of the Library of Congress, Washington, D.C. Himmler Files, Cont. No. 398, Drawer No. 2, Folder No. 35.

————, ————, Volksdeutsche Mittelstelle, Deutsche Volksgruppe Rumänien. (Schmidt). *Leistungs- und Lagebericht der Deutschen Volksgruppe in Rumänien vom 1. Juli 1942 bis 1. September 1943.* Kronstadt: [Deutsche Volksgruppe, 1944?]. T-120, Cont. 1003, frames 393139–167.

————, ————, ————, ————, Organisation der gewerblichen Wirtschaft, Wirtschaftsgruppen. *Berichte über das dritte Vierteljahr 1942 der Wirtschaftsgruppen in der Organisation der gewerblichen Wirtschaft der deutschen Volksgruppe in Rumänien.* [Nov., 1942]. T-71, roll 66, frames 565566–76.

————, Reichsministerium des Innern. *Reichsgesetzblatt.* Teil I. Berlin: Reichsverlagsamt, 1941.

————, Reichstag. *Der Grossdeutsche Reichstag 1938. IV. Wahlperiode (nach dem 30. Januar 1933).* Edited by E. Kienast. Berlin: Deckers Verlag, G. Schenk, 1938.

————, ————. *Der Grossdeutsche Reichstag. IV. Wahlperiode. Beginn am 10. April 1938 verlängert bis zum 30. Januar 1947.* Edited by E. Kienast. Berlin: Deckers Verlag G. Schenck, 1943.

————, Statistisches Reichsamt. *Statistisches Jahrbuch für das Deutsche Reich 1938.* Berlin: Verlag für Sozialpolitik, Wirtschaft und Statistik, 1938.

Great Britain. *Documents on British Foreign Policy 1919–1939.* Third Series. Vol. III. *1938–39.* London: His Majesty's Stationery Office, 1950.

————, Ministry of Economic Warfare. *Who's Who in Germany and Austria.* London: Ministry of Economic Warfare, 1945. Restricted.

International Institute of Agriculture. *Yearbook of Agricultural Statistics 1941–42 and 1945–46.* Rome: Bureau of the FAO, 1947.

International Military Tribunal. *Trial of Major War Criminals Before the International Military Tribunal. Nuremberg 14 November 1945–10 October 1946.* 42 vols. Nuremberg: [International Military Tribunal], 1947–49.

League of Nations, Economic Intelligence Service, Economic, Financial, and Transit Department. *Europe's Trade. A Study of the Trade of European Countries with Each Other and with the Rest of the World.* Geneva: League of Nations, 1941.

Lemkin, Raphael, editor. *Axis Rule in Occupied Europe.* Washington: Carnegie Endowment for International Peace, 1944.

Nationalsozialistische Deutsche Arbeiterpartei, Gauleitung Wien, Gaupresseamt, Archiv. *Reichsleiter Baldur von Schirach. Tätigkeit als Reichsstatthalter und Gauleiter in Wien August 1940–November 1942.* Vienna: Gaupresseamt, 1942 [?]

Pfundtner, Hans and Warnack, ?, editors. *Taschenbuch für Verwaltungsbeamte.* 60th edition. Berlin: Heymann, 1943.

Poliakov, Leon and Wulff, Josef, editors. *Das Dritte Reich und seine Diener.* Berlin: Arani, 1956.

Royal Institute of International Affairs. *Documents on International Affairs, 1938.* Edited by Monica Curtis. 2 vols. Oxford: Oxford University Press, 1942–43.

Six, Franz A., editor. *Dokumente der deutschen Politik.* Vol. VIII. *Der Kampf gegen den Westen.* Edited by Hans Volz. Berlin: Junker and Dünnhaupt, 1943.

United States, Department of State. *Documents on German Foreign Policy, 1918–1945.* Series C. Vol. III (English edition). *The Third Reich: First Phase, June 14, 1934–March 31, 1935.* Washington: Government Printing Office, 1959. Series D. Vol. V (German edition). *Polen, Südosteuropa, Lateinamerika, Klein- und Mittelstaaten, Juni 1937–März 1939.* Baden-Baden: Imprimerie Nationale, 1953. Vol. VI (German edition). *Die letzten Monate vor Kriegsausbruch. März bis August 1939.* Baden-Baden: Imprimerie Nationale, 1956. Vol. VIII (English edition). *The War Years, September 4, 1939–March 18, 1940.* Washington: Government Printing Office, 1954. Vol. IX (English edition). *The War Years, March 18–June 22, 1940.* Washington: Government Printing Office, 1957. Vol. X (English edition). *The War Years, June 23–August 31, 1940.* Washington: Government Printing Office, 1957.

———, ———. *Das Nationalsozialistische Deutschland und die Sowjetunion, 1939–1941.* Edited by E. Malcolm Carroll and Fritz T. Epstein. Berlin: Druckhaus Tempelhof, 1948.

———, ———. *Nazi Soviet Relations 1939–1941.* Edited by Raymond J. Sontag and James S. Beddie. New York: Didier, 1948.

———, Nürnberg Military Tribunals. *Trial of War Criminals Before the Nuernberg Military Tribunals under Control Council Law*

No. 10. Case 6. Vol. VIII. *United States against Carl Krauch et al.* Washington: Government Printing Office, 1953.

————, Office of United States Chief for the Prosecution of Axis Criminality. *Nazi Conspiracy and Aggression.* Supplement A. Washington: Government Printing Office, 1948.

Yugoslavia, Government of the Federative People's Republic of Yugoslavia. *Memorandum of the Government of the Federative People's Republic of Yugoslavia on Slovene Carinthia, the Slovene Frontier Areas of Styria and the Croats of Burgenland.* Annex No. 1, "Participation of Austria in Hitler's Aggression Against and Occupation of Yugoslavia." Belgrade: n.p., 1946 [?]

Secondary Sources
Books

Backe, Herbert. *Um die Nahrungsfreiheit Europas.* Leipzig: Goldmann, 1942.

Basch, Antonin. *The Danube Basin and the German Economic Sphere.* New York: Columbia, 1943.

Bathe, Rudolf, and Glodschey, Erich. *Der Kampf um den Balkan.* Oldenburg: Stalling, 1942.

Bengtson, John R. *Nazi War Aims.* Rock Island, Illinois: Augustana College Library, 1962.

Bettelheim, Charles, *L'Economie allemande sous le Nazisme.* (Bibliotheque General d'Economie Politique.) Paris: Rivière, 1946.

Bilimovich, Alexander D., Vegh, Jenö, and Zagoroff, Slavcho D. *The Agricultural Economy of the Danubian Countries, 1935–1945.* (Food, Agriculture, and World War II, No. 8.) Stanford, California: Stanford, 1955.

Bouthillier, Yves. *Le Drame de Vichy.* 2 vols. Paris: Plon, 1951.

Brandt, Karl et al. *Management of Agriculture and Food in the German-Occupied and other Areas of Fortress Europe.* (Germany's Agriculture and Food Policies in World War II, No. 2.) Stanford, California: Stanford, 1953.

Brausse, Hans B. *Die Führungsordnung des deutschen Volkes.* Hamburg: Hanseatische Verlagsanstalt, 1940.

Brecht, Arnold and Glaser, Comstock. *The Art and Technique of Administration in German Ministries.* (Harvard Political Studies, No. 19.) Cambridge, Massachusetts: Harvard, 1940.

Bullock, Alan. *Hitler, A Study in Tyranny.* New York: Harper, 1951.

Celovsky, Boris. *Das Münchner Abkommen von 1938.* (Quellen und Darstellungen zur Zeitgeschichte, No. 3.) Stuttgart: Deutsche Verlagsanstalt, 1958.

Croll, Walther. *Wirtschaft im europäischen Raum.* Vienna: Frick, 1940.

Daitz, Werner. *Der Weg zur Völkischen Wirtschaft, europäischen Grossraumwirtschaft und gerechten Weltordnung.* (Dr. Goebbels Spende für die deutsche Wehrmacht, No. 5.) 3 parts. Dresden: Meinhold, 1943.

————. *Wiedergeburt Europas durch europäischen Sozialismus.* Amsterdam: De Amsterdamsche Keurkammer [1943].

Dallin, Alexander. *German Rule in Russia, 1941–1945.* New York: St. Martins, 1957.

Delaisi, Francis. *Les Deux Europes.* Paris: Payot, 1929.

Deutsche Akademie, editor. *Reden aus Anlass der Amtseinführung des Präsidenten der Deutschen Akademie Reichsminister Dr. Seyss-Inquart.* Munich: Deutsche Akademie [1944].

————. *Die Wissenschaft im Lebenskampf des deutschen Volkes.* Munich: Deutsche Akademie, 1940.

Deutsches Institut für Aussenpolitische Forschung, editor. *Europa, Handbuch der politischen, wirtschaftlichen und kulturellen Entwicklung des neuen Europas.* Introduction by Joachim von Ribbentrop. Leipzig: Helingsche Verlagsanstalt, 1943.

Deutsches Institut für Wirtschaftsforschung (Rolf Wagenführ). *Die deutsche Industrie im Kriege 1939–1945.* Berlin: Dunker & Humblot, 1954.

Diederich, Clemens, editor. *Die Kroaten.* Zagreb: Verlagsbuchhandlung Velchit, 1942.

Dietzel, Karl H., Schmieder, Oskar, and Schmitt, Heinrich, editors. *Lebensraumfragen europäischer Völker.* 2 vols. Leipzig: Quelle & Meyer, 1941.

Düssel, Carl. *Europa und die Achse.* Essen: Essener Verlagsanstalt, 1940.

Einzig, Paul. *Bloodless Invasion. German Economic Penetration into the Danubian States and the Balkans.* London: Duckworth, 1938.

————. *Hitler's "New Order" in Europe.* London: Macmillan, 1941.

Epting, Karl, editor. *Cahiers de l'Institut allemand. No. 5. Economie continentale.* Paris: Sorlot [1942].

Erbe, René. *Die nationalsozialistische Wirtschaftspolitik 1933–39 im Lichte der modernen Theorie.* (Basle Centre for Economic and

Financial Research, Series B, No. 2.) Zurich: Polygraphischer Verlag, 1958.

Fainsod, Merle. *How Russia is Ruled.* Cambridge, Massachusetts: Harvard, 1953.

Festgabe für Heinrich Himmler. Darmstadt: Wittich, 1941.

First International Conference on the History of the Resistance Movements Held at Liège-Bruxelles-Breendonk 14–17 September 1958, editor. *European Resistance Movements, 1939–1945.* New York: Oxford, 1960.

Forst de Battaglia, Otto. *Zwischeneuropa.* Frankfurt a. M.: Verlag der Frankfurter Hefte, 1954.

Fox, Annette B. *The Power of Small States.* Chicago: University of Chicago Press, 1959.

Friedrich, Carl J. and Brzezinski, Zbigniew K. *Totalitarian Dictatorship and Autocracy.* Cambridge, Massachusetts: Harvard, 1956.

Ganzer, Karl R. *Das Reich als europäische Ordnungsmacht.* 3rd edition. Hamburg: Hanseatische Verlagsanstalt, 1941/42.

Gebhardt, Gerhard. *Europas Wirtschaftsreiheit.* (Das Neue Europa— Schriftenreihe der Gesellschaft für europäische Wirtschaftsplanung und Grossraumwirtschaft, No. 3.) Essen: Glückauf, 1941.

Germany, Deutsche Arbeitsfront, Arbeitswissenschaftliches Institut. *Das Arbeitswissenschaftliche Institut der Deutschen Arbeitsfront, 1935–1942.* Berlin: Deutsche Arbeitsfront [?], 1943.

———, ———, ———. *Sozialwissenschaftliche Aussprachetagung des Arbeitswissenschaftlichen Instituts der Deutschen Arbeitsfront in Bad Salzbrunn vom 14. bis 18. März 1944—Schlussprotokoll.* [Berlin: Deutsche Arbeitsfront, 1944?]. T-71, roll 60, frames 558209–16.

———. [Reichsarbeitsgemeinschaft für Raumforschung], Arbeitsgemeinschaft für Raumforschung Wien. *Wegweiser zu den in Wien vorhandenen Hilfsmitteln für die Raumforschung in den Gebieten der Ostmark, den Sudetenländern und im Südostraum: 1. Nachtrag (Ergänzungen und Berichtigungen. 1943).* [Vienna: AG für Raumforschung, 1943]. T-71, roll 68, frames 567538–73.

———, Reichsgruppe Handel. *V. Länderbericht—Ungarn.* [Berlin: Reichsgruppe Handel], 1941. T-84, roll 136, frames 1438993– 1439234.

———, Reichsnährstand. *Übersichten über die Entwicklung der deutschen Ernährungswirtschaft.* Berlin: Reichsnährstand-Verlag, 1944.

Gesellschaft für europäische Wirtschaftsplanung und Grossraumwirtschaft. *Jahrbuch: Nationale Wirtschaftsordnung und Grossraumwirtschaft.* Dresden: Meinhold, 1941.

Great Britain, Foreign Office and Ministry of Economic Warfare, Economic Advisory Branch. *Austria Basic Handbook.* [London]: n.p., 1944.

Gross, Hermann, editor. *Mittel- und Südost-Europäische Wirtschaftsfragen.* Leipzig: Böttger, 1931.

Grothe, Hugo. *Das deutsche Volkstum in der Slowakei in Vergangenheit und Gegenwart.* Wiesbaden: Grothe, 1943. T-71, roll 78, frames 579855–580029.

Gruchmann, Lothar. *Nationalsozialistische Grossraumordnung.* (Schriftenreihe der Vierteljahrshefte für Zeitgeschichte, No. 4.) Stuttgart: Deutsche Verlagsanstalt, 1962.

Hartmann, Hans W. *Die auswärtige Politik der Türkei 1923–1940.* Zurich: Leomann, 1941.

Hassel, Ulrich von. *Südosteuropa—Bemerkungen zum Ausgleich der deutschen und italienischen Wirtschaftsinteressen.* [Berlin: MWT], 1941. T-84, roll 79, frames 1367246–304.

Hayler, Franz. *Die Reichsgruppe Handel, Aufgaben und Aufbau* (Schriften zum Staatsaufbau, No. 49.) Berlin: Junker and Dünnhaupt, 1940.

Hedemann, Justus W. *Deutsches Wirtschaftsrecht.* 2nd edition. Berlin: Junker and Dünnhaupt, 1943.

Heinrichsbauer, August. *Das Bergbaumonopol.* Essen: Deutsche Bergwerkszeitung, 1919.

———. *Harpener Bergbau-Aktiengesellschaft 1856–1936.* Essen: Glückauf, 1936.

———. *Industrielle Siedlung im Ruhrgebiet in Vergangenheit, Gegenwart und Zukunft.* Essen: Glückauf, 1936.

———. *Die Kohlennot, der Ruin Deutschlands.* Berlin-Zehlendorf: Zeitfragen-Verlag, 1920.

———. *Kommunismus, Sozialismus, Zentrum.* Munich: Knorr, Hirth, 1931.

———. *Der Sozialismus im Endkampf um die Kommune—Weitere Erfolge der Novemberwahlen?* Essen: Girardet, 1929. [Copies of these publications by Heinrichsbauer are available in the library of the Hamburgisches Weltwirtschaftsarchiv in Hamburg.]

Herre, Paul. *Deutschland und die europäische Neuordnung.* Berlin: Deutscher Verlag, 1941.

Herzog, Robert. *Grundzüge der deutschen Besatzungsverwaltung in den ost- und südosteuropäischen Ländern während des 2. Weltkrieges.* (Studien des Instituts für Besatzungsfragen in Tübingen zu den deutschen Besetzungen im 2. Weltkrieg, No. 4.) Tübingen: Institut für Besatzungsfragen, 1955.

Hilberg, Raul. *The Destruction of the European Jews.* Chicago: Quadrangle, 1961.

Hillgruber, Andreas. *Hitler, König Carol und Marschall Antonescu.* (Veröffentlichungen des Instituts für Europäische Geschichte Mainz, No. 5.) Wiesbaden: Steiner, 1954.

Höhn, Reinhard, editor. *Das Ausländische Verwaltungsrecht der Gegenwart: Wesen, Aufgabe und Stellung der Verwaltung in Italien, Frankreich, Grossbritanien und USA.* Berlin: Decker, 1940.

———. *Rechtsgemeinschaft und Volksgemeinschaft.* Hamburg: Hanseatische Verlagsanstalt, 1935.

Hoffmann, Walter. *Lebensraum oder Imperialismus: eine wirtschaftspolitische Studie Südosteuropas.* (England ohne Maske, No. 27.) Berlin: Deutsche Informationsstelle, 1940.

Hory, Ladislaus and Broszat, Martin. *Der kroatische Ustascha-Staat.* (Schriftenreihe der Vierteljahrshefte für Zeitgeschichte, No. 8.) Stuttgart: Deutsche Verlagsanstalt, 1964.

Huber, Ernst R., editor. *Idee und Ordnung des Reiches.* 2 vols. Hamburg: Hanseatische Verlagsanstalt, 1941–43.

Hunke, Heinrich, editor. *Hanse, Downing Street und Deutschlands Lebensraum.* Berlin: Haude und Spenersche Buchhandlung Max Paschke, 1940.

Institut für Zeitgeschichte (Paul Kluke), editor. *Das Dritte Reich und Europa.* (Veröffentlichungen des Instituts für Zeitgeschichte.) Munich: Selbstverlag des Instituts für Zeitgeschichte, 1957.

Inter-Allied Information Committee. *Conditions in Occupied Territories.* No. 9. *Penetration of German Capital into Europe.* London: His Majesty's Stationery's Office, 1942.

I. G. Farben, Volkswirtschaftliche Abteilung. *Organe und Grundsätze der staatlichen Wirtschaftsorganisation- und Lenkung in Bulgarien.* [Berlin: I. G. Farben?], 1942. T-71, roll 62, frames 561128–46.

———, ———. *Überblick über die Wirtschaft Grossbulgariens.* [Berlin: I. G. Farben?], 1942. T-71, roll 62, frames 561147–64.

Janeff, Janke. *Südosteuropa und der deutsche Geist.* Berlin: Fritsch, 1943.

Jong, Louis de. *Die deutsche fünfte Kolonne im Zweiten Weltkrieg.* Translated by Helmut Lindemann. Stuttgart: Deutsche Verlagsanstalt, 1959.

Kamenetsky, Ihor. *Secret Nazi Plans for Eastern Europe.* New York: Bookman Associates, 1961.

Kerner, Robert J., editor. *Yugoslavia.* (The United Nations Series.) Berkeley, California: University of California Press, 1949.

Kertesz, Stephen D. *Diplomacy in a Whirlpool. Hungary Between Nazi Germany and Soviet Russia.* (International Studies of the University of Notre Dame.) Notre Dame, Indiana: University of Notre Dame Press, 1953.

Kiesewetter, Bruno, editor. *Probleme des europäischen Grosswirtschaftsraumes.* Berlin: Junker and Dünnhaupt, 1942.

Kiszling, Rudolf. *Die Kroaten.* Graz: Böhlaus Nachfolger, 1956.

Klein, Burton. *Germany's Economic Preparations for War.* (Harvard Economic Studies, No. 109.) Cambridge, Massachusetts: Harvard, 1959.

Klinkmüller, Erich, and Ruban, Maria E. *Die wirtschaftliche Zusammenarbeit der Ostblockstaaten.* Berlin: Duncker and Humblot, 1960.

Koehl, Robert L. *RKFDV: German Resettlement and Population Policy, 1939–1945.* (Harvard Historical Monographs, No. 31.) Cambridge, Massachusetts: Harvard, 1957.

Kornhauser, William. *The Politics of Mass Society.* Glencoe, Illinois: Free Press, 1959.

Korte, Heinrich. *Lebensrecht und völkerrechtliche Ordnung.* Berlin: Duncker & Humblot, 1942.

Kraus, Felix. *Für Grossdeutschland—60 Jahre völkische Schutzarbeit.* Berlin: Asmus, 1940.

Krüger, Karl. *Der Ostblock.* Berlin: Safari, 1960.

Krugmann, Robert W. *Südosteuropa und Grossdeutschland.* Breslau: Breslauer Verlags- und Druck G. m. b. H., 1939.

Laeuen, Harald. *Marschall Antonescu.* Essen: Essener Verlagsanstalt, 1943.

Leibrock, Otto. *Der Südosten, Grossdeutschland und das neue Europa.* Berlin: Volk und Reich, 1941.

————. *Weltwirtschaft oder Grossraumwirtschaft?* Leipzig: Deutsche Wissenschaftliche Buchhandlung, 1933.

Leverkuehn, Paul. *German Military Intelligence.* Translated by R. H. Stevens and Constantine FitzGibbon. New York: Praeger, 1954.

Lukacz, John A. *The Great Powers and Eastern Europe.* New York: American Book Company, 1953.

Lunelli, Italo. *Pagina della nostra fede—Italia e Germania di fronte all'Europa.* Varese: PNF, 1942.

Macartney, Carlile A. *October Fifteenth, a History of Modern Hungary, 1925–1945.* (Edinburgh University Publications of History, Philosophy, and Economics, No. 6.) 2 vols. Edinburgh: University of Edinburgh Press, 1956–1957.

März, Josef. *Gestaltwandel des Südostens.* Berlin: Frundsberg, 1942.

Markert, Werner, editor. *Osteuropa-Handbuch: Jugoslawien.* Cologne: Böhlau, 1954.

Mayer, Theodor, and Platzhoff, Walter, editors. *Das Reich und Europa.* Leipzig: Koehler and Amelang, 1941.

Medlicott, William N. *History of the Second World War. United Kingdom Civil Series: The Economic Blockade.* 2 vols. London: His Majesty's Stationery Office, 1952.

Meyer, Henry C. *Mitteleuropa in German Thought and Action, 1815–1945.* (International Scholars Forum.) The Hague: Nijhoff, 1955.

Mickwitz, Eugen von, editor. *Vierjahresplan und Grossraumwirtschaft.* Hamburg: Verlag der Veröffentlichung "Aussenhandel unter Zwang," 1941.

Mitteleuropäischer Wirtschaftstag. *Südosteuropa als wirtschaftlicher Ergänzungsraum für Deutschland.* [Berlin: MWT], 1939. Strictly confidential. T-71, roll 60, frames 557728–988.

———. *Südosteuropa, Vorschläge für eine neue deutsche Kapitalpolitik.* Berlin: MWT, 1940.

———, Rumänische Gruppe. *Sitzungsbericht der Gründung der Rumänischen Wirtschaftsgruppe des Mitteleuropäischen Wirtschaftstages.* Bucharest: MWT, 1942. T-84, roll 88, frames 3460835–62.

Molden, Otto. *Der Ruf des Gewissens. Der österreichische Freiheitskampf 1938 bis 1945.* (Beiträge zur Geschichte der österreichischen Widerstandsbewegung.) Vienna: Herold, 1958.

Müllenbusch, Josef. *Die Organisation der deutschen Ernährungswirtschaft.* Berlin: Reichsnährstand Verlags-Gesellschaft, 1941.

[Nationalsozialistische Deutsche Arbeiterpartei, Gau Wien], Gauwirtschaftsberater. *Grundlagen zum Gauwirtschaftsplan von Wien— Teilausarbeitung I—Ausbau der Wiener Hafenanlagen.* Vienna: n.p., 1942. Secret. T-84, roll 201, frame 1568340 to roll 202, frame 1568476.

Neidenbach, Karl. *Die Volksdeutsche Landwirtschaft im Banat.* Breslau: Osteuropa-Institut, 1942. T-71, roll 78, frames 580030–240.

Neumann, Franz L. *Behemoth, the Structure and Practice of National Socialism.* New York: Oxford, 1942.

———. *The Democratic and the Authoritarian State.* Edited by Herbert Marcuse. Glencoe, Ill.: Free Press and Falcon's Wing Press, 1957.

Neusüss-Hunkel, Ermehild. *Die SS.* (Schriftenreihe des Instituts für Wissenschaftliche Politik in Marburg/Lahn, No. 2.) Hanover: Norddeutsche Verlagsanstalt O. Goedel, 1956.

Nordische Gesellschaft, editor. *Wirtschaft im Neuen Europa.* Lübeck: Reichskontor der Nordischen Gesellschaft, 1941.

Oestreich, Paul. *Walther Funk, ein Leben für die Wirtschaft.* Munich: Eher, 1940.

Pasvolsky, Leo. *Economic Nationalism of the Danubian States.* New York: Macmillan, 1928.

Picht, Werner *et al. Bilanz des Zweiten Weltkrieges.* Oldenburg: Stalling, 1953.

Ploetz Verlag, A. G., editor. *Geschichte des Zweiten Weltkrieges.* 2nd edition. 2 vols. in 1. Würzburg: Ploetz, 1960.

Quecke, Hans. *Das Reichswirtschaftsministerium.* (Schriften zum Staatsaufbau, No. 57/58.) Berlin: Junker and Dünnhaupt, 1941.

Rafelsberger, Walter *et al. Wirtschaftsbetreuung in der Ostmark.* Berlin: Deutscher Rechtsverlag, 1939.

Ratenieks, Adolf. *Was bringt die Neuordnung Europas den Europäischen Völkern.* Dresden: Meinhold, 1942.

Reichs-Kredit-Gesellschaft A. G. *Rumänien: Die wirtschaftliche Lage im Frühjahr 1939.* Berlin: Reichs-Kredit-Gesellschaft, 1939.

Reischle, Hermann and Saure, Wilhelm. *Der Reichsnährstand.* Berlin: Reichsnährstand Verlags-Gesellschaft, 1940.

Reithinger, Anton et al. *Probleme des europäischen Grosswirtschaftsraumes.* Berlin: Junker and Dünnhaupt, 1943.

Reitlinger, Gerold. *The House Built on Sand, the Conflicts of German Policy in Russia 1939–1945.* New York: Viking, 1960.

Roberts, Henry L. *Rumania, Political Problems of an Agrarian State.* New Haven, Connecticut: Yale, 1951.

Romanik, Felix. *Der Leidensweg der österreichischen Wirtschaft 1933–1945.* Vienna: Österreichischer Bundesverlag, 1957.

Roucek, Joseph S. et al. *Central Eastern Europe: Crucible of World Wars.* New York: Prentice-Hall, 1946.

Royal Institute of International Affairs, Information Department. *South-Eastern Europe: A Brief Survey.* (Royal Institute of International Affairs Information Department Papers, No. 26.) London: Royal Institute of International Affairs, 1940.

————, ————. *South-Eastern Europe: A Political and Economic Survey.* London: Royal Institute of International Affairs, 1939.

Sattler, Wilhelm. *Die deutsche Volksgruppe im Unabhängigen Staat Kroatien.* (Schriften des Südostdeutschen Institutes, Graz, No. 9.) Graz: Steirische Verlagsanstalt, 1943.

Schechtmann, Joseph B. *European Population Transfers, 1939–1945.* (Studies of the Institute of World Affairs.) New York: Oxford, 1946.

Schirach, Baldur von. *Das Wiener Kulturprogramm.* Vienna: Eher [1941].

Schmitt, Carl. *Völkerrechtliche Grossraumordung.* (Politische Wissenschaft.) 4th edition. Berlin: Deutscher Rechtsverlag, 1941.

Schneefuss, Walter. *Donauräume und Donaureiche.* 2nd edition. Vienna: Braumüller, 1944.

Schramm von Thadden, Ehrengard. *Griechenland und die Grossmächte im Zweiten Weltkrieg.* (Veröffentlichungen des Instituts für Europäische Geschichte, Mainz, No. 9.) Wiesbaden: Steiner, 1955.

Schürmann, Arthur [?] W. *Der deutsche Osten ruft.* Hamburg: Hanseatische Verlagsanstalt, 1942.

Schüssler, Wilhelm. *Vom Reich und der Reichsidee in der deutschen Geschichte.* Leipzig: Teubner, 1942.

Schulmeister, Otto. *Werdende Grossraumwirtschaft, die Phasen ihrer Entwicklung in Südosteuropa.* Berlin: Junker and Dünnhaupt, 1943.

Seabury, Paul. *The Wilhelmsstrasse.* Berkeley, California: University of California Press, 1954.

Seraphim, Hans-Jürgen, editor. *Jahrbuch des Osteuropa-Instituts zu Breslau 1942.* Breslau: Schlesien-Verlag, 1943.

Seton-Watson, Hugh. *The East European Revolution.* 3rd edition. London: Methuen, 1956.

Sölter, Arno. *Das Grossraumkartell.* Dresden: Meinhold, 1941.

Tagung der Südosteuropa-Gesellschaft und der Deutschen Gesellschaft der Wirtschaft in Böhmen und Mähren. Prague: Volk und Reich, 1942.

Thierfelder, Franz. *Schicksalsstunden des Balkans.* Vienna: Wiener Verlagsgesellschaft, 1941.

Thomas, Georg. *Geschichte der deutschen Wehr- und "Rüstungswirtschaft (1918–1943/45)*. Edited by Wolfgang Birkenfeld. (Schriften des Bundesarchivs No. 14.) Boppard a. Rh: Harald Boldt Verlag, 1966.

Thompson, Victor A. *Modern Organization.* New York: Knopf, 1961.

Towster, Julian. *Political Power in the USSR.* New York: Oxford, 1948.

Toynbee, Arnold and Veronica M., editors. *Survey of International Affairs, 1939–1946: Hitler's Europe.* London: Oxford, 1954.

Toynbee, Arnold and Ashton-Gwatkin, Frank T., editors. *Survey of International Affairs 1939–1946: The World in March, 1939.* London: Oxford, 1952.

Ulshöfer, Otfried. *Einflussnahme auf Wirtschaftunternehmungen in den besetzten nord-, west- und südosteuropäischen Ländern während des 2. Weltkrieges insbesondere der Erwerb von Beteiligungen (Verflechtung).* (Studien des Instituts für Besatzungsfragen in Tübingen zu den deutschen Besetzungen im 2. Weltkrieg, No. 15.) Tübingen: Institut für Besatzungsfragen, 1958.

United States, Department of the Army, Office of the Chief of Military History. *Department of the Army Pamphlet.* No. 20-243. *German Antiguerrilla Operations in the Balkans (1941–1944).* [Washington]: Government Printing Office, 1954.

———, Military Government of Germany, Finance Division. *Dresdner and Deutsche Banks.* [Washington]: n.p., 1947.

———, ———, ———. *Report on the Investigation of the Dresdner Bank.* [Washington: n.p., 1947?].

Verein Berliner Kaufleute und Industrieller and Wirtschaftshochschule Berlin, editors. *Europäische Wirtschaftsgemeinschaft.* Berlin: Paschke, 1942.

Verein Deutscher Wirtschaftswissenschaftler, editor. *Europäische Grossraumwirtschaft.* Leipzig: Meiner, 1942.

Vogel, Rudolf, editor. *Südosteuropa-Jahrbuch.* 5th edition. Munich: Südosteuropa-Verlagsgesellschaft, 1961.

Wagemann, Ernst. *Der neue Balkan—altes Land—junge Wirtschaft.* Hamburg: Hanseatische Verlagsanstalt, 1939.

Wagner, Curt, *Grossraum-Technik.* Berlin: Elsner, 1944.

Walew, L. B. *Aus der Geschichte der Vaterländischen Front Bulgariens (Juli 1942–September 1944).* Berlin: Dietz, 1952.

Warriner, Doreen. *Economics of Peasant Farming.* London: Oxford, 1939.

Weber, Max. *The Theory of Social and Economic Organization.* Edited by Talcott Parsons. Translated by A. M. Henderson and Talcott Parsons. New York: Oxford, 1947.

Weinberg, Gerhard L. *Germany and the Soviet Union, 1939–1941.* (Studies in East European History, No. 1.) Leiden: Brill 1954.

Weissleder, Goetz. *Donauraum und Rhein-Main-Donau-Kanal.* (Verkehrswissenschaftliche und volkswirtschaftliche Arbeiten, No. 3.) Jena: Fischer, 1944.

Welter, Erich. *Falsch und richtig planen, eine kritische Studie über die deutsche Wirtschaftslenkung im zweiten Weltkrieg.* (Veröffentlichungen des Forschungsinstitutes für Wirtschaftspolitik an der Universität Mainz, No. 1.) Heidelberg: Quelle and Meyer, 1954.

Wilmovsky, Karl von and Ilgner, Max, editors. *Aufgaben und Ziele des MWT, Deutschland und die Intensivierung der südosteuropäischen Länder.* Vienna: MWT [?], 1940.

Wilmovsky, Tilo von. *Gedanken über den Umbruch der Landwirtschaft Mitteleuropas.* [Berlin: MWT, 1941?]. T-71, roll 74, frames 574739–46.

Wilson, Duncan R. *Germany's "New Order."* Oxford: Clarendon, 1941.

Wiskemann, Elizabeth. *The Rome-Berlin Axis.* London: Oxford, 1949.

Wittstock, Oskar. *Die Siebenbürger Sachsen und der gasamtdeutsche Gedanke.* Brno: Rohrer, 1943.

Woermann, Emil. *Europäische Landwirtschaft.* (Heidelberger Studienhefte. C. Nationalökonomie, No. 18.) Heidelberg: [Kraus], 1943.

Wolff, Robert L. *The Balkans in Our Time.* Cambridge, Massachusetts: Harvard, 1953.

Zeck, Hans F. *Die deutsche Wirtschaft und Südosteuropa.* (Macht und Erde, Hefte zum Weltgeschehen, No. 14.) Leipzig: Teubner, 1939.

Secondary Sources
Periodicals and Newspapers

Acikalin, Cevat. "Turkey's International Relations," *International Affairs,* XXIII (Oct., 1947), 477–91.

"Albanische Gäste in Wien," *Donauzeitung,* 4 June 1944, p. 5.

Amery, Julian. "Of Resistance," *Nineteenth Century,* CXLV (March, 1949), 139–49.

Arzet, Robert. "Die Kapitalstruktur der europäischen Wirtschaft," *Zeitschrift für Politik,* XXXI (Feb., 1941), 65–81.

"Aussenhandel—Deutsch-ungarische Wirtschaftsverhandlungen," *Südost Economist,* IV (24 April 1942), 170–71.

"Die Balkanidee und ihre politischen Grundlagen," *Zeitschrift für Politik,* XXXI (May, 1941), 316–19.

Barche, Heinz. "Der Mitteleuropäische Wirtschaftstag—zur Ost- und Südosteuropa-Politik des deutschen Imperialismus in Vorbereitung des Münchener Abkommens," *Deutsche Aussenpolitik,* V (1960), 1294–1302.

Becker, Theodor. "Die Grossraumwirtschaft Europas," *Nationale Wirtschaft,* XI (Aug.–Sept., 1943), 161–75.

Beer, Bedrich. "The Industrialization of Central and South-Eastern Europe," *Central European Observer,* XX (29 Oct. 1942), 334–35.

"Das Beispiel der europäischen Wirtschaftszukunft," *Völkischer Beobachter* (Norddeutsche Ausgabe), 12 March 1944, p. 2.

Berend, I. and Ranki, Gy. "Die deutsche wirtschaftliche Expansion und das ungarische Wirtschaftsleben zur Zeit des zweiten Weltkrieges," *Acta Historica* [Budapest], V (1958), 313–59.

Best, Werner. "Nochmals: Völkische Grossraumordnung statt 'völkerrechtliche' Grossraumordnung," *Deutsches Recht,* XI (19 July 1941), 1533–34.

———. "Völkische Grossraumordnung," *Deutsches Recht,* X (22 June 1940), 1006–07.

Bodensieck, H. "Volksgruppenrecht und nationalsozialistische Aussenpolitik nach dem Münchener Abkommen," *Zeitschrift für Ostforschung,* VII (1958), 481–500.

"Böhmen und Mähren im europäischen Wirtschaftsraum," *Völkischer Beobachter* (Norddeutsche Ausgabe), 20 Dec. 1941, p. 4.

Boettner, Johannes. "Europäische Gemeinschaftsarbeit im Gartenbau," *Vierjahresplan,* VI (15 March 1942), 128–30.

Brecht, Arnold. "How Bureaucracies Develop and Function," *Annals of the American Academy of Political and Social Science,* CCXCII (March, 1954), 1–10.

Brenneisen. "Grossraum-Grosswirtschaftsraum-Grossraumwirtschaft," *Nationalsozialistische Wirtschaftspolitik,* n. vol. (10 Sept. 1943), 269–73.

Brodbek, Walter. "Die Zukunft der Volkskräfte im Südosten," *Südost-Echo,* 10 May 1940, p. 9.

Brown, MacAlister. "The Third Reich's Mobilization of the German Fifth Column in Eastern Europe," *Journal of Central European Affairs,* XIX (July, 1959), 128–48.

Brummenbaum, Albert. "Die Intensivierung der europäischen Landwirtschaft als Gemeinschaftsaufgabe," *Deutsche Agrarpolitik,* I (April–May, 1943), 218–22.

Brunner, Max. "Vom Sinn der Grossraumwirtschaft," *Zeitschrift für die gesamte Staatswissenschaft,* CIII (1943), 119–36.

Campus, Eliza. "Die hitlerfaschistische Infiltration Rumäniens 1939–1940," *Zeitschrift für Geschichtswissenschaft,* V (1957), 213–28.

Casper, Karl. "Zur Frage des Ausbaus der Textilwirtschaft junger Industrieländer-V-Die Textilindustrie Rumäniens," *Weltwirtschaftliches Archiv,* LI (Jan., 1940), 217–44.

Christiansen, Walter. "Der Südosten in der europäischen Grossraumwirtschaft," *Wirtschaftsdienst,* XXVI (Heft 25/26, 1941), 518–21.

Daitz, Werner. "Die europäische Grossraumwirtschaft-geschichtliche Grundlagen und natürliche Voraussetzungen," *Vierjahresplan,* III (20 Nov. 1939), 1278–79.

———. "Lebensstil und Raum als Strukturelemente der Verwaltung," *Deutsches Recht,* XII (9 and 16 May 1942), 698–99.

"Das neue Europa, seine Lebenseinheit und Rechtsordnung," *Deutsches Recht,* X (7 Dec. 1940), 2081–84.

———. "Völkischer Sozialismus-europäischer Sozialismus," *Nationalsozialistische Monatshefte,* XIV (July–Aug., 1943), 345–49.

"Deutsch-Ungarische Handelskammern," *Vertrauliche Wirtschaftsnachrichten der Südosteuropa-Gesellschaft,* I (Wochenbericht 19–26 May 1941), 3.

"Deutsche Clearingschuld im Südosten," *Donauzeitung,* 29 Sept. 1944, p. 4.

"Devisenkurse in der Preispolitik," *Donauzeitung,* 7 Nov. 1943, p. 5.

Deyanowa, Milka. "Die staatlichen Massnahmen zur Förderung der Ausfuhr der Agrarprodukte Bulgariens," *Weltwirtschaftliches Archiv,* LI (March, 1940), 403–36.

Dietze, Hans-Helmut. "Deutschland-der Feind des Völkerrechts? Entwicklung und Widerlegung einer westeuropäischen Ideologie," *Deutsches Recht,* X (9 and 16 Nov. 1940), 1905–12.

———. "Junges Europa," *Deutsches Recht,* XII (28 Nov. 1942), 1569–72.

———. "Vom deutschen Verfassungsrecht zum europäischen Verfassungsrecht," *Deutsches Recht,* XI (12 and 19 April 1941), 801–13.

"Dr. Funk's Progress," *The Times* (London), 20 Oct. 1938, p. 15.

"Donau als Rückgrat im Verkehrsnetz," *Donauzeitung,* 3 June 1944, p. 5.

Dudinsky, I. "Wirtschaftliche Zusammenarbeit der Länder des sozialistischen Lagers," *Sowjetwissenschaft, Gesellschaftswissenschaftliche Beiträge,* VI ([Sept.], 1956), 1083–1100.

Edwards, A. C. "The Impact of the War on Turkey," *International Affairs,* XXII (July, 1946), 389–400.

Egert, Franz. "Die Mittlerstellung der Ostmark im Güteraustausch und Verkehr des neuen Europas," *Weltwirtschaftliches Archiv,* LV (March, 1942), 259–300.

"Erfolg der Grossraumwirtschaft," *Donauzeitung,* 31 July 1943, p. 3.

"Erweiterung der deutschen Wirtschaftsinteressen in Südosteuropa," *Südost-Economist,* III (28 Feb. 1941), 67–69.

"Europa baut mehr Ölpflanzen," *Donauzeitung,* 29 Oct. 1942, p. 5.

Evola, Julius. "Gedanken über europäische Führung," *Aktion,* II (July, 1941), 401–07. [*Aktion* was a journal issued under the auspices of Daitz' research institute. An incomplete set of the publication (Vol. II, and V complete, and the June, October, and August issues of Vol. IV) is available in the Hamburgische Staats- und Universitätsbibliothek in Hamburg].

Fick, Harald. "Die Wirtschaftspolitik der Achse," *Zeitschrift für Politik,* XXXI (June, 1941), 360–69.

F[ischer], R[udolf]. "Europas erstes Jahr—zur Rede Funks auf der Tagung der Südosteuropa-Gesellschaft," *Südost-Echo,* 13 June 1941, pp. 1–2.

"Fischreicher Donauraum—Gute Aussichten für die Zukunft-Tagung der Südosteuropa-Gesellschaft in Wien," *Donauzeitung,* 16 Dec. 1942, p. 5.

Flottmann, Erich. "Die Preispolitik in der europäischen Zusammenarbeit," *Vierjahresplan,* VI (15 Jan. 1942), 26–28.

Franges, Otto von. "Die Donaustaaten Südosteuropas und der deutsche Grosswirtschaftsraum," *Weltwirtschaftliches Archiv,* LIII (March, 1941), 284–320.

Frank, Hans. "Das Recht und die europäische Neurodnung," *Deutsches Recht,* XII (11 and 18 July 1942), 993–94.

Fuchs. "Die deutsche Verwaltung im Protektorat Böhmen und Mähren," *Zeitschrift der Akademie für Deutsches Recht,* VII (15 March 1940), 91–3.

[Funk, Walther]. "Deutschland und der Südosten," *Völkischer Beobachter* (Norddeutsche Ausgabe), 16 Oct. 1938, p. 19.

———. "Wirtschaftsordnung gegen Währungsmechanismus," *Monatshefte für Auswärtige Politik,* XI (Sept., 1944), 491–508.

218																																																																																																																																																											Nazis in the Balkans

Gadolin, Axel von. "Probleme der wirtschaftlichen Neuordnung in Nordeuropa," *Zeitschrift für die gesamte Staatswissenschaft*, CII (1942), 628–53.

Gehrold, Heinz. "Deutsche Kaufleute eigener Prägung," *Südost-Echo*, 26 April 1940, pp. 5–6.

"Gemeinsame Grossraumpolitik," *Donauzeitung*, 28 June 1942, p. 5.

"Generalbebauungsplan für Wien," *Südost-Echo*, 23 Feb. 1940, p. 1.

"Genossenschaftliche Beziehungen zu Südosteuropa," *Hamburger Fremdenblatt*, 12 Feb. 1944.

Gilbert, Felix. "Mitteleuropa—the Final Stage," *Journal of Central European Affairs*, VII (April, 1947), 58–67.

Grävell, Walter. "Die Statistik im Grosswirtschaftsraum," *Weltwirtschaftliches Archiv*, LVI (Nov., 1942), 457–89.

Gross, Hermann. "Die Donau im Güterverkehr zwischen Ost und West," *Osteuropa-Wirtschaft*, I (Aug., 1956), 51–60.

"Die grossdeutsche Sendung der Deutschen Akademie," *Völkischer Beobachter* (Norddeutsche Ausgabe), 30 June 1942, p. 6.

Guilleband, C. W. "Hitler's New Economic Order in Europe," *Economic Journal*, L (Sept., 1940), 449–60.

Hassel, Ulrich von. "Deutschland und der Südosten im Rahmen der zukünftigen europäischen Wirtschaft," *Vierjahresplan*, V (5 March 1941), 322–24.

———. "Deutschlands wirtschaftliche Interessen und Aufgaben in Südosteuropa," *Zeitschrift für Politik*, XXXI (Aug., 1941), 481–88.

Haushofer, Heinz K. "Niederdonau—Agrarpolitische Fragen eines Reichsgaues," *Deutsche Agrarpolitik*, I (Sept., 1943), 368–73.

Hedemann, Justus W. "Der Grossraum als Problem des Wirtschaftsrechts," *Deutsche Rechtswissenschaft*, VI (1941), 180–203.

Heinrichsbauer, August. "Kapitalspekulation und Industriebeteiligungen," *Ruhr und Rhein*, XXII (18 April 1941), 258–60.

———. "Die Niederlande und Südosteuropa," *Ruhr und Rhein*, XXI (27 Dec. 1940), 661–66.

———. "Die Schweiz und Südosteuropa," *Ruhr und Rhein*, XXII (7 Nov. 1941), 718–19.

———. "Der Südostraum und die Niederlage der Westmächte," *Deutsche Bergwerks-Zeitung*, 21 June 1940. T-81, roll 517, frame 5281418.

———. "Wiener Messe und Südostindustrialisierung," *Donauzeitung*, 20 Sept. 1941, pp. 17–18.

"Herrenschicht oder Führungsvolk?" *Reich, Volksordnung, Lebensraum,* III (1942), 122–41.

Heydrich, Reinhard. "Auszüge aus der Rede Heydrichs vor den Naziokkupanten," *Dokumentation der Zeit* (5 Oct. 1957), cols. 75–79.

Hösel, Ulrich. "Breslauer Messe im Zeichen der Landwirtschaft und der neuen Kontinentalbeziehungen," *Vierjahresplan,* IV (5 May 1940), 376–77.

Hoffmann, Emil. "Die Volkwerdung der Deutschen im Südosten," *Zeitschrift für Politik,* XXX (March, 1940), 100–04.

"Hohe deutsche Exportleistung—der Reichswirtschaftsminister in Wien vor der Südosteuropa-Gesellschaft," *Donauzeitung,* 12 March 1944, p. 5.

Howard, Harry N. "Germany, the Soviet Union and Turkey During World War II," *Department of State Bulletin,* XIX (18 July 1948), 63–78.

Huber, Ernst R. "Herrschaft und Führung," *Deutsches Recht,* XI (27 Sept. 1941), 2017–24.

———. "Positionen und Begriffe—eine Auseinandersetzung mit Carl Schmitt," *Zeitschrift für die gesamte Staatswissenschaft,* CI (1941), 1–44.

Hunke, Heinrich. "Die Landwirtschaft in der europäischen Wirtschaftsgemeinschaft," *Deutsche Agrarpolitik,* I (July, 1943), 291–96.

Imhoff, Ludwig. "Europas neue Wirtschaftsordnung im Entstehen," *Schulungsbrief,* IX (Nos. 4/5/6, 1942), 23–27.

"Ein Jahr Südost-Genossenschaftsinstitut Wien," *Hamburger Fremdenblatt,* 26 May 1944.

Jedlicka, Ludwig, ed. "Ein unbekannter Bericht Kaltenbrunners über die Lage in Österreich im September 1944," *Österreich in Geschichte und Literatur,* IV (No. 2, 1960), 82–87.

Jentsch, Gerhard. "Lebensraum," *Monatshefte für Auswätige Politik,* VII (Feb., 1940), 79–90.

"Jugoslawische Menschen," *Südost-Echo,* 29 Nov. 1940, pp. 12–13.

Kallay, Tibor von. "Wege zur deutsch-ungarischen Zusammenarbeit," *Südost-Economist,* IV (8 May 1942), 179–80.

Karvas, Imrich. "Industrialisierung als Grundlage des Aufbaues," *Südost-Echo,* 24 Jan. 1941, p. 5.

Kluke, Paul. "Nationalsozialistische Europaideologie," *Vierteljahrshefte für Zeitgeschichte,* III (July, 1955), 240–75.

Knejowitch, R. L. "Prince Paul, Hitler and Salonika," *International Affairs*, XXVII (Jan., 1951), 38–44.

Koehl, Robert. "Feudal Aspects of National Socialism," *American Political Science Review*, LIV (Dec., 1960), 921–33.

Koenigs, Gustav. "Wasserstrassen im künftigen Europa," *Donauzeitung*, 5 Jan. 1943, p. 5.

"Konjunkturloses Europa als Folge künftiger Grossraumwirtschaft unter deutscher Führung," *Vierjahresplan*, IV (5 Aug. 1940), 664–65.

"Konturen einer Wirtschaftsneuordnung in Südosteuropa," *Vierjahresplan*, IV (5 Oct. 1940), 853–54.

Krieck, Ernst. "Germanische Rechtsgesinnung," *Deutsches Recht*, X (10 Feb. 1940), 217–20.

Krugmann, Robert W. "Südost-Wirtschaft 1943," *Donauzeitung*, 1/2 [sic] Jan. 1944, p. 6.

Lepawsky, Albert. "The Nazis Reform the Reich," *American Political Science Review*, XXX (April, 1936), 324–50.

"Landwirtschaftliche Zusammenarbeit," *Donauzeitung*, 19 Dec. 1942, p. 3.

"Leistungsgrenzen der Handelsmonopole," *Südost-Echo*, 25 April 1941, pp. 1–2.

Leon Gheorge, N. "Der Begriff der Produktivität und die Zusammenarbeit zwischen Agrar- und Industrieländern," *Weltwirtschaftliches Archiv*, LVIII (Nov., 1943), 435–50.

———. "Die Kriegswirtschaft in Rumänien," *Weltwirtschaftliches Archiv*, LII (Sept., 1940), 301–29.

———. "Die wirtschaftlichen Grundlagen eines dauerhaften Friedens," *Weltwirtschaftliches Archiv*, LV (Jan., 1942), 34–52.

Lippisch, Anselm. "Südosteuropas Bauern arbeiten mit—ein Jahr Genossenschaftsinstitut der Südosteuropa-Gesellschaft, Wien," *Donauzeitung*, 29/30 [sic] April 1944, p. 7.

März, Josef. "Der deutsch-rumänische Wirtschaftsplan," *Osteuropa*, XIV (July, 1939), 647–56.

Magistris, Luigi F. de. "Noi e l'Africa," *Geopolitica*, IV (31 March 1942), 115–19.

Mallmann, Walter. "Idee und Ordnung des Reiches," *Zeitschrift der Akademie für Deutsches Recht*, IX (1 Oct. 1942), 273–75.

Manoilesco, Mihail. "Probleme des Industrialisierungsprozesses in Südosteuropa," *Weltwirtschaftliches Archiv*, LXI (Jan., 1945), 1–12.

Mehlan, Arno. "Die wirtschaftliche Aussenhandelsverflechtung Südosteuropas," *Osteuropa*, XIII (May, 1938), 524–40.

Meran, Karl von. "Soll der Südosten Europas Wetterwinkel bleiben?" *Aktion*, IV (June, 1943), 275–80.

Moltmann, Günter. "Goebbels' Rede zum totalen Krieg am 18. Februar 1943," *Vierteljahrshefte für Zeitgeschichte*, XII (Jan., 1964), 13–43.

Murgas, Karol. "Der neue Weg der Slowakei," *Aktion*, II (April, 1941), 277–84.

Muthesius, V. [sic]. "Was ist eine Reichsvereinigung," *Die Bank*, XXXV (13 May 1942), 313–14.

"Nationale Freiheit in der europäischen Gemeinschaft," *Aktion*, V (Oct., 1943), 1–5.

Neumann, Erich. "Deutsch-ungarische Industriebesprechungen und Mitwirkung der Industrie bei der Intensivierung der Landwirtschaft," *Donaueuropa*, II (Nov., 1942), 801–09.

Nonnenbruch. "Macht Deutschland eine Wirtschaftsoffensive in Südosteuropa?" *Völkischer Beobachter* (Norddeutsche Ausgabe), 12 Oct. 1938, p. 11.

Oberascher, Leonhard. "Nach 126 Jahren: Der neuen Heimat entgegen," *Südost-Echo*, 27 Sept. 1940, p. 7.

Perroux, Francois, "Entwurf einer Theorie der dominierenden Wirtschaft," *Zeitschrift für Nationalökonomie*, XIII (1950), 1–25, 242–68.

Pietzsch, Alfred. "Europäische Grossraumwirtschaft," *Südost-Echo*, 20 Dec. 1940, p. 23.

"Planvolle Kontinentalwirtschaft," *Donauzeitung*, 16 March 1943, p. 5.

Polacek, Adalbert. "Die Zolleingliederung des Protektorats Böhmen und Mähren in das Grossdeutsche Reich," *Weltwirtschaftliches Archiv*, LV (March, 1942), 232–58.

"Das Portrait des Tages-Baldur von Schirach, Reichsleiter für Jugenderziehung der NSDAP, Reichsstatthalter und Gauleiter von Wien," *Donauzeitung*, 10 Sept. 1941, p. 3.

"Das Portrait des Tages-Reichsminister Funk-Schirmherr der Südosteuropa-Gesellschaft," *Donauzeitung*, 15 July 1941, p. 3.

"Preisstop im Handel mit Bulgarien," *Donauzeitung*, 10 June 1943, p. 5.

"Preisstop—Vereinbarungen Ungarn-Reich," *Donauzeitung*, 2 Oct. 1943, p. 5.

Presseisen, Ernst L. "Prelude to 'Barbarossa': Germany and the Balkans, 1940–1941," *Journal of Modern History*, XXXII (Dec., 1960), 359–70.

Rafelsberger, Walter. "Wiens Entwicklung zum Handelszentrum," *Südost-Echo*, 26 April 1940, p. 5.

————. "Wirtschaftsplanung im Reichsgau Wien," *Deutsche Volkswirtschaft*, IX (21 April 1940), 376–80.

Raschhofer, Hermann. "Entwicklung und Funktion des neuen Volksgruppenrechts," *Zeitschrift für ausländisches öffentliches Recht und Völkerrecht*, IX (1 Oct. 1943), 418–44.

Rehbeck, Hans. "Wiener Messe—Tor zum Südosten," *Vierjahresplan*, IV (5 March 1940), 188.

————. "Wiens grössere Aufgaben," *Südost-Echo*, 19 Sept. 1941, pp. 1–2.

"Reichsvereinigung und Grossraumkartell," *Chemische Industrie*, LXV (12 June 1942), 233.

Reischle, Hermann. "Schicksalsgemeinschaft," *Südost-Echo*, 28 June 1941, p. 6.

Reithinger, Anton. "Die europäische Wirtschaftskraft bei planvoller Zusammenarbeit," *Zeitschrift für Politik*, XXXIII, (March, 1943), 141–53.

Ringel, Karlrobert. "Währungspolitik und zwischenstaatlicher Zahlungsverkehr in der Grossraumwirtschaft," *Weltwirtschaftliches Archiv*, LVI (Nov., 1942), 490–508.

Rischka, Kurt von. "Die Beziehungen der deutschen Landwirtschaft zu der des Südostens," *Wiener landwirtschaftliche Zeitung*, XCII (3 and 10 Jan. 1942), 1–2 and 7–8 respectively.

Ronke, Maximilian. "Fünf Jahre Rechtsentwicklung im Protektorat Böhmen und Mähren," *Deutsches Recht*, XIV (22 and 29 April 1944), 258–66.

Ronneberger, Franz. "Fünf Jahre slowakischer Staat," *Zeitschrift für Politik*, XXXIV (March–April, 1944), 95–100.

————. "Der politische Südosteuropabegriff," *Reich, Volksordnung, Lebensraum*, VI (1943), 53–107.

————. "Die Stunde der Entscheidung," *Wille und Macht*, VII (15 Dec. 1940), 16–19.

Rosenberg, Alfred. "Unterdrückte Völker und Revisionen," *Völkischer Beobachter* (Norddeutsche Ausgabe), 15 Nov. 1936, pp. 1–2.

Rühle von Lilienstern, Hans. "Der holländische Getreidehandel in der europäischen Grossraumwirtschaft," *Aktion*, IV (Dec., 1942), 75–81.

Ruhe, Ernst. "Kartelle in neuem Gewande," *Donauzeitung,* 17 Jan. 1943, p. 5.

"Saatgutaustausch im Südosten—eine Gründung im Rahmen der Südosteuropa-Gesellschaft," *Donauzeitung,* 31 March 1944, p. 5.

Schiller, Karl. "Meistbegünstigung, Multilateralität und Gegenseitigkeit in der zukünftigen Handelspolitik," *Weltwirtschaftliches Archiv,* LIII (March, 1941), 370–406.

Schippel, Hans. "Deutsche Bankinteressen im Südosten," *Südost-Echo,* 4 Oct. 1940, p. 5.

Schröder-Steinegger, Hubertus. "Neue Frachtverkehrsverhältnisse auf dem Balkan," *Vierjahresplan,* IV (20 Dec. 1940), 1085–86.

———. "Jugoslawien—neue Phase der Entwicklung," *Vierjahresplan,* IV (5 Dec. 1940), 1049.

Schürmann, Arthur [?] W. "Rumäniens Industrialisierung," *Donauzeitung,* 10 Dec. 1942, p. 5.

Selvi, Giovanni. "Die Grundlagen der Neuen Ordnung." *Reich, Volksordnung, Lebensraum,* III (1942), 9–39.

Seraphim, Hans-Jürgen. "Probleme des südosteuropäischen Bauerntums," *Deutsche Agrarpolitik,* I (April–May, 1943), 237–39.

Simon, Herbert. "Notes on the Observation and Measurement of Political Power," *Journal of Politics,* XV (Nov., 1953), 500–16.

Stuckart, Wilhelm. "Internationale Zusammenarbeit auf dem Gebiet der Verwaltung," *Deutsches Recht,* XI (26 April 1941), 903–06.

———. "Die Neuordnung der Kontinente und die Zusammenarbeit auf dem Gebiete der Verwaltung," *Reich, Volksordnung, Lebensraum,* I (1941), 3–28.

"Südostaufgaben des Protektorats," *Donauzeitung,* 8 Jan. 1942, p. 5.

"Der Südostauftrag Wiens—Gespräch des Reichsleiters Baldur von Schirach mit dem Hauptschriftleiter der 'Donauzeitung,'" *Donauzeitung,* 9 Aug. 1942, pp. 1–2.

"Südostinstitut für Holzforschung," *Donauzeitung,* 19 Dec. 1942, p. 5.

Suranyi-Unger, Theo. "Deutsch-ungarische Zusammenarbeit im Krieg und Frieden," *Ungarn,* III (June, 1942), 321–35.

———. "Entwicklung des ungarischen Aussenhandels mit Deutschland," *Mitteilungen des MWT,* VIII (25 July 1942), 9–11.

Suthoff-Gross. "Deutsche Grossraumlehre- und politik," *Deutsches Recht,* XIII (5 and 12 June 1943), 625–28.

Thalheim, Karl C. "Die Entwicklung der Wirtschaftsintegration im Ostblock," *Osteuropa-Wirtschaft,* I (Aug., 1956), 3–11.

———. "Die langfristige Entwicklungsplanung in den europäischen Ostblockstaaten," *Osteuropa-Wirtschaft,* II (Aug., 1957), 13–25.

Thierack, Otto. ["Leitworte anlässlich seiner Ubernahme der Präsidentenschaft der Akademie für Deutsches Recht,"] *Zeitschrift für Deutsches Recht,* IX (1 Sept. 1942), 241.

Treue, Wilhelm. "Das Dritte Reich und die Westmächte auf dem Balkan,' *Vierteljahrshefte für Zeitgeschichte,* I (Jan., 1953), 45–64.

Tsvetkovitch, Dragisha. "Prince Paul, Hitler and Salonika," *International Affairs,* XXVII (Oct., 1951), 463–69.

Tuka, Vojtech. "Europas werdende Neuordnung," *Südost-Echo,* 22 March 1940, p. 1.

Ulbrich. "Europas Wirtschaftskraft," *Völkischer Beobachter* (Norddeutsche Ausgabe), 14 June 1941, p. 2.

"Unbehinderte Industrialisierung," *Südost-Echo,* 29 Nov. 1940, pp. 1–2.

Vegh, Jenö. "Deutsch-ungarische industrielle Zusammenarbeit," *Volk und Reich,* XVIII (July–Aug., 1942), 464–66.

————. "Nach den deutsch-ungarischen Industriebesprechungen," *Südost-Economist,* IV (25 Sept. 1942), 363–64.

Voss, Wilhelm. "Die Donau als Grossdeutschlands Verkehrsweg zum Südosten," *Vierjahresplan,* III (5 Feb. 1939), 320–21.

Walter, Alex. "Die nationalsozialistische Agrarpolitik und die Neuordnung Europas," *Deutsche Agrarpolitik,* I (Jan., 1943), 123–25.

Wannenmacher, Walter. "Die europäische Wirtschaftsidee," *Böhmen und Mähren,* III (Jan., 1942), 8–9.

"Was das Reich lieferte," *Donauzeitung,* 12 Sept. 1944, p. 4.

Wehler, Hans-Ulrich. " 'Reichsfestung Belgrad'—Nationalsozialistische 'Raumordnung' in Südosteuropa," *Vierteljahrshefte für Zeitgeschichte,* XI (Jan., 1963), 72–84.

Wells, Roger H. "The Liquidation of the German *Länder,*" *American Political Science Review,* XXX (April, 1936), 350–76.

Wiehl, Emil K. "Das Reich und die Zukunft des Ostens," *Südost-Echo,* 28 Feb. 1941, p. 506.

"Wien als südosteuropäisches Zentrum," *Das Reich,* 23 April 1944, p. 9.

"Wien—Südosten, die Gründung der Südosteuropa-Gesellschaft," *Südost-Echo,* 5 April 1940, p. 2.

Wilhelmini, Walter. "Die Rechtspflege in den besetzten Ostgebieten," *Zeitschrift der Akademie für Deutsches Recht,* XI (10 Feb. 1944), 20–24.

"Wirtschaftsraum ersetzt nicht Lebensraum," *Wirtschaftspolitische Parole,* V (5 Aug. 1940), 472–73.

Woermann, Emil. "Die Notwendigkeit der Selbstversorgung und ihr Einfluss auf die landwirtschaftliche Produktionsausrichtung," *Deutsche Agrarpolitik,* I (April–May, 1943), 209–17.

Wohltat, Helmuth. "Der neue deutsch-rumänische Wirtschaftsvertrag," *Vierjahresplan,* III (20 April 1939), 560–63.

Zeck, Hans F. "Ein Weg ins Europa der Zukunft—der Rhein- Main-Donau-Kanal und Frankreichs ehemalige Ambitionen," *Südost-Echo,* 21 June, 1940, p. 6.

Zotschew, Theodor. "Der 'Rat für Gegenseitige Wirtschaftshilfe' (Comecon) als Instrument für die wirtschaftliche Integration und weltwirtschaftliche Expansion der Ostblockländer," *Südosteuropa-Jahrbuch,* III (1959), 107–36.

"Zukunftsreicher Gartenbau im Donauraum—Ausschüsse der Südost-europa-Gesellschaft tagten in Wien," *Donauzeitung,* 3 Dec. 1942, p. 5.

"Zusammenarbeit mit Deutschland—Gespräch mit bulgarischem Landwirtschaftsminister Bagrianow," *Südost-Echo,* 22 March 1940, p. 2.

▲▲ Index

▲▲ Index

229